LOU AND JONBENÉT

A Legendary Lawman's Quest To Solve A Child Beauty Queen's Murder

JOHN WESLEY ANDERSON

WILDBLUE
PRESS

WildBluePress.com

LOU AND JONBENÉT published by:
WILDBLUE PRESS
P.O. Box 102440
Denver, Colorado 80250

WILDBLUE PRESS is registered at the U.S. Patent and Trademark Offices.

ISBN 978-1-957288-82-6 Trade Paperback
ISBN 978-1-957288-83-3 eBook
ISBN 978-1-957288-81-9 Hardback

Interior Formatting and Cover Design by Elijah Toten
www.totencreative.com

LOU AND JONBENÉT

Other Books by John Wesley Anderson

A to Z Colorado's Nearly Forgotten History, 1776-1876
Sherlock Holmes in Little London, 1896 The Missing Year
ZacBox and the Pearls of Pleiades
R.S. Kelly, A Man of the Territory
Native American Prayer Trees of Colorado
Rankin Scott Kelly, First Sheriff, El Paso
County, Colorado Territory
Ute Indian Prayer Trees of the Pikes Peak Region

Dedication

To Lou Smit and Dave Spencer – well done, friends, well done.

Table of Contents

Foreword   11
Preface   13

Part I   19
Chapter 1 – Shoes   21
Chapter 2 – Partners   31
Chapter 3 – Careers   69

Part II   105
Chapter 4 – Boulder   107
Slides From Lou Smit's Presentation   145
Chapter 5 – Scene   165
Chapter 6 – Evidence   179

Part III   195
Chapter 7 – Jury   197
Chapter 8 – Legacy   215
Chapter 9 – Team   250

Conclusion   264
Shoes   269
Eulogy   272

Acknowledgements   277
About the Author   278
Index   279

Foreword

John Anderson spent a career in law enforcement protecting our community and standing in the shoes of crime victims. In the course of his long career, he has accumulated an impressive resumé of roles, responsibilities, skills, training, and experiences from a cadet in the police department all the way up to the office of Sheriff, the highest elected office in the county. His credentials and background give him significant credibility in conducting, analyzing, and assessing homicide investigations.

Lou Smit was born to be a detective. Ask virtually anyone who knew him and they will tell you the same thing. He was an exceptionally gifted, dedicated, and hardworking detective. His long list of accomplishments speaks for itself. He officially investigated hundreds of homicide cases, including the JonBenét Ramsey murder case. He always did his best to protect the dignity and interests of the victims. He worked for them. Beyond that, he was an amazing human being. We know this because Lou was our father. We had a front row seat as his life and career unfolded in front of us. We can say confidently that he was put on this earth to be a homicide detective.

John and Lou crossed paths at the Colorado Springs Police Department. What started out as a professional acquaintance developed into a deep friendship that only police partners and those who work on society's sharp edge can fully appreciate. We watched as John and Lou spent years together as partners in the detective bureau investigating homicides and pursuing some of the most brutal and dangerous people imaginable. John knows Lou, his methods, his capabilities and what he stood for—both professionally and personally.

Combining his knowledge of Lou and his deep background in law enforcement, John can provide a perspective on the JonBenét Ramsey murder investigation that few other people can offer. Lou spent years of his life trying to advance that case. When Lou passed away, John and a team of dedicated individuals picked up where Lou left off. They continue to advocate for JonBenét. This book summarizes John's perspectives on Lou, on the investigation, and on exciting next steps that could help advance that case to resolution. We are grateful for John's persistence in seeking justice for JonBenét and for his inspirational dedication to his friend, Lou. We are grateful for his friendship as well.

Lori, Cindy, Mark, and Dawn – The Children of Andrew (Lou) Smit

Preface

I have been trained to believe an investigation is a search for the truth. It is a process of inclusion and exclusion, based upon the objective examination of physical evidence. Physical evidence can be discovered at a crime scene through the proper application of the "Transfer Theory" which states, "Whenever a crime is committed the suspect either takes something or leaves something at the scene." I have also been taught that in homicide investigations the full spectrum of forensic science must be thoroughly exploited in an attempt to extract information from the evidence which can lead to the identification of suspects or the exclusion of innocent persons. Evidence itself does not lie—only the misrepresentation of evidence is a lie.

When homicide detective Lou Smit was hired by the Boulder District Attorney's Office to join the Ramsey Task Force, he was shocked to discover the investigation was flawed from a series of mistakes made from the moment the Boulder police first arrived at the crime scene. The Ramsey home had not been thoroughly searched for the victim's body which was not discovered until seven hours later. The crime scene had not been secured and was not processed properly for vital clues which were overlooked. There was abundant evidence of intrusion into the home, through a previously broken basement window left standing wide open, with a suitcase propped up beneath the window; a black scuff mark was visible below the window. The suspect even left a note.

This suspect had brought items into the crime scene which were needed to accomplish the abduction, including black duct tape he put over JonBenét's mouth to muffle her screams and parachute cord to bind her wrists and fashion a garrote. Lou Smit would later prove that a stun gun had also been brought into the home and used twice on the six-year-old little girl—once on her face and a second time on her back. This suspect had intentionally targeted this Boulder family and methodically planned this kidnapping to happen on Christmas night. Included in his deliberate planning were the items he would need to carry in his "kidnapping kit."

Consistent with the Transfer Theory, the suspect had taken items from the scene; including the roll of duct tape, unused parachute cord, the stun gun, and a section of a paintbrush handle he had used to construct the murder weapon—a garrote. And, he had left items behind; including a Hi-Tec boot print, a piece of duct tape that could be mated to the end of the roll it came from, and the parachute cord he used to construct the ligatures and garrote. But the most critical piece of evidence the suspect left at the scene, and also took with him, was himself—his DNA. And where was this DNA discovered? Underneath the little girl's fingernails. This genetic material was transferred as JonBenét struggled to breathe, and on the crotch of her panties, deposited there when she was sexually assaulted—and the autopsy would later confirm she was brutally sexually assaulted.

And what did the Boulder police detectives do with this critical DNA evidence? They dismissed it; choosing simply to ignore the findings in the DNA lab report. The facts of this case are these: within three weeks of the murder the Boulder police received a lab report from the Colorado Bureau of Investigation (CBI) which confirmed the presence of DNA under JonBenét's fingernails, found to be consistent with the DNA on the crotch of her panties. This DNA was that of an unknown male and was NOT consistent with anyone in the Ramsey family. A year after the murder, a Boulder detective commander taking over the investigation from John Eller, Mark Beckner, announced publicly the parents remain under "an umbrella of suspicion."

For the past quarter century, the Boulder police have ignored the DNA evidence that exonerated the Ramseys and could be used to identify her killer. But why would they do such a thing? While we may never know for sure, there may have been a combination of factors, including inexperience, lack of training, poor supervision, fear of civil litigation, and perhaps some degree of arrogance. Tragically, this homicide investigation was not "a search for the truth." In an unforgivable breach of law enforcement ethics, Boulder police detectives attempted to withhold JonBenét's body so she could not be buried, in an attempt to coerce a confession or admission from a Ramsey family member, any family member. Disinformation was deliberately leaked to the media in another failed attempt to pressure a confession or admission from JonBenét's grieving parents.

The Ramsey family was vilified by the tabloids, which biased the public's opinion of this innocent family for the past quarter century. The paparazzi were merciless in their competition for "news," which led to a feeding frenzy for photos and headlines surpassed only by the death of Princess Diana in August 1997. At least one Boulder area law enforcement peace officer—who was not with the Boulder Police Department—accepted money in exchange for information and crime scene photos that were fed to the tabloids. Mainstream news sources competing for ratings, and traditional news outlets and reporters, struggled to feed the public's unquenchable demand for information, any information. Source verification and fact-checking became optional.

Tips flowing into the Boulder police were generally ignored if the information did not support the lead detectives' investigative theory "The Ramseys did it." Despite there being no prior reported incidents of domestic violence or child abuse within the Ramsey family, some Boulder police detectives came to the bizarre conclusion that the mother had accidently killed her daughter after becoming enraged over a reoccurring bedwetting incident, while the father helped stage the crime scene to look like kidnapping. Other detectives believed the father had killed his daughter and the mother helped stage the crime scene to look like a kidnapping, including her sitting down to write a rambling three-page ransom note.

When the Boulder police were notified of the presence of the unknown male DNA found under the victim's fingernails and on the crotch of her underwear—evidence which eliminated all Ramsey family members—this inconvenient truth was simply dismissed. One fundamental investigative principle cautions, "Do not allow the theories to dictate the facts, allow the facts to dictate the theories"—but this warning, too, was ignored. Investigative incompetence, inexperience, and a command failure, fueled by an intense politically charged environment, contributed to one of the worse miscarriages of justice in American history.

Twenty-five years, a critical milestone, has passed since the death of JonBenét Ramsey, and yet, despite the undeniable DNA evidence proving this crime was committed by an unknown male, most people around world still believe, "The Ramseys did it." The only person the Boulder police ever publicly cleared was JonBenét's older brother, Burke Ramsey. More than a dozen years have passed since the death of Lou Smit, the only man bold enough to step forward and say publicly, "The Ramseys didn't do it!" Since the passing of Lou Smit, his family and a handful of retired police detectives, including Dave Spencer, Kurt Pillard, Dick Reisler, and me, have stepped in to fill Lou's shoes and fulfill his last dying wish to find justice for JonBenét.

One of the unique features of this book is the 36 slides from Lou Smit's slide presentation. These 36 slides are being published here for the first time. The slides have been carefully down-selected from Lou's original 632 slide deck, several of which were shown by Lou to the Boulder Grand Jury. These 36 slides include crime scene, autopsy, and evidence photographs, along with Lou's original investigative notes. My comments also help serve as photo captions in this book. While many of these crime scene and autopsy photos have been published, and may be considered in the public domain, several of Lou's photos, including his stun gun photos, are being shown here for the first time.

I have organized this book into three parts: a beginning, middle, and an end. Part I, Chapters 1-3, explains why Lou Smit was so uniquely qualified to investigate this kidnap-murder which led him to conclude the Ramseys were innocent and why I am uniquely qualified to write this book. Part II, Chapters 4-6, explains Lou Smit's view of the crime scene and evidence which led him to develop his "Intruder Theory." Part III, Chapters 7-9, begins when Lou Smit resigned from the DA's Ramsey Tasks Force in protest over a grand jury being convened to indict JonBenét's parents and tells how he dedicated the rest of his life to solving this case. The last chapter ends by sharing what Lou Smit's family and friends have done since his passing in 2010 to fulfill his dying wish to continue his work to solve this case and find the killer of JonBenét.

I have written this book in hopes that: 1) lessons can be learned and best practices adopted by law enforcement agencies to prevent such a miscarriage of justice from reoccurring, 2) the truth coming out will help exonerate the Ramsey family, 3) advancements being made in DNA technology will be applied to help identify the killer through the analysis of the unknown male DNA found on JonBenét's body and her clothing, 4) this story being told now will assist in the passing of legislation requiring DNA evidence collected during criminal investigations of violent crimes to be ruled an open public record, and lastly, 5) one day there will be justice for JonBenét.

John Wesley Anderson, Author, Colorado Springs, Colorado December 26, 2021

Part I

Chapter 1 – Shoes

Lou Smit was not like all the other detectives I waited on at the front counter of the Identification Bureau in the Colorado Springs Police Department. He was more personable, detail-oriented, and engaging. The ID Bureau was where all the mug shots, fingerprints, criminal records, case reports, and traffic tickets were filed. It was the summer of 1972 and I was an 18-year-old police cadet, fresh out of high school with dreams of turning 21 and becoming a police officer. I never imagined the detective standing on the other side of the counter, with a toothpick tucked in the corner of his mouth, would become my best friend and a law enforcement legend.

Andrew Louis "Lou" Smit was born April 14, 1935, in Denver, Colorado. He was the second of four children born to his parents, Andrew and Henrietta Smit. Born during the Great Depression, Lou's family moved many times as his father looked for work. Lou enlisted in the U.S. Navy at age 17, where he travelled to many exotic places, including Japan and Hawaii. Part of his job, as a navigator on an airplane, was to learn Morse code. After the Navy he married his sweetheart, Barbara DeRuiter. They would have four children: Lori, Cindy, Mark, and Dawn.

Lou had earned an associate degree in electronics from DeVry Technical Institute, but struggled to find work to support his family. His cousin, Bill Thiede, a Colorado

Springs police officer, talked Lou into applying for the Department in 1966. The problem was the 5-foot 9-inch minimum height requirement—Lou was only 5 feet 8 ¾ inches. Lou really wanted to be a police officer and told Bill to whack him over the head with his nightstick. Later, at his medical exam, Lou measured exactly 5-feet 9-1/4 inches tall, including the bump on his head.

The ID Bureau, where I worked, was across the hall from the Detective Bureau. Whenever I saw Detective Smit coming up to the counter, I would race the other cadets to see what Lou needed.

"Hey, Johnny," Lou would say, "Can you check if this guy's got a record?"

Besides my mother and one other cadet, Rich Radabaugh, no one ever called me Johnny. I didn't necessarily like the name, but had to admit it sounded pretty good whenever Lou, my mom, or Rich called me Johnny. Lou had an older brother named John, whom I never met, and a brother, Larry.

Police work can offer abundant opportunities for laughter, which serves as a much-needed reliever of stress. However, police humor can come across as highly inappropriate, especially in polite societies, such as in church. But Lou was always comfortable in church. He and Barb regularly attended the Cragmor Christian Reformed Church after moving to Colorado Springs in 1966. Physical exercise was another important stress reliever for Lou. He belonged to the YMCA and worked out early in the mornings. Lou also loved to play racquetball and golf. He was great fun on a racquetball court or golf course and was good at most things. However, he was a lousy shot and struggled every quarter to qualify on the pistol range.

Although I was not with Lou at the time, I was aware he had shot and killed a man who had broken into city hall. Lou was on patrol at the time the burglar alarm came into police headquarters. One of the responding officers went to police headquarters, located across the alley from city hall, to retrieve a key to the building and as they started searching the building the suspect attacked an officer and then ran out the front door. Lou chased him across the street and, as he wrestled the burglary suspect to the ground, the man tried to take Lou's .357 magnum revolver away. During the struggle, Lou's gun went off and the suspect was shot and killed.

Years later, Lou would tell me, when no one was around to hear, what it was like to be inches away from the other man's face and watch, "as the fire went out of his eyes." Lou was a devoutly religious man and I know it bothered him, taking another man's life. In this case, the suspect had brought about his own death in trying to disarm the arresting officer. Suspects don't take your gun away and then simply hand it back to you—they intend to kill you with your own gun. Bottom line—although Lou was a gentleman, he could be one of the toughest men I would ever know and was determined to go home to Barb and his children at the end of the day.

I spent the first 18 months of my 22-½ year career with Colorado Springs Police Department (CSPD) as a police cadet assigned to the ID Bureau. In the middle of the night, when all of my paperwork was finished, I read every unsolved homicide case on file. I would talk with Lou about these unsolved murders. I studied the crime scene diagrams and autopsy photos. I memorized the victims' and suspects' names and studied the killers' modus operandi (M.O.). Today, these old unsolved homicide cases are referred to as "cold cases," but Lou always believed it was the detective's responsibility to keep these cases from growing cold. If nothing else, Lou would always say, "You have to stir the pot."

When Lou arrested someone for murder, I would read his reports to learn how he solved the case. What physical evidence led him to this suspect? How did he notify the victim's family the case had been solved? What questions did he ask the suspect? Lou always tied the suspect to the evidence and the evidence to the suspect. He would ask the suspect what clothing he was wearing, where he got the weapon, where it was now, where he was before committing the crime and where he went afterwards. Lou always wanted to develop additional witnesses or suspects, find additional evidence, and would ask a suspect who else knew about this crime?

If the suspect denied committing the crime and offered an alibi, Lou set out to either prove or disprove what the person said. In fact, there were times I wondered if he worked just as hard to prove someone hadn't committed the crime as he did to prove they did commit the crime. But what Lou's approach did was to strip away criminal defenses that often surface during a trial. In Lou's cases, defense attorneys had a difficult challenge attempting to establish the innocence of their clients. Lou had already eliminated most defenses: such as mistaken identify, self-defense or defense of others, or trying to prove a suspect lacked the mental capacity to formulate intent.

Lou's honesty, thoroughness, and objectivity earned him respect with prosecutors, defense attorneys, and the courts alike. Lou was the only police officer I knew to have his name and home address listed in the phone book. One time, Lou got a call from a defense attorney who asked Lou to go jogging together the next day in Monument Valley Park. As they were jogging, the defense attorney casually indicated to Lou where a witness was waiting. The defense attorney jogged on and Lou went to talk with the witness who was afraid to speak with the police and thought they were being followed. That person told Lou who had committed a recent murder and afterwards went on to become one of Lou's most reliable confidential informants.

Like most uniformed patrol officers, cadets in the ID Bureau worked 8-hour shifts, 21 days in a row and then were given 7 days off. When we returned from our days off, we rotated shifts: midnight shifts rotated to days, days to evenings, and evenings to mids. Twice a year, our rotation schedule created a "short-shift" and we worked 42 days in a row, without a day off, but no one ever complained. Many of the Department's top brass, when they were 18, had stood in line to volunteer to fight in the military at the beginning of WWII. Some were gone from home for three or four years. All of the "old guard" knew 17- or 18-year-olds who never made it home at all.

Before or after our shifts, or on days off, cadets were allowed to ride with uniformed officers. We weren't old enough to carry a gun or make arrests, but it was a great way to learn the job and the back alleys of the city. Some officers didn't want to be bothered with having a cadet as a rider, but most officers made time to "teach us the ropes." We all had our favorite patrol officers and learned which districts offered the most excitement. Sergeants were great fun to ride with because they covered half the city and didn't get stuck filling out a lot of paperwork.

One of our favorite patrol sergeants to ride with was Jerry Busemeyer. I had met Jerry when I was in high school. He raised cattle near our ranch in eastern El Paso County. I had helped Jerry work his cattle and always admired his physical strength. Three months into the job, on a hot September night in 1972, I was assigned to work the midnight shift in the ID Bureau. Since my shift didn't start until midnight, I showed up at the Department early hoping to get in a ride-along with Sergeant Busemeyer. When I arrived at the Department I found my buddy, Rich Radabaugh, had beaten me to the station and was already out riding with Jerry.

Reluctantly, I found myself riding with another officer, a nice enough guy, but I soon found myself standing in the middle of a busy intersection at Platte Avenue and Weber Street, directing traffic, while the patrol officer sat in a parked patrol car and filled out the paperwork on a traffic accident. He had the windows rolled down in the cruiser and I heard the excited voice of my friend Rich, on the radio reporting "shots fired" and calling for assistance. Sergeant Jerry Busemeyer had been shot. They had pulled over a suspicious vehicle in a rough part of town and while Jerry was walking up to the car, the driver jumped out and a gunfight erupted.

Rich was in the front passenger seat of the patrol car when he got on the radio to report shots fired. Then the dispatcher asked Rich their location. There was silence on the radio for a few seconds, and then Rich got back on the radio and reported their location. Rich later told me he didn't know where they were and had to get out of the police car and run to the nearest corner to read the street sign and then run back to the police car to report their location, all while the gunfight was underway. Although Jerry was shot, he was able to handcuff the suspect with Rich's help. It turned out the suspect was an escaped armed robber and the car had been reported stolen. Jerry was transported to the emergency room of the closest hospital.

Shortly before midnight, I reported for duty at the Police Department, as one of my heroes, Sergeant Jerry Busemeyer underwent emergency surgery at Saint Francis Hospital. The suspect who had shot Jerry was in a small holding cell near the booking desk and was refusing to give his name or be fingerprinted. Suspects being booked into jail always had their mugshots and fingerprints taken and one set of fingerprints—called a "Ten Print," along with the palmprints, called a "Flat Set"—sent to the FBI for identification purposes. Our booking clerks were not police officers; they were civilian employees and most were older WWII veterans. Police cadets often relieved the booking clerks when they took their lunch break or if they called off sick.

I liked working the booking desk, especially on a Friday or Saturday night, because there was always a lot of action. Sometime after midnight, the shift lieutenant came into the ID Bureau with two men wearing dark suits and ties. The lieutenant said they were FBI agents and had a federal court order directing the suspect's fingerprints be taken, with or without his cooperation. The lieutenant ordered me to go with the two agents and assist them in fingerprinting the man who had shot Sergeant Busemeyer. What I don't remember is where the regular on-duty booking clerk was at the time, but wondered afterwards if the shift lieutenant had told him to take a break.

I do remember escorting these two FBI agents to the gun locker, where they secured their handguns and then leading them to a small holding cell where the suspect was seated. We brought the suspect from the holding cell to a small room, about the size of a walk-in closet, where the fingerprint equipment and camera were located. The two agents showed the suspect their badges and the federal court order. The suspect continued his belligerent behavior and told the FBI agents where they could shove their court order and their badges. The two agents calmly took off their suit jackets, laid them aside, closed the door behind us, and the fight was on.

The suspect was not a small man, and this was obviously not his first fight. The fingerprint room had been built for two; the booking clerk and whoever was being fingerprinted, not four men now engaged in a heated brawl. I don't remember all the fights I was in during my thirty years in law enforcement, but I do remember that one! Both federal agents were fast and we were all three in good physical condition; however, the suspect was determined he was not going to be fingerprinted. But it was three against one and soon all four of us were wrestling on the floor.

We finally got the suspect flipped over on his stomach, with one arm bent up behind his back, and I sensed he was starting to tire. I know I was. His fists were clenched, but I pried one of his fingers loose and smeared black fingerprint ink on a fingertip and then tried to roll his print onto a white fingerprint card. The suspect saw what I was doing and intentionally smeared the ink on the card, making it illegible. The two agents managed to get both of the suspect's arms bent behind his back and applied more pressure. I started over again, inking his fingers while he continued to kick and scream. Eventually, the suspect gave up and agreed to cooperate. I decided right then and there—I am going to like working with the FBI!

A few days later, I stopped by Saint Francis Hospital to visit Jerry Busemeyer. He was out of intensive care by then and when I walked into his hospital room he was propped up in the bed. Jerry had tubes running everywhere, but seemed happy to see me. Maybe he was just happy to be alive, but he managed to talk in short breaths. He pulled the sheet down and showed me where the bullet, a .22, had entered his stomach. The bullet had bounced around inside his rib cage, perforating his intestines and other vital organs before finally coming to rest in a place where the doctors thought it best to leave it alone, rather than try to remove it surgically.

Jerry told me he felt intense pain when he got shot, but what kept him in the gunfight was knowing the cadet in the police car was unarmed. Jerry explained that during the shootout, when the suspect was on one side of the patrol car shooting over the hood at him, he was crouched down on the other side of the cruiser and fired a couple shots under the car trying to bounce the bullets off the pavement into the suspect. Sergeant Busemeyer eventually returned to duty, but never fully recovered from his wounds and was later medically retired. The suspect's fingerprints revealed a long criminal record and he was sent back to prison for first degree assault on a peace officer. One of Jerry's sons, Jerome, grew up to become an FBI agent.

Thirty-eight years after visiting Jerry in Saint Francis Hospital, I would return to visit my best friend, Lou Smit, as he lay dying in hospice care. But during those intervening years, my personal and professional life was enriched beyond anything I could ever have imagined through Lou's friendship. When it came to homicide investigations, I never met anyone more capable or more dedicated than Lou. While I continued with my dreams of wearing a blue uniform, working patrol and experiencing the thrill of driving red lights and siren across town, my dreams began to also include the thought of one day becoming a homicide detective and Lou Smit's partner.

One of the investigative fundamentals Lou understood well is Locard's exchange principle, or the Transfer Theory, which states, "The perpetrator of a crime will bring something into the crime scene and leave with something from it, and that both can be used as forensic evidence." In the JonBenét Ramsey murder, Lou pointed out that the duct tape, cordage, and stun gun had been brought into the Ramsey home, by the suspect, and this evidence proves the perpetrator's motive and intent: to immobilize and tie someone up so they can be controlled. Lou knew full well the key to solving the JonBenét case was what the suspect took with him—his DNA.

In the book, *Death of Innocence*, written by John and Patsy Ramsey, John tells how he and Patsy met Detective Lou Smit. John Ramsey told about Lou sharing a philosophy he developed as a young homicide detective. Lou told JonBenét's father how he felt at three o'clock in the morning looking down at the victim's lifeless corpse and wondering, "Who is he? How was he killed? Who did it? Why?" Lou shared how his attention was drawn to the victim's shoes. Lou wrote down these words, which he shared with his partners and JonBenét's father, "Shoes, shoes, the dead man's shoes, who will stand in the dead man's shoes?" Lou believed, "The detective stands in the dead man's shoes to protect 'his' interest against anyone else in the world."

Far too often the minds of the dedicated men and women in policing become seared with indelible memories experiencing the darker side of life. Cops see things and learn to use words that should not exist, such as erotic asphyxiation, petechia, and rigor mortis. Tragically, suicide is not uncommon in policing. I have probably read hundreds of Lou's reports, but one really stands as a testament of Lou's attention to detail. It was a murder-suicide where a police patrol sergeant, involved in a domestic argument with his wife, shot and killed her, and then called 911 before turning his 9mm handgun on himself. Lou's crime scene description alone was 26 pages long.

I asked Lou why he had written such an amazingly detailed crime scene description, while commenting at the time the case seemed rather open and shut; this was obviously not a homicide case that would be going to court. Lou replied that since this was a police officer, he wanted to ensure the scene was investigated impartially. If anyone ever read his report they would feel as if they were there and he just wanted to make sure he didn't leave any questions unanswered.

Those three investigative principles; 1) unbiased objectivity, 2) thoroughness, and 3) leave no questions unanswered, became part of the foundation upon which I, and so many of Lou's other homicide partners, built our careers upon. Sadly, the reason the JonBenét Ramsey homicide was not solved within weeks of her murder is that the foundation of that investigation was flawed from the very first day. JonBenét's homicide was: 1) not investigated impartially, 2) the crime scene was not secured and processed properly, and 3) there were far too many questions that remained unanswered—until now.

Chapter 2 – Partners

Boulder and Colorado Springs are geographically located less than 100 miles from one another, yet from a cultural and political perspective they are worlds apart. Nestled at the foot of Pikes Peak, Colorado Springs has served as the county seat for El Paso County for more than 150 years. With a strong business, religious, and military presence, El Paso County has historically been considered conservative. The City and County of Boulder, with the University of Colorado at its core, has always been guided by more liberal philosophies.

I was born on January 20, 1954, in Wayne, Nebraska, the second of three children born to my parents, Margie and John Reid Anderson. When I was two years old, my parents moved to Colorado Springs. They divorced the following year. My mother, Margie, found herself a single mom, struggling to raise three small children. She worked as a waitress at Michelle's, a nice restaurant in downtown Colorado Springs, popular with many police officers who dropped in frequently for coffee. They encouraged my mother to apply for one of the new "meter maid" positions being created. Two "civilian" women were to be hired to write parking tickets in the downtown area, freeing up uniformed police officers for other law enforcement duties.

Sergeant Harold "Red" Davis, a former U.S. Marine who had fought in the South Pacific during WWII, had recently returned from the Northwestern Traffic Institute in Chicago, Illinois. He presented a plan to Police Chief Irving

B. "Dad" Bruce to create a Traffic Division. Included was a recommendation to "civilianize" parking enforcement duties. In 1957, my mother applied for the position and was hired by Sergeant Red Davis. She was not only the first meter maid for the CSPD, but was the first hired in the State of Colorado. I still have her small brass uniform badge– Meter Patrol 1.

The Department was small at the time, less than one hundred officers, and everyone knew everyone, plus most of their families. My mother rented the basement of Captain Jess Spears's home. She later confided with me that when times were tough, Chief Dad Bruce loaned her money to make ends meet until payday, which was only once a month. During inclement weather, meter maids worked various jobs inside police headquarters. Mom often worked the telephone switch board located in a small room adjacent to the ID Bureau. I learned to operate the switch board when I was a cadet and thought of her every time I sat at that switchboard.

As a small boy, I would be dropped off at the Colorado Springs Day Care Nursery by my mother on her way to work. I remember clinging to the wrought iron fence encircling the playground, watching my mother, in her brown uniform, drive past on a 3-wheel Harley Davidson motorcycle. I couldn't believe anyone could get paid for doing such a fun job! My first bicycle came from the CSPD Impound Lot. I spent countless hours pedaling my bike down the street, pretending it was a police motorcycle. Before I was in kindergarten, I knew what I wanted to be when I grew up—a Colorado Springs Police Officer.

One day, Sergeant Red Davis approached my mother and told her he had a younger brother, Gary, who he wanted her to meet. The Davis' came from a large family, six boys and one girl, and Gary liked kids. They started dating and were soon married before a Justice of the Peace. When my mom and stepfather left on a short honeymoon, Gary's older brother Les Davis came to babysit us three kids. Les was also a Colorado Springs police officer and would become Lou's and my lieutenant in homicide. My mother and stepfather had two daughters together and then adopted my younger brother. We were a blended family of "yours, mine, and ours."

One day in 1962, my mother told us kids that President John F. Kennedy was in Colorado Springs. She made us put on our church-going clothes and loaded us up in the car. She drove to the east side of town and made us stand on a street corner for what seemed like hours. In reality, I'm sure it was less than an hour, but I would have rather been riding my bike. I remember seeing the President's motorcade coming slowly down the street, escorted by a dozen police motorcycles and patrol cars with flashing red lights. My Uncles Red and Les Davis were part of that police escort for President Kennedy. He sat on the trunk of his black convertible limousine.

There must have been hundreds of people lining both sides of the street to catch a glimpse of JFK. As the motorcade headed east on Boulder Street, President Kennedy waved and smiled at the crowd. As they passed by the corner where we stood, President Kennedy turned and looked right at me, waved, and smiled. I vividly remember his brilliant red hair, ablaze in the sun; his was the same color as Uncle Red's hair. It was not until I was much older that I learned the President's visit to Colorado Springs was connected to the Cuban Missile Crisis. I was only eight years old at the time, two years older than JonBenét Ramsey when she was murdered.

My stepfather worked for the Mountain Bell Telephone Company. As he moved up in the phone company, we moved to Cañon City. Three years later, he was promoted again and my parents bought a 160-acre ranch in eastern El Paso County. Pikes Peak was visible on the western horizon and Colorado Springs sat at its base. My sisters and I went to school in Ellicott. My favorite memories growing up were playing with our cousins and visiting our grandparents, Charles and Betty Davis. My grandfather was the caretaker of 11-Mile Dam for 33 years. They lived in the stone caretaker's house below the dam. During the holidays, my cousins and I would hide under the dining room table, listening to our uncles' war stories of being on the Department.

My first day as a police cadet was an evening shift assigned to the ID Bureau. I was told to report to Captain Jess Spears. He pointed to an older cadet, 20-year-old Mike Bowers, and said, "He'll show you what to do." After spending the first year and a half in the ID Bureau, I was assigned to the Impound Lot. I worked alongside my friend and fellow cadet, Rich Radabaugh, impounding abandoned or stolen cars and bicycles. Rich and I learned how to identify altered vehicle identification numbers (VIN). I became a court-qualified expert on altered Harley Davidson motorcycle VINs, while waiting for my 21st birthday to finally arrive.

In the 1960-70's, whenever police cadets tested for the CSPD, we were required to take the same Civil Service exam Lou had taken to become a police officer. Over 700 high school seniors crowded into the City Auditorium with me, in 1972, to take the written test for only five cadet openings. The written test was followed by a physical agility test, a polygraph examination, an interview panel and then a medical exam. I weighed 178 pounds and fortunately stood 6 feet tall, so I didn't have to be wacked over the head with a nightstick to meet the minimum 5-feet 9-inch height requirement. I placed number three on the list; Rich Radabaugh finished first.

Rich and I, along with three other cadets, were hired on July 16, 1972. Since we had already passed all the Civil Service tests to be police officers, the only other requirement when we turned 21, and were old enough to be sworn in as police officers, was to retake the medical exam with the City's doctor. Included were back X-rays to make sure we hadn't been injured since our last medical exam; back injuries were, and remain today, a major reason for medical retirements with police officers and firefighters, but retirement was the last thing on my mind. After waiting nearly all my life, I was finally going to be a Colorado Springs police officer.

Three days after my 21st birthday, I was told to report to Assistant Chief Red Davis in the police administration office on the second floor of the Department. Uncle Red issued me a new .357 magnum Smith & Wesson Model 19 six-shot revolver, handed me a box of ammunition and a silver patrolman's badge. The inventory control number engraved on the back, A3, identified it as having been worn by Bill Thiede, Lou's cousin, who had been promoted to Sergeant. Unlike some departments, we didn't use badge numbers when we wrote tickets or made arrests. We were identified by three-digit IBM numbers. These numbers were followed by a one letter designator, indicating where we were assigned.

That day I traded in my cadet badge and my previous IBM number 589C (C indicated Cadet), for my new IBM number, 122, previously issued to Captain Jess Spears, who had recently retired from the Department. I was honored to wear the badge Bill Thiede had worn on his uniform shirt and to have been reissued Captain Jess Spears's IBM number; I felt like they helped anchor me to the Department's storied past. I was determined to make my mother and the Davis family proud every day that I pinned that badge on my uniform and reported for duty.

For the next twenty years, I wrote the number 122P at the bottom of hundreds of traffic tickets and arrest reports; P indicated I was assigned to patrol. When I became a detective, I typed 122D at the bottom of my arrest warrants, booking sheets, and investigative reports. I was also issued a new detective's silver flat badge. When I worked with Lou as his partner in Homicide, he was one of the few detectives who knew that Les Davis was my uncle. With different last names, few people knew I was his nephew and I didn't want people thinking I was shown any favoritism on the Department-I wasn't. Like the other cadets, I didn't start on the "bottom rung of the ladder"-I started in the basement and worked my way up just to reach the bottom rung!

The first year on the CSPD, all Fourth Class Police Officers are considered "probationary employees"— meaning we can be terminated at any time, without an appeal. After the first year, when we became Third Class Police Officers, we received our first pay raise and became Civil Service employees, which meant we could have an administrative review for serious disciplinary matters, including demotions or terminations. Those of us who wanted to test for detectives were required to wait until we were First Class Officers. I never wanted to be a detective—until I met Lou Smit. My rookie year, 1975, was a particularly deadly year for the community and CSPD.

On May 14, 1975, the CSPD Lieutenant in charge of the Police Academy interrupted our class to announce our department's police helicopter had just gone down. The pilot, Officer Bernard Livingston Carter, had been killed, along with an unidentified passenger. The chopper burst into flames as it hit the ground and the two bodies on board were burnt beyond recognition. We waited hours, calling our friends to learn who among us was missing, before hearing the other man killed in the crash was an unauthorized passenger, a Division of Wildlife Officer.

Bernie Carter had been a homicide detective and was highly respected for having solved the case of the Candlelight Killer, along with his partner Neil Stratton. Homicide partners Killa and Trapp were another well-respected pair of detectives on the Department. Harry Killa and Kenny Trapp had been involved in a shootout near Saint Francis Hospital and both went on to have distinguished careers. Smit and Spencer emerged as another pair of respected homicide partners. Dave Spencer was from Goodland, Kansas. He had joined the Department on February 14, 1972. I continued to dream of one day being Lou's partner in homicide, but first I had to survive my first three years in Patrol.

The Police Department had not lost an officer in the line of duty since Patrolman Richard Stanley Burchfield was shot and killed on Thanksgiving Day, November 26, 1953. Sergeant Red Davis had drawn the crime scene diagram and the FBI assisted in the manhunt for the killer. The murder of Officer Burchfield became a cold case. Tragedy struck again on August 7, 1975, when motorcycle officer Dennis John Ives crashed on his police motorcycle while traveling southbound on I-25 at a high rate of speed. Officer Ives left behind two small boys; one went on to become a CSPD officer, the other a deputy with the El Paso County Sheriffs Office.

Before 1975 had ended, another traffic officer, Harry Lee Allen, was killed December 22, 1975, three days before Christmas. He had been investigating a traffic accident and was taking measurements for a diagram when he was struck by a hit and run driver. I knew these men. Their names are engraved on the Pikes Peak Region Peace Officer Memorial in Colorado Springs, located in Memorial Park. It is illuminated by a low blue light, a thin blue line that is meant symbolically to separate "Good from Evil." Unfortunately, more names will be added to this memorial and the police will not always be able to separate good from evil.

Evil came to Colorado Springs in 1975, in the form of Freddie Lee Glenn and Michael Corbett, responsible for at least five murders. Corbett and Glenn's killing spree began on June 19, 1975, with the kidnapping of Daniel Van Lone, a 29-year-old cook. Corbett, a soldier at Ft. Carson, along with another African-American soldier, kidnapped Daniel Van Lone as he was headed home from work at the Four

Seasons Hotel. They drove Daniel to a remote area, made him lie on the ground, and shot him in the back of the head. Their motive was robbery and they took everything Daniel Van Lone had with him at the time—his life and 50 cents.

The following week, they met another soldier, 19-year-old Winfred Proffitt, at Prospect Lake, supposedly to sell him marijuana. The soldiers had been training with bayonets at Ft. Carson and Corbett ran Proffitt through with a bayonet just to feel what it was like. Then on July 1, 1975, Corbett and Glenn, along with two other men, decided to rob the Red Lobster restaurant on South Academy Boulevard. They failed to get any money, but on their way out they grabbed 18-year-old Karen Grammer, who worked at the restaurant and was waiting for her boyfriend to get off work. They drove Karen to an apartment the men shared, where she was repeatedly raped.

Afterward they promised Karen they were going to drive her home and sat her in their car. They put a cloth over her head and drove her to a mobile home park on South Wahsatch Avenue. When they let her out of the car, Glenn, possibly high on LSD, stabbed Karen in the throat, hand, and back, and then left her to die. Lou told me how Karen staggered to a nearby house, with one light on, and reached for the doorbell before she collapsed and died. The image of Karen's blood smeared down the white doorframe, below the doorbell, would haunt Lou for the rest of his life.

The detectives did not know for certain who Karen was, until the next week when her older brother, Kelsey Grammer, came to Colorado Springs to identify her body. I wasn't on the scene for any of those murders; however, I was one of the first officers on scene July 25, 1975, when they shot and killed 21-year-old Winslow Douglas Watson III. I was still in training at the time and we were just blocks from the scene when we got the call. My training officer told me to talk to the witnesses and put out a description of the suspect's vehicle on the police radio.

I ran to the witnesses gathered on the street, near where the young black man lay, I got a few sketchy details of the suspect's car, which I put out on the radio as my training officer began mouth to mouth resuscitation. As I aired the vehicle description and direction of travel, I glanced over at my training officer, a white officer, trying desperately to keep the victim, a young black man alive until the ambulance arrived. Black lives always mattered to us as much as white lives or any other lives. Slowly the other officer stood up, his mouth drenched in blood and accepted a towel from a woman who had called in the shooting. Winslow Douglas Watson III was gone.

Assistant Chief Red Davis showed up on the scene, along with the detectives and the crime lab. It was Detective Lou Smit who finally connected this string of vicious murders to Corbett and Glenn. Both killers were arrested and convicted of multiple murders. In 1976, Freddie Lee Glenn was sentenced to the gas chamber for the murder of Karen Grammer. Two years later, the Colorado Supreme Court overturned the death penalty in Colorado. Glenn became eligible for parole in 2009. Karen's brother, Kelsey Grammer, by then a well-known actor with television roles such as Dr. Frasier Crane, had planned to appear before the Parole Board to ask that they deny the parole for the man he accurately described as a "butcher" and a "monster."

A rain delay at New York City's JFK International Airport caused Kelsey Grammer to miss his connecting flight to Denver, where he was to testify in front of the Parole Board at the Limon Correctional Facility. Detective Lou Smit and Bob Russel, the DA who had convicted Glenn and Corbett, were there and Glenn's parole was denied. Kelsey had written a letter to DA Russel, describing his younger sister as being, "so smart and good and decent...We could laugh for hours together." Kelsey shared his grief and guilt, "I was supposed to protect her—I could not. I have never gotten over it. I was supposed to save her. I could not. It very nearly destroyed me." JonBenét's father would share similar feelings in his and Patsy's book, *Death of Innocence*.

Lou was convinced Glenn and Corbett were responsible for more murders, including a cab driver who was robbed and murdered on Fort Carson. When I was Lou's partner, he asked me to go with him to the Colorado State Penitentiary, in Cañon City, to interrogate Inmate Michael Corbett, on this and other murders. I remember when this huge man entered the small interview room it felt like the room had suddenly shrunk. Corbett had spent hours every day lifting weights in the exercise yard and was one of the most massive men I had ever seen.

Neither Corbett nor Glenn ever cooperated with Lou, nor did he expect that they would, but Lou never gave up. Inmate Freddie Lee Glenn continues to come up for parole. At his last hearing in 2017, Karen Grammer's older brother, Kelsey, continued to voice his opinion that Glenn does not deserve any freedom and should remain behind bars for the rest of his life. Parole should not even be a consideration until all of the other "cold cases" these killers committed have been cleared. The victim's families deserve to know what happened to their loved ones. On June 24, 2019, DOC inmate Michael Corbett died of natural causes in a Denver-area hospital.

Another homicide Lou and his partner Dave Spencer investigated that we often discussed was at the Antlers Hotel in downtown Colorado Springs. On December 3, 1976, the body of Janet Kate Conrad, an employee in housekeeping, was found at 6:30 p.m. on the 10th floor in a service area. Kurt Pillard was the first officer on scene. Janet was 38 years of age. She had been dead about two hours. She was found nude from the waist down, bound, gagged, and had been strangled. Janet lived four blocks from the hotel. She was survived by her second husband, Ronald Conrad and four sons: Randy, Ronnie, Rex, and Ray French of Rocky Ford.

Detectives noted bruising on Janet's arms, knees, legs, and face. Her pants and underwear had been thrown to one side and her glasses had been broken. She was bound with a vacuum cleaner cord tied around her wrists so tightly it had dug into her flesh. Her breasts were scratched and gouged, and blood was found in her vaginal area. The coroner determined she had died as a result of asphyxiation due to strangulation. The day after Janet's murder, CSPD Lieutenant Adas Talley told the press there were no suspects in custody.

The following day, Monday, December 7, 1976, the Gazette Telegraph newspaper reported, "Colorado Springs detectives said they are anticipating a 'lengthy' and drawn-out investigation." No one could have imagined how lengthy and drawn-out this homicide investigation was going to be before it was solved. Detective Dave Spencer retired in 2000, Lou passed away in 2010, and Kurt Pillard retired in 2012. Fortunately, in Colorado there is no statute of limitations for First Degree Murder and the culture of the CSPD is to never give up on cold cases, and I was not about to give up on my dream of becoming Lou's homicide partner.

In 1978, I became a First Class Police Officer and was finally eligible to test for the Detective Bureau. The Chief's Secretary, Dorothy Phillips, was the only person who typed up the list for promotions. To keep everyone from calling throughout the day or hanging around her office asking how they had done, she had a practice of always posting promotional lists on the department's bulletin board by the back door, on Friday afternoons, as she was leaving work.

I lingered around the back door, along with 12-15 other anxious cops, and finally Dorothy came down the hall, posted the one-page list on the cork bulletin board with a thumbtack and left for the weekend. We all crowded around searching for our names on the list. There were 2-3 openings in the Detective Bureau and lists were ranked in order of how we finished. When I got close enough to read the names, I was crushed. There were 17 names on the list and my name wasn't among them. Surely there must have been a mistake! I knew everyone on the list and my performance evaluations, arrests numbers, and clearance and conviction rates were outstanding.

The following week I met privately with Lou to ask for his advice. He encouraged me to make an appointment with the Captain of Detectives to ask him how I could do better the next time the test was administered—which wouldn't be for another whole year! The Captain told me, "Look, John, you were only eligible to test by a few weeks, and if we would have brought you in to the Bureau now you would have been the youngest Detective in Department history." He also pointed out how I didn't have a single college credit to my name. College credits were not required at the time. I looked out his office door, where many of the detectives sat, and commented on how, except for Lou, most of those guys didn't have one college credit either.

He explained, "You asked for my advice and it's this; go down to Pikes Peak Community College (PPCC), sign up for next semester, take as many classes as you can and retest next year." I was really disappointed; one more year seemed like an eternity. I remarked, as I got ready to leave his office, that I didn't know college was going to be required to advance in the Department. He replied simply, "Times are changing."

I followed the Captain's advice, enrolled at PPCC, and started on an Associates Degree in Police Science. I concentrated on courses that would help me do better on the next test for detectives. I took courses such as Constitutional Law, Search and Seizure, Fundamentals of Investigation, and Forensic Science. By the time the next detectives exam was administered, I had completed ten courses, had accumulated 30 credit hours, and was maintaining a 3.90 GPA, all while working full time as a patrol officer.

My favorite college professor at PPCC was Bernie Barry. At the time he was teaching, he also served as the Chief of the PPCC Campus Police. Bernie had been a Manitou Springs Police Officer and a former El Paso County deputy sheriff. Bernie had a Bachelors Degree. When I was about to graduate, he took me aside and told me he would be very disappointed in me if I didn't go on to earn at least a Bachelors Degree. I appreciated his encouragement to pursue my higher education. As a student, I was impressed with Bernie's understanding of police administration and thought it was a shame he wasn't in charge of a major law enforcement organization.

Then something memorable happened; the CSPD Police Chief announced he was retiring. There were only two Assistant Police Chiefs, Carl Petry, who was in charge of the Detective Bureau, and Red Davis, my uncle and childhood hero. Petry announced he didn't want the job because he had planned to retire himself. Everyone, especially me, knew Red Davis would be a shoe-in for the next Police Chief, but it didn't happen. I was shocked when City Council passed over the entire command staff and selected a young police lieutenant, John Taggart.

The one thing John Taggart had that my uncle did not was a college degree, a Masters in Police Administration. My uncle had a high school diploma and a Purple Heart. I was heartbroken. Red Davis announced he would be retiring from the CSPD. Then, a few months later, something else remarkable happened; Uncle Red announced he was running for El Paso County Sheriff. I was elated! However, I had not yet registered to vote; you had to be 21 at the time. I headed to the El Paso County Clerk and Recorders Office to register to vote, but realized I didn't even know which party I needed to register in to vote for Uncle Red.

I pulled over at the next phone booth, and dropped a dime in the payphone—which tells you how long ago this was–and called my mother. Her sage advice was, "If you don't register Republican, your uncle will never speak to you again!" Uncle Red won and became the 24th Sheriff for El Paso County. Red Davis served as Sheriff from 1979-1983 and passed away during his second term. Bernie Barry, who had run against my uncle, finished Red's second term and would become the 25th El Paso County Sheriff. He served from 1983-1995. I would be elected the 26th Sheriff and Lou would be my Captain of Detectives, but I'm getting ahead of myself.

In 1979, when the next Detective test rolled around, I didn't finish first or second. I came in third, but that was good enough that year. I started in the Detective Bureau being assigned to property crimes. My office was just down the hall from the Homicide Unit, where Lou and Dave Spencer worked. Dick Reisler was a senior detective and taught me a lot about being a detective. On homicide callouts, when extra help was needed, Dick and I were loaned out to the homicide detectives. One skill I had developed was drawing crime scene diagrams. My mother's brother was an engineer and had taught me how to draw blueprints when I was in elementary school.

When my parents bought our ranchland, my stepdad asked me to draw the floorplans for our ranch house. I was only in the sixth grade, but those house plans were used by the carpenter to build our ranch house. Before I graduated high school, I had been hired to draw floorplans for a small business south of Ellicott, which I got paid to help build, and another home southwest of Calhan. I was working to help build that house when I got the phone call offering me the job as a police cadet on the Department. When I was in the Detective Bureau, another Detective, Kurt Pillard, asked me to draw the house plans for his and his wife's new home.

My crime scene diagrams became popular with the prosecutors at the DA's Office. Soon I was explaining my crime scene diagrams to grand juries and began showing other detectives how to use the drafting board, T-square, and other drafting supplies our Captain had purchased. Dick Reisler was transferred to homicide, and partnered with Dave and Lou, while I continued to be called out as needed. Eventually, another opening came up in homicide and I was selected. We worked two 3-man teams. One detective was assigned to the crime scene, one to the victim, and one focused on the suspect.

Now I had a front row seat to watch and study how Detective Lou Smit investigated a homicide, from the initial call-out to the arrest and ultimately a conviction. One of the first things I noticed was Lou and Dave Spencer didn't start taking their notes on a blank sheet of notebook paper, like the other detectives and I were doing. They were filling in the blanks on preprinted forms that included the essential information they needed to collect. When they sat down with a witness or a suspect, they followed along on the Interview Form and asked all the relevant questions: name, date of birth, place of birth, address, place of employment, nearest relative, etc.

If the victim's body was in the trunk of a car, they had a form to fill out to get a complete description of the vehicle and they had another form to complete on the victim. Experienced officers know what basic information needs to be documented on a crime scene involving a car: make, model, year, license number, etc. They probably also know the basic information that is important to document on a dead body: gender, race, age, hair color, clothing, etc. However, in the middle of the night, standing in a bloody crime scene, after you've been up 24 hours, without a blank box on a form waiting to be filled in, it's easy to overlook something: postmortem lividity, was the victim wearing any jewelry, what time the coroner arrived on scene, etc.

These forms were not part of the official police report, they were simply a more organized method of notetaking while a homicide was being investigated. When we got back to the Bureau, I watched as Dave and Lou dictated or typed their supplemental reports from the investigative notes they had completed at the crime scene or during an interview or interrogation. What I realized is these forms helped them document a much more detailed crime scene description, conduct a more thorough interrogation, and write a better police report. Plus, their supplemental reports were so well organized that all the critical information was presented in a logical order, rather than randomly jotted down on a blank piece of paper and scattered throughout a case file.

Finally, I asked Dave, "Hey, where can I get those forms?" He replied, "Ask Lou, he made them." Sure enough, Lou had created a dozen or more forms to help him take his notes. Lou carried copies of the forms in his notebook and was happy to loan me the original to make my copies. Until you've gone to your first couple dozen autopsies, it's easy to get overwhelmed by the sights, smells, and the sounds and fail to document critical information (e.g., rigor mortis, post-mortem lividity, petechial hemorrhages). Once I started taking my notes on Lou's forms, I was hooked. His systematic process of notetaking and report writing took a lot of pressure off me to make sure I wasn't forgetting something, and it immediately elevated my investigative skills.

During evening shifts, Lou and I discussed how we might improve upon the functionality and appearance of his investigative forms if I used the T-square and drafting table to draw boxes around the individual note sections. Then we tailored the size of each of the boxes according to how much information we might need for the specific fields. For example, the person's name, date of birth, height, and weight didn't require as much space as place of birth or the person's nearest relative, along with their contact information. After using the T-square and templates to customize each form, I typed the heading for each box in the upper left corner of that field.

Other CSPD detectives began using Lou's forms to take their notes. Then a handful of the DA's investigators began asking for copies of Lou's forms. Suggestions from prosecutors began to come in on what they would like to see added to the ALS (Andrew Louis Smit) forms, such as a check list to remind the detectives to ask if the suspect was left or right-handed, and a Miranda Waiver that could be read to a suspect during an interrogation. As homicide detectives, we worked closely with the DA's office and were all sworn investigators for the grand jury.

Most of our homicides were presented to the grand jury and after each case we conducted an informal debriefing with the prosecutors. We freely discussed what went right and where we could do better on the next case. Once I had started on my undergraduate and graduate degrees in business, I learned that what we had been doing all along was a systematic approach for "process improvement" based upon "best practices and lessons learned."

I mentioned to Lou that I thought it would be good to add a lead sheet that could be used to keep track and prioritize leads. At a glance we could tell who on our three-man team was going to follow up on what lead, and which ones had been completed. One of the things I soon realized about working with Lou or Dave or Dick Reisler was if there were three leads that needed to be completed you better grab one quickly, otherwise they would all be gone. If we needed to check to see if a witness, suspect, or victim had a criminal record, or we needed to pull together a photo line-up, you better raise your hand and say, "I got this." And if you volunteered for something, you absolutely got it done, usually before you went home or first thing the following day.

Lou had developed a method of using black three-ring notebook binders, with dividers, to organize his homicide case files. We adopted Lou's process of using those binders for our major cases and made up an identical set of notebooks for the prosecutors. When asked, we refused to make up a third set of notebooks for public defenders; they were on their own. We also incorporated Lou's method of case-file organization into our Major Case Investigations courses we taught around the state. When I first went into homicide, all the cold cases were kept in folders or binders of various descriptions in an unlocked file cabinet in the office. As more cold cases started to pile up, someone, probably a supervisor, moved all the cold case files to the basement, most likely to make room for more recent homicide case files.

I remember coming to work one evening shift and seeing Lou hauling these case files (I think there were about 35 cold cases at the time) out of the basement, one at a time, and then organizing them into black three-ring binders and putting them back on the shelf in plain sight. He printed out labels, along with a photo of the victim, laminated them and placed them on the outside spine of the black notebooks. "Not out of sight, not out of mind," was Lou's thinking—although he never had to verbalize it. With Lou Smit, actions always spoke louder than words.

This was during a time before there was widespread use of computers, but over the course of several weeks, Lou saw me watching him organizing these old cold cases and said, "You know Johnny, I think we can solve some of these." I remember replying, "I think we can solve all of them." Lou laughed and often repeated this story to other detectives, adding, "That's when I knew I wanted to work with this guy"—referring to me as one of his newer homicide partners.

One of Lou's and my most satisfying homicide cases together was a cold case that hadn't been assigned to either of us. The brutal kidnap-murder of Cynthia McLuen happened December 7, 1982, the day after one of my best friends, CSPD Officer Mark Dabling, was shot and killed during a traffic stop. Cynthia, a 22-year-old cosmetologist at a Walgreens, was abducted in the parking lot when she got off work late one night. The case was assigned to another detective who later resigned from the Department and the case lingered.

There were extenuating circumstances in the homicide investigation of Cynthia McLuen, a single mom working extended Christmas hours at Walgreens. Her partially nude body wasn't found until three weeks after her abduction. When investigating a homicide, the body of the victim is a critical piece to the murder triad, linking the victim and the suspect and the crime scene together. Weeks turned into months as investigative resources were focused on the murder of Officer Dabling. Cynthia also deserved our best efforts, but I felt she received something less. Four years later Lou arrested James Lamar Rhodes for the murder of Cynthia McLuen.

The night Mark was killed, I was working a surveillance detail with Art Sapp, another of my CSPD Academy classmates. When the "officer down" call was broadcast on the police radio, we didn't know it had been Mark who was shot. The suspect, an escaped felon from Florida, Vernon Wayne Templeman, had robbed a bank in Boulder earlier in the day and had driven a stolen car to Colorado Springs, where he checked into the Holiday Inn North on Fillmore and I-25. After checking into the motel, the suspect decided to drive to get something to eat.

Mark spotted a car making an illegal left turn onto Fillmore Street, at a busy intersection on the north end of Colorado Springs. The intersection was notorious for accidents, often caused by cars making an illegal left turn. When Mark turned on the overhead lights of his marked CSPD patrol car, he followed procedures and called in his location and vehicle license number—it would be his last radio transmission. As Mark approached the car, the suspect leaned out of the passenger window and fired a shot from a sawed-off rifle, as Mark ran for cover.

Witnesses in a nearby fast food restaurant saw what had happened and ran out to help the fallen officer as the suspect in the stolen car drove away. Art and I couldn't leave our assigned posts and we listened to the police radio traffic as other officers arrived on the scene. Mark was rushed to the nearest hospital. Before I transferred to Detectives Unit, Mark and I had worked the street together for several years. His locker was just a few down from mine. I saw him nearly every day when we came to work or went home. It was an excruciating experience for Art and me, waiting, and praying together, that Mark would make it out of surgery. He wouldn't. Hours later, the suspect who shot Mark was arrested driving another stolen car, fleeing southbound on I-25 from Colorado Springs.

Art's and my stakeout panned out and we made an arrest at about 2 a.m. The restaurant, The Hatchcover, had been broken into the night before and one of the items stolen was the business safe, which weighed about 150 lbs. (the suspect weighed around 135 lbs). The burglar was a former cook at the seafood restaurant in southern Colorado Springs. The burglary at The Hatchcover had been on the morning of December 6th and at about noon the restaurant's safe was discovered under some shrubs in a decorative cement planter. Patrol officers determined the suspect had removed the safe from the back of the restaurant; however, he had been unable to force it open or carry it away where he could pry it open.

The safe had been discovered by the manager of a dry cleaner located in the same shopping center as The Hatchcover. The dry cleaner's manager offered to let the police hide inside the location overnight to see if the burglar returned after dark to claim the stolen safe. The detective captain had approved overtime for two detectives to set up surveillance on the stolen safe and arrest the suspect if he returned. Art had already volunteered and was walking through the Detective Bureau looking for a surveillance partner. I always liked Art, plus I was starting vacation the next day and wouldn't return until January 2nd. Any overtime at Christmas was always appreciated. I hadn't used any vacation all year and was in a "use it or lose it" situation.

When our burglary suspect returned in a car to claim the stolen safe, Art and I saw him back the car up as close as he could to the planter, pop open the trunk, and then we watched in amazement as he lifted the heavy safe out of the planter and started carrying it to his car. After we arrested him, we called in a marked patrol car to transport him to the station and then we impounded the suspect's car. We returned the stolen safe to the owner and then headed into the station. The suspect confessed to the burglary, told us where the other stolen items were located, which included a professional set of chefs' knives, and then we booked him into county jail.

As I was placing some of the evidence from our burglary into an evidence locker, I came across a handful of other detectives working Mark's homicide. The image of them hanging up Mark's blood-soaked uniform shirt on a hanger to air dry is an image I will never forget; his CSPD shoulder patch was completely saturated and stained red from his blood. I often think about Mark's and my last conversation, when he told me he had nominated me for Outstanding Young Men of America for 1986. Mark Dabling had been nominated the previous year.

I don't know that I ever measured up to being one of America's Outstanding Young Men—but Mark Lane Dabling did. During my 30-year career in law enforcement, I have known nine officers personally who were killed in the line of duty. One thing I can tell you is you always lose your best. I don't know what it is; maybe by their nature they are always first to step into the breach, to run to danger, toward the sound of the gunfire, when human nature is to run the other way. Thank God there are men and women who choose to run to danger, to confront evil.

The lead homicide detective assigned to investigate the death of Officer Mark Dabling was Dave Spencer. He was supported by Lou Smit, undeniably the best partner anyone could ever have. The homicide case file they assembled filled 12 black three-ring binders, each three inches thick and every detail was organized to where it could be found within seconds. Dave and one of the DA investigators retraced the suspect's path of violence across the nation. They drove from where the suspect escaped from prison in Florida, to Chicago, where another police officer had been shot and wounded, then to California, and on to Boulder, Colorado, where he robbed a bank.

The suspect was tried, convicted, and sentenced to life in prison, but I could tell this case took a toll on Dave. Lou said, "As a homicide detective, you die a little bit with every victim." But with every case you learn a little bit more and as a team you grow a little stronger. As more detectives and other agencies began using Lou's forms, suggestions flowed in on how to improve the forms and the investigative process. We divided the packet into three sections: the Initial Phase, the Follow-up Phase, and the Prosecution Phase.

Lou bought a Mac Plus personal computer and a laser printer. The printer weighed about as much as a Volkswagen engine, but what a game changer! Later, Lou talked me into buying a Mac Plus and a laser printer and he started using AutoCAD to draw crime scene diagrams. We copyrighted our Major Crimes Packet to prevent someone from stealing our work. I launched a small business, the Criminal Investigations Institute, and Lou was a silent partner. We talked about developing a software program so the forms could be completed in the field, at a crime scene, or during an interview by using a handheld device or a laptop computer. However, neither were affordable at the time. Lou was always ahead of his time when it came to technology.

Lou and I, and sometimes Dick and Dave, were asked to teach other detectives and prosecutors how we investigated major crimes and used our Major Case Investigation Packet. We added a glossary of terms to the back, where detectives could at a glance make sure they were spelling a word correctly and applying the term properly. We assembled slide presentations on several of our cleared homicide cases which we presented during our two-day Major Case Investigation training courses. We demonstrated how to complete the forms properly and organize their major case, such as a homicide. On the first page of our packet, Lou included a quote he always thought epitomized the role of the detective: "The investigator stands in the dead person's shoes to protect their interests against those of everyone else in the world."

There is one other enduring quality of Lou Smit that made him different from any of the other homicide detectives I've ever known, and that was his deep religious conviction. Most of the cops I worked with were spiritual in one way or another. A few were Methodists, like me; others were Baptists, or Mormons, and a few were raised Catholic or Jewish, some practicing, most were not. Then there was Lou. If we were called out on Saturday night, he would not turn in an overtime slip past midnight, because in his faith, Sunday the Sabbath was a Holy Day. Although we might be on a case, if Lou was not being paid, in his mind he was not "working."

Homicide detectives were issued take-home cars and when we were called out, we drove straight to the scene, hospital, or wherever the sergeant told us we were needed. When Lou arrived at the scene, he took his time getting out of the car. I'm sure most patrol officers thought he was just making notes, which he was prone to do using a small tape recorder, but I had ridden with him several times to crimes scenes and was personally familiar with his practice of always saying a silent prayer at each scene before starting a homicide investigation. He shared with me that his prayer was intended for the victim and their families.

Lou continually asked God for His guidance. One of Lou's quotes was to acknowledge that he was, "Just an ordinary detective with an extraordinary partner." After a case was finished, once we had a conviction, Lou would always return to the scene of the crime and say a prayer, thanking God for his guidance in solving the case. In his billfold, Lou carried a wallet-size photo of each victim of his unsolved homicides; included was a photo of JonBenét. And every night, before he went to bed, Lou prayed on his knees, mentioning each victim by name.

One of the lessons I learned early in my career as a police officer is people will lie to you—accept it, expect it, especially if they have something at risk of losing. What I learned from Lou was the importance of this lesson in solving homicides and getting a conviction in court. You must anticipate this flaw in human nature—people are going to lie. Your job is to document the falsehood and then prove it as false. If a suspect said they acted in self-defense, document it. At least they can't change their story later saying they weren't there and if you can't disprove the person acted in self-defense, perhaps they did-your job is to prove it one way or the other.

One of the first things rookies are taught on domestic violence calls is to separate and then interview the couple to find out what had happened. If one person has a fresh bruise to their right eye, ask if the spouse is left-handed and check to see if there are bruises on the children. Only 11% of the human population is left-handed and injuries to the face are usually caused by someone facing the victim while striking them with a closed fist. Eliminating 9 out of 10 possible suspects by wounds caused by left-handed people, especially if they have a history of domestic violence within the family, is a good start to a domestic violence investigation.

If a person has abrasions on their knuckles, document the wounds, take photos, and ask how the injuries happened. If a wife says she got the black eye by walking into a door, ask her if this happens to her a lot. If she says she can be rather clumsy at times, check to see if she has other injuries and if her husband is her only means of financial support. Fortunately, during my 30-year policing career, legislation was enacted which forced police officers, doctors, and teachers to become mandatory reporters of domestic violence or sexual assault on children. Issuing temporary restraining orders became required and safe houses were established. Training for mandatory reporters became widely available statewide and we learned that domestic violence and sexual assault on children were not isolated events, but patterns of violent behavior and sexual abuse that will continue without some sort of dramatic intervention.

What I learned from Lou was to lock a suspect into a lie, any lie—and then break down the false statement. On a homicide where the victim was sexually assaulted, Lou would ask the suspect if he knew the victim. Was he was ever with the victim? Was he inside the residence where the crime occurred? If he said, "No, I was never there, I didn't do it." Lou would carefully write that statement down and follow-up with questions connected to the physical evidence, "How can he explain that his fingerprints were found at the scene or his seminal fluid discovered on the victim's underwear?" If the suspect later took the stand in court and changed his story, the prosecutors can always ask him, "Were you lying then or are you lying to us now?"

Working as a team was a great learning opportunity and with each new homicide case, we rotated assignments. One team was on "call-out" for a week at a time, and then the other team took over for a week. We still worked our regular shifts, two months of 8-hour day shifts, followed by one month of evening shifts. Call-outs were frequent, especially on weekends, and we routinely worked well beyond our 8-hour shifts. Working 24 or even 48 hours in a row was not at all uncommon and I remember working 72 hours once. Overtime pay, at time and a half, was welcomed, but we were expected to produce results—measured in cases cleared by arrest.

Over the years, working dozens of homicides together, Lou and I, Dick and Dave, and the other CSPD homicide detectives became very proficient at wound pattern interpretation. We attended autopsies to document the results and other important information from the coroner (e.g., manner and cause of death, estimated time of death, internal injuries). This also gave us an opportunity to learn the medical-legal side of homicide investigations. We would compare our interpretations of an injury or a wound with the coroner, who in El Paso County almost always was a medical doctor and board-certified pathologist, in addition to being an elected official.

In time, we learned to differentiate a stab wound caused by a single-edged or double-edged knife, if the wound was caused by a person holding the weapon in their left or right hand, and if the suspect was facing the victim or attacked from behind. At a crime scene we were expected to immediately recognize patterns of post-mortem lividity on a body that were inconsistent with how the body was found lying, suggesting the body had been moved. We learned to identify stab wounds consistent with picquerism or paraphilia commonly used in acts of sadomasochism, where a person derives sexual gratification from their acts of torture and inflicting pain.

These skills cannot be learned from reading a book— they have to be acquired through years of experience, from being at one crime scene after another, from leaning over a victim's body in the middle of the night and standing alongside the autopsy table at eight o'clock the next morning. To become good at homicide investigations, you have to work for years with experienced crime scene investigators in the field, accompany expert interviewers into interrogation rooms, and watch forensic experts in the crime lab. You have to skillfully be examined on the witness stand by seasoned DA prosecutors and then be cross-examined by competent defense attorneys in the courtroom. And then, to become really good, teach these skills to someone else. When it came to homicide investigations, there was no one better to learn from than Detective Lou Smit.

One of the most memorable adventures I shared with Lou was a mysterious trip to meet Miss Lee. Miss Lee worked at a massage parlor on the south side of town, often frequented by Ft. Carson soldiers on "GI paydays." On September 19, 1974, a soldier from Ft. Carson entered the massage parlor and viciously attacked Miss Lee and another massage therapist, who also was a young Asian female. The man tied up both women, slit Miss Lee's throat with a knife, shot the other woman, robbed the business, and then set the building on fire. Miss Lee managed to untie herself and survived the brutal attack; the other woman did not.

Lou arrested the suspect, who was positively identified by Miss Lee, as the man who had slit her throat, killed her friend, and set the massage parlor on fire. Eventually, the case went to court and the suspect was convicted and sentenced to life in the Colorado State Penitentiary. This case happened before I became Lou's partner, but he talked often of Miss Lee. He admired the courage she demonstrated to survive such a vicious attack and identify the suspect in court, so he could be sentenced to life in prison and not remain free to attack anyone else in the future.

Some people might be quick to judge Miss Lee and the other victim for working in a massage parlor or think of them as prostitutes. But Lou always spoke respectfully of Miss Lee, almost as if she were royalty. I don't know if it was from Lou having spent time in Japan while he was in the Navy, but he held Miss Lee, who was born in Japan, in very high esteem. Miss Lee moved away from Colorado and eventually married. She and her husband raised a family, but she always covered up the scars on her neck with a scarf and didn't tell anyone about nearly being killed working in a massage parlor. Every year, Lou and Miss Lee exchanged Christmas cards, but he was always guarded about her whereabouts and real name.

In 1983, two serial killers, Henry Lee Lucas and Ottis Elwood Toole, began confessing to multiple murders across America. Lucas had been convicted of 11 murders and Toole of six murders. Serving multiple life sentences, the two serial killers enjoyed the notoriety as detectives, anxious to clear their unsolved cases, made trips to the prisons where Lucas and Toole were being held. The two became adept at listening to what crimes the detectives wanted them to confess to, and they picked out small details in the crime scene photos they were shown to make it appear as if they had been at the scene of the murders.

One of the murders Ottis Toole confessed to committing was the murder at the massage parlor in Colorado Springs. This false confession was brought about by the defense attorney for the Ft. Carson solider who had been convicted. The attorney claimed his client was innocent and had been misidentified by Miss Lee. This attorney paid two private investigators from Colorado Springs to go to the prison where Ottis Toole was incarcerated. They showed him photos taken by the CSPD crime lab and not surprisingly, Toole confessed to that murder as well.

When the investigators returned to Colorado Springs, the attorney shared details Toole had provided them that only could have been known by the killer. Then he demanded the prosecution make Miss Lee available to be questioned by his two investigators and shown a photo of Ottis Toole, to prove he was the real killer. The problem was Lou Smit was the only person who knew Miss Lee's real name and where she lived. The defense attorney demanded Lou reveal her real name and address, otherwise his client must be set free. This attorney had lost other cases to Detective Smit and knew Lou would never disclose Miss Lee's real name or her address.

As a compromise, the judge agreed to let Lou meet with Miss Lee to re-interview her and show her a photo of Ottis Toole, confirming he was not the man who had assaulted her and slit her throat. The two private investigators started following Lou, hoping to catch him talking with Miss Lee. They were being paid to find out who she was and where she lived, so she could be subpoenaed to appear in court—all along, hoping she would not show up and their client would be freed. Lou knew he was being followed and asked me if I would like to meet Miss Lee. He spoke so often and respectfully of her it felt as if Lou was inviting me to meet Princess Diana.

Of course I jumped at the opportunity and Lou explained he had it all arranged. He told me to pack enough clothes for three days and bring a carry-on bag to work with me the next morning because we needed to travel fast. He explained that we might have to change planes one or more times to make sure we were not being followed, and we could not risk having to wait for our luggage at baggage claims. He told me we could not carry our guns; he had that covered on the other end. He could not tell me where we were going—in retrospect I don't think our sergeant even knew where we were going, except that it was to meet Miss Lee.

I told Lou, "Count me in!" This was exactly the kind of adventure I enjoyed sharing with Lou. I didn't know where we were going or who would be meeting us when we got off the plane. However, this was in the middle of winter, so I asked Lou if he could at least tell me what to pack—were we going to need coats and warm clothes? I will always remember Lou's smile and the twinkle in his blue eyes, when he replied, "You may want to pack your swimming suit."

The next morning, I parked my detective car in the lot behind the Detective Bureau, where we normally park. I grabbed my overnight bag, went inside, locked my gun in my desk drawer, and waited. About mid-morning, Lou came up to me and asked, "Are you ready, Johnny?" I grabbed my bag and said, "Let's go." I followed Lou out the back door and saw Barb, Lou's wife, waiting in her car parked in the alley. I jumped into the back seat and helped Lou watch to make sure we were not being followed. Lou gave directions for Barb to follow a round-about route to the Colorado Springs Airport. Lou kissed Barb goodbye and we walked inside.

Lou checked to make sure our flight was on time and it was. He then bought me breakfast as we watched to make sure no one was following us. I still didn't know where we were going. After breakfast, we talked casually as departure flights and gates were being announced. "That's us," Lou announced, as I grabbed my bag and followed him down the concourse. There were several gates ahead of us and Lou waited until, "Final boarding call for flight such and such," was announced. I followed Lou. We were the last two to board the plane bound for somewhere.

Our plane pulled away from the gate and headed for the runway. It was starting to snow lightly and I listened intently as the pilot came over the intercom to welcome us on board and announced our arrival time and the current temperature in sunny Las Vegas! I turned to Lou, sitting in the seat next to me with a wide smile on his face. I asked just to confirm I had heard correctly, "We're going to meet Miss Lee in Las Vegas?"

"Yep," he said, with a toothpick clutched between his smiling lips. It was a smooth flight and when we landed, we grabbed our carry-on bags from the overhead compartment. I followed alongside Lou as he led us through the terminal to Passenger Pickup and watched to make sure we weren't being tailed. We stepped out of the airport into the warm desert air, and Lou nodded toward a newer model dark sedan parked along the curb, "There's our ride." I recognized the man popping open the trunk was none other than retired CSPD Lieutenant Ad Talley!

"Welcome to Vegas!" Ad said with a firm handshake. Talley had been legendary CSPD detectives Harry Killa and Kenny Trapp's Lieutenant in Homicide when I was a police cadet. I had waited on him countless times when he came to the counter in the ID Bureau, looking up information on a suspect or a case. Ad had been retired from the Department for a number of years. I wasn't sure he would even remember me. I think I was still just a teenager the last time we had met, but being with Lou always gave me immediate credibility with the "Old Guard."

Now, for anyone at the Department who knew Lieutenant Talley, they would agree, Ad was in his element in Las Vegas. Wearing a dark suit and brightly colored tie, he looked like a Las Vegas pit boss, and he might have been. For most people who didn't know Adas Talley, picture a stern-looking sixty-something, heavily tattooed white man, with well-groomed silver hair combed back, about 5-11 in height, weighing around 215 pounds, and smoking a cigarette. Ad had been in the U.S. Navy during WWII and had once been in a motorcycle gang.

He was tough as they come and looked like he could have been an extra in the 1953 film, *The Wild One*, riding a Harley Davidson motorcycle alongside Marlon Brando. That film became a cultural icon as the original outlaw biker film in the 1950s and helped to launch the era of motorcycle gang violence in America. I didn't ask, but knew Ad was heavily armed. He drove us around Vegas to shake off any tail, and then pulled into the valet parking in front of the 31-story Landmark Hotel and Casino, located just east of the Las Vegas Strip.

It's not there anymore, but back in its heyday The Landmark was owned by billionaire Howard Hughes and featured such entertainers as Frank Sinatra and Danny Thomas. With its huge rotating restaurant on top of the building, this architectural marvel was a cultural icon for Las Vegas, Nevada. We rode the elevator to the top floor, where the entrance to the rotating restaurant was located. It was now in the middle of the afternoon, and I wasn't sure if the restaurant was even open. It may not have been, but Ad spoke to the maître d' who led us over to a huge private booth with a magnificent view of Las Vegas.

Talley waited outside the restaurant to make sure we, "Weren't bothered," while Lou and I ordered something non-alcoholic to drink and waited for Miss Lee to arrive. When she walked in, I knew instantly who she was and saw she was every bit as beautiful as Lou had described. Dainty, impeccably well-dressed, dark sunglasses; she was obviously nervous but so happy to see Lou again. She had told her husband she was going somewhere, other than Las Vegas, to meet someone, but certainly not a homicide detective from Colorado Springs.

That moment, meeting Miss Lee in Vegas with Lou was one of the highlights of my career as a homicide detective. We three settled into the high-backed booth and talked for well over an hour. She did not recognize Ottis Toole's photo and reaffirmed her assertion that the man Lou had arrested in Colorado Springs was the man who had tried to kill her and murdered her co-worker. Miss Lee wore a beautiful silk scarf around her neck to cover the scars she would carry for the rest of her life. She pulled down her scarf just enough to reveal the healed wounds to her throat and said in her soft voice, "You never forget the face of the man who did this to you."

After Miss Lee left, Ad drove Lou and I to a different hotel casino where Lou had reserved the two of us rooms. I don't remember where we stayed; Lou and I had been to Vegas several times together and he liked staying downtown, so we may have been at the Four Queens. After we checked in and went up to our rooms, Lou began to organize his notes and write up his report while everything was still fresh in his mind. I asked what I could do to help and he assured me he had it covered. After a couple hours, he had dictated his report into a portable tape recorder; Lou always had the latest and smallest model available on the market.

After all his supplemental reports had been written and our work for the time being was finished, Lou suggested we put on our swimming suits and start enjoying Vegas by the pool. Lou might have finished with what he needed to do in meeting with Miss Lee, but I knew he wasn't finished with Ottis Toole. After we returned to Colorado Springs, Lou flew to Florida where he began a methodical search to discover where Ottis Toole was on the day Miss Lee was attacked and her coworker was murdered. Lou found and interviewed Ottis Toole's mother, who recalled her son being upset, at around that time, over a flat tire on his car. She remembered Ottis had thought someone had stabbed a knife into the sidewall of the tire, and reported it to the police.

Lou then drove over to the local police department and found they had a police report on file for the incident. The date on the police report in Florida was the same date Miss Lee was attacked in Colorado. Then Lou drove to the prison where Ottis Toole was being held and asked to speak with the convicted serial killer. They visited for a while and Ottis said he remembered two investigators from Colorado coming to see him and then told Lou he had robbed the massage parlor, stabbed the two Asian women who worked there, and then set the building on fire.

Then Lou asked Toole if he remembered the time someone punctured the tire on his car with a knife in Florida. Toole told him he does remember that incident, described which tire it was and was mad because he had to buy a new tire as the hole was in the sidewall. Lou asked him where he bought the replacement tire, how much it cost, where he went the next day, what he was doing the day before, and who might have punctured his tire. What Lou did not tell Toole at the time, was that the date the tire was flattened in Florida was the same date the murder happened in Colorado

Springs. Instead, Lou asked Ottis about where he had been in Colorado and learned Toole only had a vague recollection of Colorado for having trees and mountains.

Lou returned to Colorado Springs and told the District Attorney, Bob Russel, about the police report proving Ottis Toole was lying about committing the murder at the massage parlor. Then Lou and Bob Russel both flew back to Florida to confront Ottis Toole with the fact he could not be in two places at the same time, only this time he would be videotaped. I watched the video several times; it was a masterful interrogation. It began with Lou reconnecting with Toole, introducing DA Russel, and then locking the serial killer into a false murder confession on tape.

Then Lou got Toole to tell the DA all the details about the day the tire was sliced on his car. Lou held a copy of the police report in his hand and after going over the smallest details, he pointed to the date on the police report, and told Toole that was the same date as the murder in Colorado Springs. Ottis Toole was not the sharpest tool in the tool shed, but he was smart enough to know Lou had trapped him in a lie. In the video you see Toole lean back in his chair and smile a goofy grin at Lou. Then he admitted to Lou and Bob he had lied about the murder.

Then Lou got Toole to admit how he managed to provide details of the crime to detectives. Toole said he would look at the crime scene photos and find some small detail in the background or something unique to the victim. During the discussion he would describe what the victim was wearing or ask detectives if she had a rose tattoo on her ankle. When they said yes and showed him a photo he would say, "Yes, I remember that tattoo." In Lou's case it was a coffee can containing a handful of coins. The gig was up and the video of Toole recanting his confession made national news. It would not be the last time Lou's investigative skills made national news.

Law enforcement agencies across the country were suddenly in the precarious position of "unclearing" their homicide investigations if they had closed their case based solely upon the false confession of a serial killer. Some police agencies had the moral courage to admit they had made a mistake, others decided to "leave well enough alone." When DA Russel returned to Colorado, the judge denied the defendant's motion for a new trial and ordered the killer to serve out his life sentence—thanks to the investigative talents of one man, Detective Lou Smit.

On another homicide case, I came into the office late one afternoon and Lt. Davis assigned me a routine follow-up lead on a homicide case. He knew I was already working another murder; however, he said the other team was spent—they had been out all night and he needed me to interview a possible witness, the victim's ex-boyfriend at Ft. Carson. Lt. Davis explained the body of the victim, known as "Lady," had been found in the trunk of her car, a newer model Ford Thunderbird. She was found strangled with a pair of pantyhose wrapped around her neck.

Lt. Davis explained the last person to see Lady alive was a gardener at the apartment complex where her ex-boyfriend lived. The apartment complex was located about a mile north of where Lady's car had been found. The gardener knew the ex-boyfriend, known as "Nolle," and he also knew Lady and what her car looked like. The gardener told one of the other detectives that he saw Lady getting into the passenger side of her Thunderbird, while Nolle held the door open for her, and then he saw Nolle get into the driver's seat and drive away. The gardener said this was late in the afternoon on the day prior to Lady's body being found in the trunk of her car.

Early the next morning, Lady's car had been driven off the roadway, near the Colorado Springs Airport, where it struck a piece of heavy equipment parked along the road, and her car had been set ablaze. A newspaper delivery person, driving east on Airport Road, had nearly run over a tall, slender, light-complected black man, in his twenties, who was running north across Airport Road, away from the burning car. Lt. Davis explained Lady's ex-boyfriend, Nolle, was a soldier at Ft. Carson and was the last person seen with Lady. Nolle was described as a short, dark-complected Puerto Rican man and was confirmed to have been on guard duty at Ft. Carson at the time the victim's car had been set on fire in what appeared to be a staged traffic accident.

When I contacted Nolle on Ft. Carson, he was in the Criminal Investigations Division (CID), but was not in custody because he was only considered to be a possible witness in the murder of his former girlfriend. After I identified myself and began the interview, we talked for about 45 minutes, covering when and how they met, how long they had been intimately involved, and when and why they broke up. Nolle was friendly and cooperative, but knew nothing about her murder. He told me he and Lady had dated for several months, but ended their relationship a month ago, after his wife said she was moving to Colorado Springs to be with him at Ft. Carson.

As I wrapped up the interview, I asked Nolle when and where he had last seen Lady alive. He said he last saw Lady at a bowling alley, near Ft. Carson, several days before her death. He had just lied to me! The only reason to lie to me was to distance himself from the time of Lady's murder. But Nolle did not look anything like the tall, slender, light-complected black man in his twenties who had been seen running away from the scene—in the direction of Nolle's apartment.

Rather than confronting Nolle about why he had just lied to me, I asked him, "Do you live alone or do you have a roommate?" He said he had a roommate, another Ft. Carson soldier, who he described as a tall, slender, light-complected black man in his twenties. Nolle said they were in the same company and gave me the other soldier's name. Another problem I had to resolve was confirming Nolle was not initially considered a suspect. I hadn't advised him of his Miranda Rights and needed to make certain what he had told me was admissible in court. Plus, I was on Ft. Carson, a federal military installation, where I did not have any law enforcement jurisdiction.

I had to make certain Nolle didn't think he was in custody when he made what I believed was going to be a very incriminating statement, but I also didn't want to be accused of letting a killer go free. So I thanked Nolle for his cooperation, sat him in a chair in the hallway outside of the interview room, and walked down the hall to have a cup of coffee with a CID polygraph operator who I knew from another case. When I returned Nolle was nowhere to be seen. One of the investigative techniques I learned from Lou was that an interview or an interrogation was not a single event, but a series of interviews or interrogations. I knew I would be speaking with Nolle again, real soon, but first I needed to find, arrest, and interrogate his roommate.

At first, Nolle's roommate denied being involved in Lady's murder; but, when told we had an eyewitness who identified him as the man seen running from the scene, he decided it would be best for him to cooperate. He explained when Nolle relieved him on guard duty at Ft. Carson, he said he had Lady's car and she was dead in the trunk. Nolle asked him for a favor and they came up with the idea of making it look like Lady had died in a fiery traffic accident (he never explained how Lady's body being found in the trunk, rather than behind the steering wheel, might complicate matters). I had also made an arrest on my first case and had worked 48 hours straight, arresting three suspects for murder and clearing two separate homicide investigations.

I include these stories not to seek any self-glorification, but to qualify this statement; in my thirty years in law enforcement, I was involved in approximately 100 homicide investigations, including mass shootings and serial killers. I was lead detective on 23 murder cases and never lost a case in court. Of the 23 homicide cases assigned to me, all but one was solved. If you count the cold case of Cynthia McLuen that Lou and I took off the shelf, most people would consider mine a near-perfect record. I was involved in more homicide investigations than all the detectives in the Boulder Police Department combined. However, Lou Smit was involved in more than twice my number of homicide investigations and he too never lost a single murder case in court. BUT— Lou Smit was about to sharpen his investigative skills even more.

Chapter 3 – Careers

Joe Kenda was an intelligent and entertaining sergeant to work for, although we did have our differences. Norm Short was Lou's and my sergeant when I first went into homicide. I liked Norm; his father was a former elected Sheriff of El Paso County (1949-1954). Norm had been a Navy Seal during the Vietnam era and helped form the first CSPD SWAT Team. There are not a lot of "shrinking violets" chasing killers. When Norm rotated back to Patrol, he was replaced by Sergeant Joe Kenda, who was a homicide detective prior to me coming into the Detective Unit.

When Joe was selected to replace Norm Short, I was glad to see him coming into the Unit and we got along very well, at first. Joe had a wry sense of humor and could deliver a pithy one-liner or tell an amusing story. Cops can gain esteem in law enforcement circles by telling good war stories. Other than Joseph Wambaugh, I have never met anyone better than Joe Kenda in telling police war stories. People like being entertained and a little embellishment only adds to the drama. On more than one occasion, after hearing one of Joe's stories, a detective would comment, "I didn't realize he was talking about my case, that wasn't what happened at all!"

During a briefing on a homicide case at the DA's Office, I was with Joe and two other detectives when Joe verbally described the case to the deputy DA. It was such an amusing story that it had all of us laughing when Joe left the room. After he was gone, we told the deputy DA what had really happened and where certain facts had been exaggerated. The prosecutor chastised us for not correcting the facts of the case as they were being presented. He explained how he could have made a crucial mistake based on the misinformation.

I decided the deputy DA had a valid point and I would have to speak up the next time it happened; the other two detectives had the good sense to let it go. About a month later, the same thing happened. After Joe finished telling a much more exciting version of our case, I spoke up in front of Joe and corrected a few of the inconsistencies. Joe glared at me, but didn't say anything; he didn't need to—he was the boss and I had just ruined one of his stories.

The six years I had worked alongside Lou Smit in the Detective Bureau was a privilege I will cherish for the rest of my life. But, as the Bob Dylan song goes, "The times they are a-changin'." In law enforcement agencies there is some prestige in being a homicide detective, especially being assigned the lead detective, and there is no denying the adrenaline rush of "slapping the cuffs" on a killer. The call-outs, long hours, out-of-town trips, and time away from home can create difficulties though, both professionally and personally. Being a father, the worst homicide cases for me were those with multiple victims and dead children.

On Valentine's Day, February 14, 1985, the ex-husband of 37-year-old Cassandra Rundle stopped by her home on LaClede Street, in the quiet Ivywild neighborhood of southern Colorado Springs, to deliver valentines. He claimed he entered the house and found the body of his ex-wife, Cassie, along with the bodies of her 12-year-old son, Detrick Sturm, and 10-year-old daughter, Melanie. All three victims had been strangled and the mother and daughter had been raped. Joe Kenda was the detective sergeant in charge of the homicide investigation.

Lou and I were not involved in the initial call out for what could only be known as the "Valentine's Day Massacre." The investigative focus naturally fell immediately upon the ex-husband; after all he had found the bodies and must have had romantic thoughts on his mind when he arrived at his ex-wife's home on Valentine's Day. Following protocols, the CSPD detectives requested the DA's Office to be notified of the brutal murders. The District Attorney himself, Barney Iuppa, responded to the crime scene to guide detectives on legal matters.

When Barney Iuppa, a life-long Democrat, announced he was running against the five-term Republican incumbent, Bob Russel, no one gave Barney much hope of defeating Bob. El Paso County was a Republican stronghold. Bob had tried 29 murder cases, more than any other Colorado prosecutor. He was appointed special prosecutor against Ted Bundy, who was arrested for the murder of 23-year-old Caryn Campbell in Aspen, Colorado. However, that case didn't go to trial because Bundy escaped twice—once from the Pitkin County Courthouse and a second time from the Garfield County Jail in Glenwood Springs, Colorado. Barney won the election.

One of the lead detectives assigned to our Valentine's Day murders was Dick Reisler. Interviews with Cassie's friends and family suggested she was not interested in getting back together with her ex-husband and she was thought to have been dating and sexually active with other men. Days passed without an arrest as pressure mounted from the community on the police to apprehend whoever was responsible for this horrendous crime. Pressure inside the Department fell upon the Homicide Unit; make an arrest, the community needs to feel safe again!

Several days after the bodies had been removed, Lou and I walked through the bloody crime scene, reviewed the evidence, and volunteered at the next team meeting to help follow up leads—any leads. In addition to the ex-husband, we felt there were other potential suspects who could be pursued. It became very uncomfortable to suggest alternative theories or suspects. Joe Kenda was the sergeant in charge of the investigation and Lou and I were not told about the next team meeting. It was not our case and we were being uninvited to participate.

The Valentine's Day triple murder in 1985 was probably my most memorable experience, during a homicide investigation, of what might be referred to as "herd mentality." High-profile cases tend to attract internal and external influences which can cause an investigation to start leaning one way or another. This tendency can produce devastating consequences as investigators lose their objectivity. Individuals who speak out against the direction the herd is moving—even if it's over a cliff, as Lou would find out in Boulder–can get left out in the cold.

Thirty-five years after the Valentine's Day murders, Dick Reisler was interviewed by a newspaper reporter for *The Gazette*'s "Colorado Cold Case." He shared how that triple homicide still haunts him and how, "When crimes go cold, police are stuck with a burden that never really goes away." Dick talked about "the toll the killings had on his life for years and even now, as the killer remains unidentified. In a crime that shocked Colorado Springs and beyond, an assailant had bound, raped, and strangled" a mother and daughter and her son "was also choked to death."

Dick shared, "More than 100 items could bear clues about the identity of the family's attacker, such as hair and fibers from the home." Even today, Dick hopes to hear news about an arrest in the Valentine's Day murders. *The Gazette*'s "Colorado Cold Case" episode concluded with an acknowledgement, "thanks to improvement in DNA analysis, and details from the autopsy reports that suggest police possess multiple items that could yield crucial DNA evidence."

Looking back, I think the Valentine's Day murders may have been the first time I bumped heads with Sergeant Joe Kenda, but it wouldn't be the last. The breaking point between us was a cold case, the unsolved murder of Officer Richard Burchfield, on Thanksgiving Day, 1953 (three months before I was born). I had wanted to solve that case since I was 18 years old and now I was getting close, but Joe told me to stop spending so much time on these old unsolved murders."

Joe was firm, and the boss, so I tried to reach a compromise. I told Joe I was really getting close to clearing this case. I was certain I had established sufficient probable cause to establish that the killer of Officer Burchfield was a 17-year-old hardened juvenile delinquent who had been pulling a string of personal armed robberies in Colorado Springs.

I believed Officer Burchfield had discovered who was responsible for these robberies and evidence showed he had caught the suspect shortly after his last robbery. Officer Burchfield was shot and killed by the suspect, who was seated in the right front passenger seat of the patrol car. The officer's last radio transmission was advising the dispatcher he was headed to police headquarters. I told Joe I just needed a little more time to finish putting the case together and since I had not used much vacation time that year, and the end of the calendar year was rapidly approaching, I offered to take vacation until after New Year's Day to finish the case on my own time.

Joe said something to the effect of not being able to tell me what to do on my own time, and I felt we had reached an understanding—in retrospect, this was a huge mistake on my part! During the next three weeks, I took a trip to Denver to review the FBI files on the Burchfield murder, which did not appear to have been thoroughly reviewed for many years, perhaps in decades. Days later, I sat down with Lou and presented a comprehensive review of the facts and physical evidence in the case, and he reached the same conclusion I had. The problem was the suspect, a convicted felon, had been shot and killed during a drug deal in 1977 in Denver.

The best alternative, at least in my mind at the time, was to request a review of the case by the DA's Office. What I hoped to accomplish, by soliciting their legal opinion, was that based on the belief that if the suspect had been alive today, the DA would have agreed there was sufficient probable cause to issue a warrant for his arrest or use the grand jury to seek a return of a "True Bill" for the murder of Officer Richard Burchfield. The District Attorney, Barney Iuppa, agreed to personally attend my presentation, along with one of his senior deputies and one of his DA investigators, Ed Rogers. Ed was a retired FBI agent who had been on the scene in 1953 and was intimately familiar with the involvement of the FBI in the Burchfield homicide investigation.

At the end of my several-hours-long presentation, DA Barney Iuppa stood up, shook my hand, and said that while he would not allow the grand jury to "indict a dead man," but if the suspect were still alive, he believed there was sufficient probable cause to arrest the killer. He also felt there was a strong case for a conviction if the case were to go to trial. The DA's Chief Deputy and his senior investigator, Ed Rogers, concurred with the findings in my investigation.

My next mistake was not rushing back to the Detective Bureau and telling Joe and my chain of command what the DA had decided. I thought our meeting was in confidence, and I had time to write up my supplemental reports showing the case was not "cleared by arrest," but was an "exceptional clearance" based on the death of the primary suspect. Unfortunately, someone leaked the DA's conclusion to the press and the headline in the next morning's paper reported the police had solved the murder of Officer Burchfield. My timing could not have been worse; the Department was in transition and going through a national search for a new police chief.

When the Acting Chief of Police, Neal Stratton, asked the Captain of Detectives and the rest of my chain of command why he wasn't told about this development, I was about to learn an invaluable lesson—don't embarrass your bosses! Joe wanted me transferred out of the Detective Unit. Wisdom comes with experience, and years later, when I finally became a boss myself, I realized your job is to make your boss look good. In the corporate world, making your boss and his boss look good is especially important in the eyes of the company's shareholders and stakeholders.

In a law enforcement setting, the shareholders are the people inside the organization who have a vested interest in an outcome of your actions, and the stakeholders are the citizens in the community that you are sworn to protect and serve. I had reached a critical junction in my career and hired an attorney to buy myself a little more time to explore my options. Since I was not being demoted, and would not lose any pay or benefits, an appeal to the Civil Service Board was not an option. Lou Smit and Les Davis were both highly upset about my being rotated out of the Detective Bureau, but I asked them not to do anything that might jeopardize their positions.

I agonized over what to do and even considered leaving the Department. I applied for a DA Investigator's position in Summit County and was invited to Breckenridge to interview for the position. I knew the DA and several of his senior prosecutors and investigators. The interview was going well and about halfway into it, the Chief Deputy conducting the interview was reviewing my resume and commenting on my impressive credentials as an investigator. Suddenly, the strangest thing happened. In an instant my destiny became clear; my path was not there in the beautiful mountains of Summit County, but was back in the streets of Colorado Springs.

The Deputy DA must have thought I had gone nuts, because I leaned forward and asked for my resume. When he handed it to me across his desk, I said I would like to respectfully withdraw my application for the DA Investigators position. He said okay, but if I changed my mind to give him a call.

On the drive back to Colorado Springs, it felt like a huge weight had been lifted off my shoulders. I called my attorney and asked him not to pursue any further civil action against the Department. The only thing I would like him to negotiate was to ensure my personal record reflected that it was my decision to rotate back to the Patrol Division and my personnel record remained clean. The Acting Chief of Police, Neal Stratton, seemed anxious to avoid any controversy and went along with my request.

Weeks later, the new Police Chief, Jim Munger, asked a handful of senior and retired detectives to assemble in his office to hear me present my case. It was not a pleasant experience. Everyone who sat around the Chief's conference table had their own preconceived ideas about the Burchfield murder; most opinions were based on unsubstantiated speculation and rumors which had persisted for decades. Since there was no "smoking gun," the decision was reached that the DA could do whatever he wanted to do, but the official position of the CSPD was Officer Burchfield's homicide investigation would remain open.

Looking back, Joe Kenda and I both had strong egos, and as much as I would like to lay the blame on Joe for my eventual transfer out of the Homicide and back to Patrol, I see now that it wasn't all his fault and more importantly—he was the boss! This insight didn't start to creep into my mind until August 19, 2010, the night before Lou Smit's funeral. On behalf of Lou's family, Cindy Smit Marra, Lou's middle daughter, had asked me to deliver a eulogy for Lou at his funeral to be held at the New Life Church, in Colorado Springs, on Friday August 20, 2010.

New Life Church had been selected because it was thought to be the only venue large enough to seat the thousands of people expected to attend Lou's "Celebration of Life." I was so crushed by Lou's death, I wasn't altogether confident I would be able to speak, let alone deliver a eulogy befitting of Lou. Breaking down and crying in front of thousands of people wasn't something I was anxious to do, but Dave told me, "John, you have to do this," and so I did.

The night before Lou's funeral, his family arranged for a viewing at the Swan-Law Funeral Home. I wavered on going but decided my attendance was not optional. I felt I had to show my respect for Lou's family; besides, this might give me a chance to talk with John Ramsey, Kelsey Grammer, and Trip DeMuth, who had also been asked to deliver a eulogy for our mutual friend Lou Smit. Hundreds of Lou's friends and family crowded into the funeral home that evening for his viewing. The CSPD Honor Guard was there, standing watch over Lou in his coffin. One of the retired officers in attendance was Sergeant Norm Short, whom I hadn't seen in years.

I don't know how this happened, but Norm and I got to talking and the subject of me leaving the Detective Bureau came up and Norm shocked me by telling me he would have transferred me out of the Homicide Unit too, except he had "gotten kicked out first." Our conversation reminded me that Norm and I had also butted heads a few times when he was my sergeant. Norm passed away a few years later; Lou's funeral was the last time I talked with Norm Short. I have thought about our final conversation many times since Norm's death and finally had to face the fact that when I was a homicide detective, I had bumped heads with both of my sergeants and the only common denominator was me!

As much as Lou and I loved being homicide partners, nothing lasts forever. Dick Reisler summed it up best when he said, "John lost his position because he cared too much." Neither Lou nor I would have decided on our own to end our partnership; someone else had to make that decision for us, but I believe it was "meant to be." Fortunately, Lou's life and mine would remain intertwined and we would remain partners, even after his passing in 2010.

When I transferred out of Homicide, I rotated back to the Patrol Division and became a Master Patrol Officer. Dave Spencer transferred to Robbery and Dick Reisler transferred to a special anti-crime squad and was promoted to sergeant. I talked Lou into signing up for the next annual sergeant's test together and we committed to being one another's study partners. Along the way a change had been made with Police and Fire Civil Service promotional exams. In an attempt to promote more women and minorities into supervisory positions, candidates for promotion were grouped into "statistically equivalent bands."

The Police Chief could select anyone from the top band. The process worked, but it made it more difficult for a white male, like Lou or me, to get promoted. When the next sergeant's test was administered, Lou ended up alone in the top band—a statistically equivalent band of one! The only test for promotion Lou Smit ever took proved what his partners knew all along; Lou had no equal. When Lou was promoted, I went to his promotional ceremony and he gave me the honor of pinning his brass sergeant's badge on his blue uniform shirt. I was so proud of him and knew he would make an outstanding sergeant, especially once he worked his way back into the Detective Bureau. But Lou had been out of patrol for so long he felt like a fish out of water.

When I transferred back to Patrol, I too had a fairly steep learning curve. Fortunately, I was assigned to a senior Master Patrol Officer who "taught me the ropes." I sort of knew how Lou felt, but I had only been away for six years, Lou had been out of uniform almost twenty years and never got comfortable being a patrol sergeant. His biggest worry, I believe, was making a mistake that might cost an officer or a citizen their life. Deep down, I knew Lou missed being a detective. Then Lou did something unheard of on the Department; within a few months of being back in patrol, he gave up his sergeant's stripes and returned to the Detective Bureau.

I began to refocus my efforts on advancing my career. I realized "times were a-changing" in policing and holding just an Associates Degree wasn't going to cut it. Thanks to Dick Reisler, I found I liked teaching criminal investigation courses at the CSPD Police Academy. I tested for instructor at the Training Academy, which was across the street from Regis University, and was selected. Then I transferred as many college credits as I could from UCCS to Regis and started on a Bachelor's degree in Business Administration. While I primarily taught criminal investigation classes, I was cross-trained to teach firearms, defensive tactics, and police driving.

I was also selected to teach "Train the Trainer" courses to other police instructors across Colorado. Over time I became ranked as a Distinguished Master on the police firearms range, certified to teach advanced defensive tactics to police officers, and recognized as one of the top police driving instructors in Colorado. However, I always knew there was someone out there "better than you" and when it came to teaching homicide investigations there was no one better than Lou. Although he was good at it, Lou didn't really like to speak in front of large groups.

Occasionally I talked Lou into joining me, and sometimes Dave and Dick, in teaching Major Investigation Courses for other law enforcement agencies and forensic organizations. Our Major Crimes Packet was always well received. We taught courses for Rocky Mountain Division of the International Association for Identification (RMDIAI). The Boulder Police Department even hosted a few of my investigative courses. I went on to become a court-qualified expert in crime scene reconstruction and bloodstain pattern interpretation. I helped found the Rocky Mountain Association of Bloodstain Pattern Analysts (RMABPA) and served as President.

As a staff instructor at the Police Academy, I had gotten into perhaps the best physical condition I had been in since playing high school football. I was never one to sit on the curb and watch as police recruits ran by; I felt I needed to lead, to be out front. While I knew I was never going to be the fastest runner in a group of young people, I could go the distance and worked to improve on my endurance. The other instructors, like Art Sapp and Ron Gibson, felt the same way. Ron got me into running and we ran the 10K Bolder Boulder a few times. One summer I did the Colorado Springs Triple Crown of Running, which was a 10K in downtown Colorado Springs, a 10-mile run in the Garden of the Gods, and the Pikes Peak Marathon ascent.

Almost every morning Lou ran laps, forwards and backwards, when he worked out at the YMCA. Lou took martial arts training and learned to box. Art was a black belt in the martial arts and on several occasions he and Lou entered "tough man" competitions, usually held at the City Auditorium across the street from the Department or in the Denver area. I remember Lou coming to work once with a broken nose and several busted ribs. It hurt him just to breathe and he tried not to laugh. Not laughing was hard for Lou; he loved to laugh, especially at himself. Lou was not trying to prove how tough he was, he just wanted to get in the ring to learn better defensive skills and improve his physical conditioning. Lou Smit was a tough man.

In the Academy, we broke down our entry-level, in-service, and advanced training courses into three performance categories: knowledge, skills, and abilities or KSAs. Over time, I began to assess what KSAs I needed to acquire in order to advance in my police career. Two areas I felt I was lacking were Traffic Safety and Police Administration. I also felt I was going to need a Master's

Degree to continue advancing in my career. The times were still "a-changin'" and like the Bob Dylan song says, there are times you need to learn to swim or you sink like a stone.

After teaching three years in the Academy, I had earned my Bachelor's Degree and Police Chief Jim Munger promoted me to Sergeant. I invited Lou to pin my new brass sergeant badge on my uniform. At my promotion ceremony, Lou surprised me by pinning his sergeant badge on my chest. When Lou had given up his stripes and accompanying pay raise, he had retained his sergeant's badge; it remains one of my most prized possessions today. I absolutely loved being back in uniform and on patrol. One of the things I learned teaching at the Academy is, "If you want to get really good at something, try teaching it to someone else."

With my prior patrol and investigative experience, coupled with a greater confidence in my physical skills acquired from teaching firearms, defensive tactics, and pursuit driving, I knew I was making a positive contribution to the young police officers assigned to my patrol team. One of those young officers, Vince Niski, would go on to become the Chief of Police for the Colorado Springs Police Department. As a recently-promoted sergeant, I was assigned to the night shift, filled primarily by rookies straight out of the Academy. I always said being a CSPD patrol sergeant was the best job I had in my thirty-year career, and I had a lot of really good jobs!

I had personally gotten to know every rookie who graduated from the Academy over the last three years and knew most of these younger cops were destined to become superstars on the Department. All they needed was a little time on the streets and someone to be there to "show them the ropes," just as Lou and so many senior officers had taught me how to be a cop. As a newly-minted sergeant, I enjoyed being back on the street, leading young motivated cops and seeing them advance in their careers, fulfilling their dreams of being police officers. I understood how Lou felt, watching me advance in my career, developing my abilities, and living my dreams.

The two lessons I took to heart was keeping your boss informed on what you're doing, and whatever it is your boss asks you to do, get that done first and do it to the best of your ability. Afterward, you can work on the things you want to do, and make time to ask your bosses how they think you can improve your performance. Your relationship with your boss is as important to develop as your relationship with your coworkers and subordinates. As a police sergeant, I found there was a lot I could learn from simply asking my Lieutenant for their advice. The more confident you become, the more open you are to suggestions or recommendations.

One day, when I was a Patrol Sergeant, the CSPD Traffic Lieutenant, Don Bjornsrud (BJ), made me an offer I couldn't turn down. I had known and looked up to "BJ" since I was in first grade. His family lived just down the street and I rode my bike past his house countless times. After high school, BJ joined the Navy and became a Golden Gloves boxer. BJ's mother and my mother were lifelong friends. When he was home on leave, BJ would take his younger brother, Billy, and me to the YMCA to work out (you don't lift a lot of weights in the first grade, but it was cool for Billy and me just to be around BJ and his friends). In the Department, BJ was close friends with Lou Smit, Bill Thiede, and Bill Flanagan, who was my Lieutenant at the Academy.

My favorite BJ war story was a fight call one night at the Navajo Hogan, a biker hangout on the north side of town. On-scene officers requested backup and I heard BJ and Bill Thiede call out on scene at the bar. When I pulled up, there must have been 25-30 motorcycles parked outside and several dozen bikers preparing to fight half a dozen cops. Just as things started to get out of hand, BJ shouted, "Hold it!" He reached into his wallet and pulled out a hundred-dollar bill and tossed it on the hood of the nearest police cruiser. Then BJ announced to the bikers he had a hundred dollars on the cops winning this fight. His challenge caught the bikers completely off guard. They laughed at his bravado and dispersed; no one accepted BJ's hundred-dollar bet.

During BJ's storied career at the CSPD, he had been a motorcycle officer, traffic sergeant, and now was in charge of the Traffic Division. BJ told me he was retiring the following year and had an opening in traffic for a sergeant. He said he wanted me to take the job, because he wanted to enjoy his last year on the Department and he promised me I could have anything I wanted.

"Really? Anything?" I asked.

"Yep," he said.

I shared with BJ that I had wanted to learn how the Traffic Division functioned and I also wanted to start on a graduate degree. I asked, "Can I have a flexible schedule?"

"Absolutely! In fact, you will be making up the schedule; you can assign yourself to any shift and give yourself any sets of days off you want."

"Can I have a take-home car?"

"Yep," he said. "You will need a take-home car because you will be on call-out." One traffic sergeant was required to be on call 24-hours a day for all fatal accidents involving planes, trains, and automobiles. Plus, they were paid overtime at time-and-a-half.

Then came the clincher, "Can I ride a motorcycle?"

"Absolutely," BJ said, then added, "But you will have to wait until next summer, when the next police motorcycle training course is scheduled, and you'll have to pass the exam."

From talking with other motorcycle officers, I knew passing the test would not be easy, but I had owned motorcycles since I was in the 7th grade. The motorcycle I owned at that time was a newer model Kawasaki Z1B 900cc, which was the same make and model many of the CSPD officers in traffic were riding at the time, although there were several veteran officers, including BJ, who always preferred the more traditional police motorcycle—the Harley Davidson.

"Deal," I said, as we shook hands. BJ was a wonderful Lieutenant to work for and I did everything I could to make sure he enjoyed his last year on the Department. I learned as much as I could from him and other sergeants and experienced traffic officers about Traffic Safety. I was a court-qualified expert on bloodstain pattern interpretation and crime scene reconstruction, but I was not an expert on traffic accident reconstruction. Fortunately, we had experts in Traffic to investigate fatal accidents involving planes, trains, and automobiles.

While I was a sergeant assigned to the Traffic Division, Lou retired from CSPD and went to work for the El Paso County District Attorney's Office. Things had never been the same for him after our close-knit team had broken apart. As homicide detectives, we always attended the autopsies for each of our victims, and Lou's skills as an investigator were about to be put to the test working part time for the county coroner.

At 9:37 a.m. Sunday, March 3, 1991, I was the CSPD on-call Traffic Sergeant. United Airlines Flight 585 was cleared for a visual approach from the south to land at the Colorado Springs Municipal Airport. Suddenly, the Boeing 737, carrying 20 passengers and 5 crew members, rolled to the right and crashed nose-first into a park a few miles south of the runway. There would be no survivors. When the 911 dispatcher called me, I instinctively looked toward the airport to see if I could spot any smoke coming from the crash. Seeing none, I asked her if this was a training exercise; she assured me it was not.

The dispatcher advised that we had two of our motorcycle officers, called "solos," running Code 3 (red lights and sirens) to the scene. As the on-call Traffic Sergeant, I was being called out to respond to and assume supervisory control over the crash site. I threw on my uniform, jumped into my marked police car, and ran Code 3 to the crash site. When I turned on my police radio, I heard my two solos call 10-97 (on scene) and within seconds reported back, "No survivors."

I had been on a few plane crashes, and from experience knew a debris field can be strewn out for hundreds of yards. I questioned, at the time, how they could determine there were no survivors so quickly—until I arrived at the scene. The airliner, traveling at 245mph, crashed nose-first, straight down into Widefield Park, less than four miles from the runway. It dug a crater into the soft ground, 15 feet deep and 39 by 24 feet wide, and exploded upon impact. A huge fireball erupted when it first hit the ground. An eight-year-old girl playing in the park sustained minor injuries when she was knocked to the ground from the force of the explosion.

As I got within a half mile of the park, smoke led me to the accident site. When I parked my cruiser, I could see flames shooting up from this huge pit, but I couldn't see the plane! I thought there must be some mistake; this can't be a 737 that had gone down—there was not enough debris. As I started walking gingerly across the grass, to avoid stepping on crash debris and body parts, to where my two motorcycle officers were standing near the smoking pit, I walked past a huge wheel standing upright. It was taller than I was—"This wasn't a Cessna," I immediately concluded. The 737 had collapsed into itself as if it had been an enormously long aluminum can, standing on end, which had been stomped on by a giant.

A state patrol officer arrived on scene as bystanders started to gather. We established a perimeter to protect the impact site. More first responders started to arrive. While the airport runway was inside the city limits of Colorado Springs, Widefield Park was in the County. I confirmed that our dispatcher had notified the El Paso County Sheriff's Office and the El Paso County Coroner's Office. The National Transportation Safety Board (NTSB) was notified and later determined the cause of the crash was a defective 737 rudder control unit. Lou was one of the deputy coroners who had the dismal task of working with the NTSB to recover bodies.

Of the 25 "souls on board" United Flight 585, there were no survivors. However, the Coroner's Office needed to account for 26 bodies. In an odd twist of fate, a man who had been killed in a head-on traffic accident in Kansas was being transported back to Colorado Springs where he was to be buried. His body lay in a coffin down in the plane cargo hold when the plane went down. I often thought of what bad luck he had, being killed in a car crash in Kansas and while flying back to attend your own funeral, you're in a plane crash with no survivors. Even though Joe Kenda wasn't there, I have no doubt he could tell that story better than me.

Fifteen hours after the worst plane crash in Colorado Springs history, the worst fire disaster in the City happened at a nursing home. Nine elderly residents were unable to escape the inferno. An employee of the home discovered the fire about 12:30 a.m. in a room where smoking was allowed. After battling the blaze for six hours, Colorado Springs firefighters were still putting out hot spots. Residents, ranging in ages from 70 to 98-years-old, were asleep in their beds at the Crystal Springs Estate home when the fire broke out. Eight residents died at the scene; one later at the hospital. Six people, including four firefighters, were admitted to hospitals.

Six engine companies along with two ladder companies battled the fire at the one-story brick building that had two wings and a basement. The building had been built in the 1950's and did have the required smoke and heat detectors—both were functional. According to code, sprinklers were required in the basement; but not on the main floor where most of the residents perished (city fire codes were changed as a result of this fire). Firefighters were able to contain the fire in the exit ways but many residents were confused and didn't want to leave their rooms. Once the fire got into the attic it raced out through both wings. The building was a total loss.

I was not one of the first responders on the initial call to the nursing home; however, my team of traffic officers and I were assigned to protect the scene the next day. Lou Smit was one of the members of the Coroner's Office who did respond to the scene of the nursing home fire to help identify the bodies. The Coroner established a temporary morgue in Colorado Springs to hold the bodies and body parts from the United Flight 585 and the elderly residents from the Crystal Springs Estates nursing home. Over the next several weeks, the families from both these deadly disasters trickled into the temporary morgue to attempt to identify their loved ones.

I appreciated being in the Traffic Division, an important part of the CSPD, established by my Uncle Red, where my mother once worked. However, after BJ retired, an opening came up for a sergeant at the Police Academy. I applied and was selected. While I loved teaching police officers, part of my motivation was the Regis University campus, which I could see across the street every time I looked out my office window. Both my undergraduate and graduate degrees were in Business Administration, which most people would think had little to do with law enforcement, but I knew would prove invaluable in running a large law enforcement agency.

While Lou Smit worked at District Attorney's Office and part time for the Coroner's Office, we met to keep in touch. Lou's cousin, Bill Thiede, retired as a captain with the CSPD. Bill's son, Travis, was hired by the Department and I was his first sergeant when he reported for duty at the CSPD Police Academy. Travis was a bright young officer and you could tell early on this young man had a promising future ahead of him in law enforcement.

As was the custom, CSPD Police Academy graduates were issued a new silver police officer badge, which they clutched in the palm of their left hand as they raised their right hand to be sworn in as police officers. At their graduation, recruits are encouraged to invite a member of the family or close friend to come up and pin their new badge on their uniform shirt. Lou had asked me to pin his badge on him when he was promoted to sergeant and I had invited Lou to pin his sergeant's badge on me at my promotion ceremony.

At Travis' Academy graduation ceremony, he was issued a new shiny police officer's badge. Before his family came up to pin his badge on his shirt, I handed him my CSPD Patrolman badge, engraved with A3 on the back, and said, "Here, I want you to have my old CSPD badge; it was worn by your father before me, when he was a police officer." I know Travis, his dad, and Uncle Lou appreciated this professional courtesy. Travis worked for the CSPD several years and then became an FBI agent, where he is still employed today. Travis' sister, Susan, also graduated from the CSPD Police Academy and she and her husband both later retired from the CSPD.

After serving two years as the Sergeant at the Police Academy, I was one of two sergeants selected to attend an 8-hour Time Management course in Golden, Colorado. The other sergeant was Lou Velez, a former CSPD Academy classmate of mine, who went on to earn a Ph.D. and become the Chief of Police for the City of Colorado Springs and later for Pueblo, Colorado. The course was one in a series of corporate management training courses, titled "Operation Bootstrap." Available openings were customarily offered to police officers free of charge.

I was reluctant to take a day away from work to attend a time management course; I felt I didn't have enough time to do the work I needed to do, let alone attend a time management course. My Lieutenant had decided I was going to be there and so I was, but I don't think he ever knew what a game-changer that class turned out to be for me and my career. Halfway into the day, the instructor introduced what he called a "three-minute drill," where we took a blank sheet of paper and divided it into four equal squares. In the upper left corner, we wrote Short Term Professional Goals, and in the upper right, Long Term Professional Goals. In the lower left, we wrote "Short Term Personal Goals," and "Long Term Personal Goals" in the lower right.

The instructor said we were to jot down, as fast as we could, our goals in the appropriate boxes. Abbreviations were encouraged, as were drawing symbols, and spelling wasn't important. Then he said, "Go!" I was less than enthusiastic, but went ahead with the exercise. When the instructor announced only one minute remained, I was shocked. I had been writing like a man possessed! My short-term professional box was overflowing with things I needed to be doing back at the Academy; however, I had almost nothing written in any of the other three boxes.

At the last second, I jotted down one or two personal goals and then quickly drew a pair of captain's bars in the box for my long-term goals, but that wasn't my long-term professional goal; I just had never written down or shared with anyone that my long-term goal was to lead a large law enforcement organization. The instructor presented statistical data supporting the premise of how people who wrote down their goals were much more likely to accomplish them; and conversely, people like me, who had a general idea where they wanted to go but had not written their goals down or devised a strategy how to get there, were much less likely to be successful.

Then came the punchline—the instructor encouraged us to ask ourselves, "Are your short-term goals leading you to where you want to be long term, both personally and professionally?" In other words, "If your short-term goals, what you are doing today, are NOT leading you to where you want to be tomorrow, then why are you doing them?" The instructor finished the exercise by encouraging us to take the time to write down, refine, and work to accomplish our goals for the next three to five years. He said if you do this, what you'll find is your long-term goals will happen more quickly than you expected and you will have to "dream bigger dreams."

Having already experienced my career dream come true in being Lou's homicide partner, I now had an intriguing invitation to "dream bigger dreams." I spent the next weekend refining my goals on my Mac Plus and developing a strategic step-by-step plan on how to make my short-term goals happen. I soon realized most of the work waiting for me back at the Academy was self-imposed. Very few projects had been assigned to me by my Lieutenant. I shifted all those assignments to the forefront, reprioritized the work I had assigned to myself, and deleted any of those projects which would not lead me to my long-term goals.

That weekend I made time to "dream bigger dreams" and realized I had some pretty lofty ambitions. I wanted to be internationally recognized by my peers as an expert in forensic science, write a book, and lead a major law enforcement agency, consisting of several hundred peace officers, in the noble pursuit of justice. I also committed to working on my personal goals; unfortunately, my marriage was in trouble and could not be salvaged.

I graduated with my BBA in 1990 and started on my graduate studies. To close the gap in my professional career, I applied for a sergeant opening on the Chief's Staff in Professional Standards. Lorne Kramer had been selected Police Chief to replace Jim Munger, who had been promoted to Deputy City Manager for the City of Colorado Springs. Both Kramer and Munger were retired from LAPD. One of the police chief finalists was Tom Koby, who was, at the time, one of Houston's five assistant chiefs. I met Koby briefly during the selection process for CSPD. In June of 1991, Tom Koby was hired to be the Boulder Police Chief.

Both Lorne Kramer and Jim Munger greatly enhanced the professionalism of the CSPD, and I became a student of their approach to leadership and policing. Although their backgrounds were similar, their management styles were quite different and both were very effective. Munger was of German descent and his approach was very business-like and authoritarian. Kramer was more personable; he was very outgoing and loved to laugh. One of the attributes they both shared was an unwavering commitment to Community Oriented Policing, based on the philosophy, "Policing is something you do with a community, not something you do to a community."

My first assignment as a sergeant in Professional Standards was in Community Relations. My office was on the fourth floor of the Police Operations Center (POC), just down the hall from Chief Kramer's office. When I headed home at the end of the day, I would knock on his door to ask if there was anything I could help him with so he could go home. Occasionally he'd ask me to drop something off downstairs, but most of the time he'd just say, "Thanks, I got it covered."

One afternoon Chief Kramer invited me to sit down in his office and asked if I had ever heard of The Hundred Club. I had not but Chief Kramer explained The Hundred Clubs consisted of one hundred community members who contributed financially to fallen officers' widows and orphans. LAPD had a Hundred Club and he had decided to start one in Colorado Springs. Chief Kramer handed me a slip of paper with three names and phone numbers for the Board of Directors of the Hundred Club in Denver. He told me to go meet with them so we could model our nonprofit organization after their program.

I made arrangements to meet the following week with the three officers in the Denver Hundred Club. They made reservations for us to meet at the famed Denver Athletic Club in downtown Denver. All three were successful community leaders. Over lunch they each gave me their advice and a copy of their bylaws. One of the intriguing membership rules strictly prohibited members from announcing publicly that they belonged to the Hundred Club.

When I reported back to Chief Kramer, he gave me another sheet of paper with three names and phone numbers of community leaders in Colorado Springs. He directed me to contact them individually and said they would help start up our Hundred Club. The goal was to cap membership at one hundred and within weeks over 120 community members had sent in their checks to join. Every year, the Colorado Springs Police Chief, Fire Chief, and El Paso County Sheriff would host an annual Hundred Club dinner where nominees from each of these three first-responder organizations would be recognized and fallen officers honored.

One of my assignments as the Sergeant in Community Relations was to represent Chief Kramer at various community events and minority nonprofit organizations, such as the National Association for the Advancement of Colored People (NAACP), Hispanic Chamber of Commerce, and League of United Latin American Citizens (LULAC). This turned out to be an extraordinary learning experience for me because I got to see policing through the lens of our local minority communities. Some of my closest friends today were leaders in those organizations.

Another invaluable learning experience was a collateral assignment I held to relieve the Department's Public Information Officer (PIO). Whenever this PIO Lieutenant was called out, they would respond to the scene or the Department to collect information first-hand, and then reduce the event down to a succinctly written press release. The press release was faxed to media outlets in our community and the PIO was available to answer questions, often on live TV.

As homicide detectives, one of our duties was to write and fax press releases on our call outs. This responsibility had to be done as early in the investigative process as possible, usually within hours of being called out or making an arrest for murder. One of the most valuable lessons I learned was, "If you don't control the media, the media will control you." As PIOs we were taught to be cognizant of which facts the media needed and when. We were expected to be respectful of their news deadlines, maintain a positive working relationship with members of the media, and help keep the community informed of newsworthy public safety activities.

In writing press releases, we were instructed on what information needed to be safeguarded so we did not compromise any follow-up criminal investigations or prosecutions. Facts had to be verified and personal opinions or speculations on motive were strictly prohibited. In most violent crimes, the question of motive often comes up; "why" did this suspect commit such a horrible crime? My personal opinion that there is evil in this world, or that Michael Corbett and Freddie Lee Glenn, who murdered Karen Grammer and Winslow Douglas Watson III, were evil people might be my opinion, but it doesn't belong in a media release or repeated in front of a camera.

One of the most vicious kidnap-murders in my and Lou's law enforcement careers was committed by a truly evil man. On the evening of September 17, 1991, 13-year-old Heather Dawn Church went missing from her home on Eastonville Road, in northeastern El Paso County. Suspicion fell upon her parents, Michael and Diane Church, who were going through a divorce. The father had moved out of the home where his daughter and infant son lived with their mother. On the evening of the kidnapping, Diane left the home to attend an event at her church, leaving Heather alone to babysit her younger brother.

When the mother returned home, she found her daughter missing. After calling a few of her daughter's friends to see if they had heard from Heather, Diane Church called the El Paso County Sheriff's Office to report her daughter missing. Sheriff's deputies responded, including Search and Rescue members, a K9 Unit, detectives, and the crime lab. Detectives pointed out no forced entry into the home and suspected that Heather had run away or perhaps there had been a parental or grandparental abduction. However, civilian crime scene technician, Elinor McGarry, suggested an unlocked window in the mother's bedroom may have been used to gain entry.

The search for any signs of Heather Dawn Church garnered community interest as the case dragged on and days turned into months. The FBI joined in the search to find Heather and pored over the evidence. A latent fingerprint that CSI Technician, Elinor McGarry, had lifted from the aluminum frame of the window in the mother's bedroom was submitted to the Colorado Bureau of Investigation (CBI). No match was found in the database. Months turned into years as Heather's case grew cold. In fairness, without a body—the third component of the murder triad—the chances of solving a homicide are greatly diminished.

Two years to the day of Heather's disappearance, a human skull and a handful of scattered skeletal remains were found off a remote mountain road northwest of Colorado Springs. Forensic odontology was used to confirm the remains were those of 13-year-old Heather Dawn Church. Now a confirmed homicide investigation, investigative efforts were renewed by El Paso County Sheriff's homicide detectives. While neither Lou Smit nor I had any investigative jurisdiction over this case we, along with the entire law enforcement community, wondered if the killer was still at large in the community. He was; in fact, he lived just down Eastonville Road.

I was still working on the Chief's staff in Professional Standards and had completed my MBA from Regis University. I had also placed in the second band on the Lieutenants exam that year and was confident I would test better the following year. I had already written down my long-term goal of one day being elected the El Paso

County Sheriff, following in my Uncle Red's footsteps, but the unsolved kidnap-murder of Heather Dawn Church weighed heavily on my mind. The murder hadn't happened on my watch, it wasn't even under my jurisdiction, but this unsolved murder was part of my motivation to make my long-term goal a short-term objective.

In wanting to keep my boss informed, and to make sure he heard the news from me that a member of his staff was going to run for Sheriff, I dropped by Chief Kramer's office on my way home. I had thought through how my decision might impact him in his position, as Chief of Police, and my position in Community Relations. When I told Chief Kramer my decision, I shared with him that some people might consider my position in Community Relations to be a conflict of interest. I told him if he needed to transfer me to midnights at the airport, I would understand and I promised not to do any political campaigning in uniform or on duty.

The next day Chief Kramer called me into his office and said to avoid any potential conflict of interest, he had decided to transfer me to Internal Affairs (IA). Not only did this assignment isolate me from the community and the responsibility of filling in for the PIO when he was not available, but IA was the one missing piece that I felt I was still lacking in my skill set. I felt I needed a better understanding of the internal investigative process and the appellate review process over disciplinary actions. El Paso County Sheriff's personnel were not Civil Service employees; they served at the "will and pleasure" of the elected sheriff.

I welcomed the move to Internal Affairs, a process requiring an objective examination of all the facts regardless of who is involved. The other full-time sergeant in IA was Bill Lidh. Our lieutenant, when I first transferred in, was Kurt Pillard. There could not have been two better people for me to learn the IA process from than Bill and Kurt. While I had investigated minor IA complaints as a patrol sergeant, and had been involved in the investigation of a half dozen officer involved shootings, IA handled all the serious complaints and investigated officer-involved shootings to determine if there had been any violations of departmental policy and procedures.

Every week, the IA Lieutenant would meet with the Chief of Police to update him on the status of our personnel investigations and present our investigative findings, including disciplinary recommendations from the accused officer's chain of command for sustained policy violations. The IA Lieutenant would present the cases to Chief Kramer, while Bill and I attended to answer any questions the Chief might have, or to investigate further if he thought it necessary. What a timely and invaluable opportunity for me, wanting to become a police executive, learning the IA and appellate process from a nationally respected police executive—Lorne Kramer.

The other person whom I greatly respected and felt I had to meet with personally, to inform him of my decision to run for El Paso County Sheriff, was my mentor from PPCC, Bernie Barry, the sitting El Paso County Sheriff. This meeting did not go well. Sheriff Bernard Barry had yet to announce his intention to seek another 4-year term; however, four other candidates had already entered the Sheriff's race. Sheriff Barry was in his sixties and most people, including me, thought he was looking to retire rather than to start another four-year term in office.

I knew all four candidates running against Sheriff Barry and did not feel any of them had the best interests of the community in mind. Two of these candidates had run against Sheriff Barry four years earlier, in a very heated political campaign, and had nearly unseated the incumbent in that election. I knew nothing about politics, but felt if the Office was going to change hands, I wanted to make sure the position once held by my Uncle Red wasn't run into the ground. What I had hoped in requesting a coffee meeting with Sheriff Barry is that he would welcome my decision and endorse my soon-to-be announced candidacy.

When Sheriff Barry and I met, I told him of my decision. Our conversation and our coffees both grew cold. He told me he was going to seek another term; he had just not announced his decision. He asked me why I wanted his job and pointed out how I already had a job. What I didn't tell Sheriff Barry, and hadn't told Chief Kramer, is that my decision to run now was made in part to take on the kidnap-murder investigation of Heather Dawn Church. The one person I would tell was Lou Smit. I also told Lou that if I were elected Sheriff, I needed him to join me at the Sheriff's Office as my Captain of Detectives. Lou said, "First, we have to get you elected."

While the General Election wasn't until the coming fall, and it was now late spring of 1994, I knew I would have to win the Primary Election that was to be held late summer. I registered as a candidate and picked the date to make my announcement. I decided to make my announcement from El Paso County Republican Headquarters, in Colorado Springs, and then spent hours putting together a detailed Press Kit with my resume, vision, and goals for the office.

When the date and time came for my announcement, only three people showed up: Lou and two other friends. I double checked my press release to make sure there had not been a mistake on the date, time, and location; there wasn't—there was just no interest in my announcement that I, a political outsider, was joining an already overcrowded field. When it came time for me to make my announcement, I stalled for a couple more minutes and glanced down the hall, hoping to see a newspaper reporter or one TV crew rushing down the hall to report on my entering the political arena.

No media came to my announcement—none. I looked out into the hallway, hoping to spot anyone with the news headed toward me and the only person walking my way was a young man whom I did not recognize. Like all anxious politicians, I pumped his hand while introducing myself, and thanked him for attending my announcement. He explained that he couldn't stay, he was on his lunch hour, and then he spotted the Press Kits I had laid out on a nearby table. The man picked one up, glanced through it briefly, and asked if he could take one. I said sure; what I didn't know until later was this man was a spy with Sheriff Barry's campaign committee!

He left and I walked to the front of the room. Lou Smit sat in the front row, while my other two friends spread out, making the room look less empty. I said I had prepared a speech about a battleship and a lighthouse, but I wasn't sure if I should give it now. Lou clapped his hands enthusiastically and said, "Come on, Johnny, we want to hear your speech!" When I made my announcement, I had no campaign manager, no treasurer, no campaign money, and no committee.

I commented to Lou after my announcement for Sheriff, "Geez Smit, I'm not off to a very good start with my political career, am I?" He smiled and said that he was reminded of this one man who started off with only twelve followers and that turned out okay. Not that Lou was comparing me to Jesus Christ, but he did make the point that, if this was what He wanted, no one could stop me. Lou and my other two friends each wrote me a check for my first campaign contributions. *The Gazette Newspaper* ran a short 2-inch column reporting I was running and word started to trickle out of my announcement wanting to be the next Sheriff of El Paso County.

A cop friend stepped forward to congratulate me on my announcement and said to let him know if there was anything he could do to help. I handed him the three checks and asked if he would be my campaign treasurer. One of the detectives from the Sheriff's Office introduced me to a woman whose husband had been the victim of a murder, and she became a terrific campaign manager. Her father, Charlie Hess, was a racquetball friend of Lou's. Charlie had been with the CIA and was a former FBI agent under J. Edgar Hoover. Charlie was destined to play an important role in the Sheriff's Office Cold Case Unit working with Lou Smit.

Despite my late start, with the help of family and friends, I managed a respectable showing at the Republican County Assembly. I had asked my Uncle Les Davis to second my nomination. Les delivered a great speech, telling the crowd he had known me since I was a little boy and he had every confidence I would serve the County honorably, the same way his brother Red had served. Sheriff Barry did not win enough votes to advance onto the Primary Election and eventually endorsed my candidacy. I deeply appreciated his political and personal support as I faced off against two other opponents in the general election.

After winning the General Election in November 1994, I met privately with Lou and he accepted my invitation to become my Captain of Detectives. I told him I only had two requests, to catch whoever killed Heather Dawn Church and to reorganize the Detective Bureau. I promised him anything he needed; he would have complete control over the investigation, along with my unwavering support, including unlimited overtime, training, and travel expenses.

Between Thanksgiving and Christmas of 1994, Lou obtained a complete copy of the Heather Dawn Church homicide case file. He began to sift through the hundreds of pages of supplemental reports, crime scenes photos, diagrams, and inventory of the physical evidence. He asked me to join him at a meeting he had arranged with Elinor McGarry, the CSI technician who had processed the crime scene four years earlier. Lou told Elinor he was convinced the one latent fingerprint which she had developed on the aluminum window frame was the key to solving the kidnap-murder of 13-year-old Heather Dawn Church. Elinor replied, "What took you so long?"

On January 10, 1995, I was sworn in as the 26th Sheriff for El Paso County, Colorado. I took over a law enforcement organization consisting of 404 civilian and sworn personnel and Captain Smit took over the Heather Dawn Church homicide investigation. One of the hardest decisions for me to make was what to do with the former Captain of Detectives, a previous classmate of mine from the Police Academy. I considered him a friend, but he had already been in charge of the cold case for four years and I couldn't have two Captains of Detectives. He never complained about his demotion to Lieutenant or being transferred to midnights in the jail.

On March 28, 1995, eleven weeks after Lou Smit took over the Heather Dawn Church kidnap-murder investigation, he called me at 2:30 a.m. to tell me he knew who killed Heather. The latent fingerprint Elinor lifted at the crime scene, from the aluminum frame of the window in the mother's bedroom, had been matched to Robert Charles Browne, a convicted felon from California. Lou told me on the phone that they didn't know where the killer was, but now that they knew who he was, Lou promised, "We will find him."

After Lou's phone call, I was so excited I couldn't go back to sleep! I got up, took a shower, put on a suit and tie, and drove down to the Sheriff's Office. The sun had not come up yet, but the Detective Bureau was abuzz with activity. In the Captain's office, I found Lou sitting behind his desk with a big smile on his face. I said, "You found him, didn't you?"

Lou replied, "Yep, and you're not going to believe this but he lives just down Eastonville Road. You want a cup of coffee? I just made a fresh pot and I can tell you how this happened." Over coffee, Lou told me how he had brought his team together on his first day as Captain and focused them on his one main goal—finding the killer of Heather Dawn Church. He learned that the CBI fingerprint database was not integrated with the other 92 fingerprint systems in the U.S. and Canada. Lou directed copies of the unidentified latent fingerprint to be submitted 92 times, for comparison purposes, to every Automated Fingerprint Identification System (AFIS) in North America. California was the first state to reply with a "hit." Louisiana would be the second, a few days later, to confirm a fingerprint match to convicted felon Robert Charles Browne.

Lou told me Browne was one of the closest neighbors to where the Church family lived on the fringe of the Black Forest in rural El Paso County. Lou's detectives were busy all day putting together search and arrest warrants, along with a Rule 41.1 (Court Order) to obtain the fingerprints that our lab experts would independently confirm matched the latent fingerprint Elinor collected from the crime scene. Lou established surveillance on the suspect's residence and coordinated plans with the Patrol Division to arrest the killer of Heather Dawn Church.

Assuming Robert Browne could be armed and might resist being arrested for murder, Lou's detectives suggested we continue surveillance on the residence and try to catch him in a car away from his home. Browne also had two large Pit Bull guard dogs and SWAT units prefer not to have to put guard dogs down if it can be avoided. Surveillance teams throughout the night confirmed someone was inside the residence, and his car was parked in the driveway.

Early the next morning we assembled the takedown team, which included SWAT team members, search detectives, transport deputies, crime lab personnel, and supervisory personnel. We staged on Eastonville Road about a half mile north and out of sight of the suspect's house. I rode out to join the arrest team with Lou in his unmarked detective car. At sunrise, there were over a dozen Sheriff's marked and unmarked cars that lined up on Eastonville Road just over a hill north of the suspect's residence.

The surveillance team reported seeing movement in front of the house and thought the suspect might be getting ready to leave in his car. We waited patiently and eventually he got into his car and drove away from his home toward Colorado Springs. The surveillance team followed Browne's car and as soon as it was out of sight, detectives swooped in on the suspect's residence to execute the search warrant. An animal control officer came to take custody of the two Pit Bulls, who were not happy to be leaving their home. Lou and I headed to Colorado Springs in his car and listened on the police radio for updates of the suspect's location and direction of travel.

The surveillance team did a great job on not being spotted, and followed Robert Charles Browne to an art supply store in Colorado Springs. I got on the radio and gave the order to arrest the suspect when he came out of the store, before he could get in his car and drive away. Lou and I were still a couple miles away and I turned to Lou and said, "Come on, Smit, you're driving like an old lady; step on it or we're going to miss out on this arrest!" Lou laughed and stepped on the gas. We arrived at the art supply store just as the suspect was being handcuffed and led to an awaiting Sheriff's marked patrol car.

The art supply store was only three blocks from the Sheriff's Office and within minutes Robert Charles Browne was being advised he was under arrest for the murder of Heather Dawn Church. He was read his Miranda Rights, which he waived. Browne told detectives that they had made a mistake; he had not killed the little girl across the road and in fact he had never met any of the Church family or ever stepped foot on their property. To lock Browne into his false statement, Detectives asked him specifically if he had ever been in or near the home of the Church family. He denied ever touching or looking into the mother's bedroom window.

Browne emphatically denied ever being on the Church property and insisted he didn't know anything about the murder. He had not killed the little girl and insisted we had arrested the wrong person. Then detectives asked how he could explain his fingerprints being found at the crime scene. Browne insisted detectives made a mistake; it was impossible his fingerprints were found in the Church home. Then he accused detectives of planting the fingerprint in an attempt to pin the murder on him because he had a prior criminal record and lived across the street.

That evening, after Lou had called Heather's parents to tell them the man who had murdered their daughter was in jail, I called a press conference at the Sheriff's Office to announce the man who had kidnapped and murdered Heather Dawn Church had been taken into custody. The local media interrupted TV shows to air the press conference live. Standing by my side was Detective Lou Smit and his team of detectives. On May 25, 1995, Robert Charles Browne stood in front of a District Court Judge and pleaded guilty to First Degree Murder.

In a plea agreement with prosecutors, Browne accepted a life sentence, without the possibility of parole, in exchange for us dropping the death penalty. None of the homicide detectives nor I were anxious to give up the death penalty on Browne. However, Lou had talked to Heather's parents, both very religious people who were not in favor of the death penalty. They also wanted to avoid the agony of a long trial and taking the witness stand. The conviction of the man who had kidnapped and murdered their daughter would not bring closure. However, it would mark a new chapter in their lives where they could finally look ahead to the future, rather than looking back over their shoulder to see if the killer was stalking them or Heather's brother.

Within three months, Lou and his team had solved one of the most high-profile murder cases in El Paso County history and had arrested the killer with essentially the same investigative information and physical evidence that had been there all along. By the end of the year, Lou and his team had cleared two more cold cases, committed by another killer who had moved to New Mexico. One of these cold cases was in the City of Colorado Springs; the other was in El Paso County. However, this suspect would plead not guilty and demanded his day in court. He was convicted by a jury on two counts of First Degree Murder and given two life sentences.

In 1996, after serving 18 months as my Captain of Detectives, Lou retired from the Sheriff's Office to spend more time with his wife, Barb, who had been diagnosed with cancer. By the time my second term was up, the homicide unit had surpassed my personal clearance rate of 97%, accumulating an unprecedented 105% clearance rate. Like Lou and me, they too maintained a perfect 100% conviction rate on all murders. I respected Lou's decision to retire, but I was saddened to see my friend's legendary law enforcement career, spanning four decades in four different law enforcement agencies, come to an end. What I could not have known was Lou Smit's finest work as a homicide detective was yet to come—in Boulder, Colorado.

Part II

Chapter 4 – Boulder

The frantic 911 call Patsy Ramsey, JonBenét's mother, made at 5:52 a.m. on December 26, 1996, the morning after Christmas, is heart-wrenching to listen to as she desperately pleas for help from the police. What is even more painful for law enforcement professionals like Lou, Dave Spencer, and me is the awareness her desperate plea for help went unanswered. Harder still, is seeing how Patsy and her husband, John, were falsely accused by the Boulder Police of murdering their own daughter. Patsy and John Ramsey, along with their immediate family, would become victims of one of the worst miscarriages of justice in American history.

The verbatim transcript of the 911 recording begins with the police dispatcher answering the call, "911 Emergency." Patsy, with obvious panic in her voice says, "Police." The police dispatcher asks, "What's going on (sic) ma'am?" Without being asked, Patsy excitedly blurts out their address, "755 15th Street." The dispatcher calmly repeats, "What's going on there (sic) ma'am?"

Patsy: "We have a kidnapping. Hurry, please."

Police dispatcher: "Explain to me what's going on. Ok?"

Patsy: "There (). (sic) We have a, there's a note left and our daughter's gone."

Dispatcher: "A note was left and your daughter's gone?"

Patsy: "Yes!"

Dispatcher: "How old is your daughter?"

Patsy: "She's 6 years old. She's blonde, 6 years old."

Dispatcher: "How long ago was this?"

Patsy: "I don't know. I just got the note, and my daughter's gone."

Dispatcher: "Does it say who took her?"

Patsy: "What?"

Dispatcher: "Does it say who took her?"

Patsy: "No! I don't know. There's a, there's a ransom note here."

Dispatcher: "It's a ransom note?"

Patsy: "It says SBTC. Victory! Please!"

Dispatcher: "Okay, what's your name? Are you Kath…?"

Patsy repeats: "Patsy Ramsey. I'm the mother. Oh my God! Please!"

Dispatcher: "Okay, (sic) I'm sending an officer over, OK?"

Patsy: "Please!"

Dispatcher: "Do you know how long she's been gone?"

Patsy: "No! I don't! Please, we just got up and she's not here. Oh my God! Please!"

Dispatcher: "Okay, Cal…"

Patsy: "Please send somebody."

Dispatcher: "I am (sic) honey."

Patsy: "Please."

Dispatcher: "Take a deep breath and…Patsy? Patsy? Patsy? Patsy?"

This frantic call for help lasts just 1 minute and 41 seconds. It will become one of the most heavily scrutinized and misconstrued emergency phone calls ever made to an emergency 911 call center. The first Boulder Police Officer to arrive at the scene was Patrol Officer Rick French. The Ramsey home is located on the west side of the 700 block of 15th Street. It is a large brick single-family home with three stories above ground and a partial basement. The 100-year-old Tudor style home was decorated for Christmas with large red and white striped ornamental candy canes lining the walkway which led from the street to the front door.

Snow lay on the ground in front of the house, as well as on the north and west sides of the house. However, crime scene photos taken the morning of December 26, 1996, will show that much of the snow on the south side of the house had melted. During the winter months, in Colorado, the snow melts more quickly, being warmed by the sun, for buildings with a southern exposure.

The main entrance to the residence faces 15th Street. Walking around the residence, in a counterclockwise direction, to the north side of the home, is another exterior entrance leading to a butler's kitchen. This entrance may be important, as it was found to be unlocked the next morning; however, Mr. Ramsey thought the door had been locked the night before and he suggested it might have been unlocked by one of the neighbors or police officers while searching for JonBenét.

Similar to the Lindbergh Baby kidnapping, on March 1, 1932, both crime scenes were contaminated by police officers, family members, and friends of the family during the search for the missing children. Both victims, 20-month-old Charles Augustus Lindbergh, Jr., and 6-year-old JonBenét Ramsey, were asleep when they were abducted from their second floor bedrooms. The Lindbergh home, Highfields, located in East Amwell, New Jersey, had been accessed using a wooden ladder, which was found beneath the baby's bedroom window. In both abductions, the killer or killers had written unusual ransom demand letters, and sadly, neither victim would be found alive.

On the north side of the Ramsey home, a black aluminum baseball bat was found lying on the concrete foundation near the butler door. A second aluminum baseball bat was found in the yard on the southside of the home. The Ramseys did not believe either baseball bats belonged to them; however, they could not rule out the bats were left behind by neighborhood children who often came over to play with JonBenét and her nine-year-old brother, Burke.

Lou Smit later documented in his investigative notes, that the black aluminum bat had been photographed with a small pink colored fabric material attached to the surface, consistent with the pink duvet found in the green suitcase propped up against the broken open basement window on the southside of the house. Inside the green suitcase was a Barbie doll, belonging to JonBenét, and one of her favorite Dr. Seuss children books. Lou also noted that the autopsy report and photographs documented a severe 8-inch depressed skull fracture, running from the front to the back, along the right side of the skull, which had to have been inflicted by a massive blow from a blunt object, possibly a baseball bat.

Two additional pieces of physical evidence, located just inside the butler's door, of importance that Lou points out in his slide presentation, was the three-page ransom note found on the bottom step of the spiral staircase. This staircase is located immediately inside and to the west of the butler door, and the note pad, used to write the ransom note, was found on top of a small desk within view of the spiral staircase.

There is another set of stairs, located inside the front entrance, that lead up to the second floor, where JonBenet and Burke slept in separate bedrooms. In a later interview, Patsy Ramsey would mention that the front stairs were rarely used by the family, and since the ransom note was found on the bottom step of the spiral stairs, whoever had left the note must have known the habits of the parents, who would be coming down the spiral staircase that morning and find the note.

Continuing the exterior examination of the crime scene, as one continues to walk counterclockwise around the north side of the residence, there is another door, on the north side of the residence. On the west side of the home, is a garage door allowing access to an attached two-car garage. The garage is accessible from the alley which runs north-south behind the home. The residence can be entered through the attached garage, which leads to the kitchen. Lou Smit's crime scene diagram shows a second exterior door which leads from the garage to the south side of the house, where the second aluminum baseball bat was found in the yard.

Continuing to examine the exterior of the Ramsey home, walking from the back alley, along the south side of the home, is a study, which juts out from the home, and on the east side of the study is another entrance leading into the kitchen. Just outside this entrance is a BBQ grill, positioned along with west wall, and immediately to the left of this outdoor grill is a green metal grate covering a basement window well.

Lou Smit's crime scene diagram has an arrow pointing to the grate, located below a room he labeled as the "North Dining" room located closest to the kitchen. This heavy metal grate is of importance, as Lou points out in his notes, as it allows access to the basement through a broken window which was found standing open. The green suitcase, with the pink duvet inside, was found just below this broken basement window. John and Patsy Ramsey described how the house had been purchased with an alarm system; however, it had not been used for months, following an accidental alarm incident which they didn't want repeated.

Completing the exterior crime scene examination, walking from the southside of the house, toward the street, is a set of French doors which lead into a second dining room. Lou labeled this room as the "South Dining," on his crime scene diagram. Walking further to the east is a solarium, and it too has an exterior door on the southside of the house. Several exterior crime scene photos taken, by the Boulder crime lab, on the morning of December 26, 1996, of the southside of the house, showing that there is no snow on the ground.

Walking around to the front of the house, Lou Smit's slide presentation shows a street-view of the Ramsey home. Below and to the left (south) of the front entrance, Lou drew an orange circle around the "Outside location of the boiler room window" where the door leading into the wine cellar is located. JonBenet's body would be found by her father, lying on the floor of the wine cellar, seven hours after the arrival of the Boulder Police Department. Officer French, the first police officer to arrive at the scene, was handed the ransom note, which he read and handed back to the parents. He then searched the home, failing to find the victim's body in the wine cellar.

Lou Smit's crime scene diagram shows, as one enters the front entrance to the home, a door, straight ahead, which leads to the kitchen. On the left is an opening to the living room, which leads to the solarium and from there into the south dining room. The north dining room, accessible from the south dining room, leads to the kitchen. To the north of the main kitchen, is a butler's kitchen, and a hallway which leads to the study, the attached two-car garage, and the spiral staircase leading to the second and third floors.

As you ascend the spiral stairs, to the second floor, is a guest bedroom, with a full bathroom. The bedroom was once used by JonBenét's older brother, John Andrew Ramsey, who was away at college on the night of the murder. Lou Smit's investigating notes draw attention to this guest bedroom as it overlooks the garage; the Ramsey's were away from the home, attending a Christmas dinner with friends, in Boulder, who had children of similar ages to JonBenét and Burke. Lou's slides also show distant and close-up views of the dust ruffle for the bed in this guest bedroom as having been disturbed. The drawers in the adjoining bathroom were unusual, for they had been left open and a long rope was found in a "sack or bag" in the guest bedroom.

The closest bedroom to the guest bedroom is JonBenét's bedroom. It too has a full bathroom and was furnished with two twin beds with the headboards positioned against the east wall. There is an exterior door that leads from her bedroom out to a balcony overlooking the yard on the south side of the house. Down the hall is a play room, another bathroom, and a set of additional stairs that lead up to the third floor or down to the front of the house. On the far east side of the second floor is another bedroom used by Burke. This bedroom was also furnished with two twin beds. Burke was asleep in one of these beds when JonBenét was abducted.

The computer generated crime scene diagram, created by Lou Smit, shows the stairs near Burke's bedroom, go up to where the parent's bed was located. The upper, or third floor, is a large master suite with a study, a dressing area, and two full baths. One of these bathrooms leads out on to a deck. A stairway, which Lou labeled as the "Back Stairs," leads down to the second level. This back stairway is where the spiral staircase is accessed, on the second floor, which can also be descended to the first floor, where the ransom note was found by Patsy Ramsey on the bottom step.

Lou Smit's crime scene diagram of the basement, shows a half bath, at the bottom of the stairs, is a laundry room, storage area, and a boiler room. The wine cellar is accessed from the boiler room. This is where JonBenet's body was found. Nearby is a room that the Ramsey family referred to as the "Train Room" because Burke and JonBenét had a model train set up to play with in the basement. Lou's crime scene diagram shows an arrow pointing, from the outside of the house, to the metal grate covering the window well. This window was found standing wide open and was photographed by the crime lab on the morning of December 26, 1996, before JonBenét's body was discovered.

John Ramsey explained that he had broken the upper pane of this window several months earlier when he had been accidently locked out of the home. He unlocked and crawled through this window to gain entrance into the home and to his regret, failed to have this broken window repaired. When Boulder police detective said there was no forced entry into the home, they told Lou Smit that no one could have used this basement window to enter the home. Lou Smit then had himself photographed and video recorded crawling in and out of this broken window. The Boulder police never retracted their statement of there being no forced entry into the home; but clearly they were wrong.

From his personal experience, in crawling through this basement window on several occasions, Lou said it was difficult to step up into the window well without something to stand on, and he came to the conclusion the killer had positioned the green suitcase, upright below the broken window, to climb out of the window after JonBenét had been killed. Lou also shared with me, that he thought the killer had placed JonBenet, alive, inside the large green suitcase, in an attempt to remove her from the home. However, the suitcase was too large for him to push the suitcase up and out of the basement through the broken window well.

Lou's crime scene diagram shows the Boiler Room being located adjacent to the train room. He drew an arrow to where a paint tray had been found on the floor near the door leading into the wine cellar. JonBenet's body was found on the floor, just inside the cellar door, a few feet from the paint tray. Inside the paint tray was the bristle end of the broken paintbrush handle. The middle portion of the paint brush handle had been used to fashion the garrote using white parachute cord. The upper third portion of the paintbrush handle, opposite the bristled end, has never been found. Lou theorized that the killer may have kept this item as a trophy.

Seven hours after the ransom note was discovered, Detective Linda Arndt instructed JonBenet's father, to take one friend and search the house again. They started in the basement. John Ramsey pointed to the broken window, explaining that he had broken that window, months earlier, when he had been locked out of the house without a key, and the green suitcase had been moved from another part of the basement. When John Ramsey opened the door leading into the wine cellar, he found JonBenet lying on the floor with a piece of black duct tape over her mouth. Attempting to help his daughter, he removed the duct tape, and tried to untie the white cord binding her wrists.

When that failed, John Ramsey said he picked up his daughter, cradling her in his arms, screamed, and ran up the stairs with her in his arms. He carried her to where the Boulder detective was, hoping she would be able to help JonBenét, and laid her motionless body on the floor, near the Christmas tree. Detective Linda Arndt found no pulse and called for assistance and for the crime lab to return. John Ramsey covered his daughter's body with a blanket, but when Patsy Ramsey saw her daughter, lying on the floor, she pulled the blanket back, trying to comfort her daughter, further contaminating the crime scene.

When the crime lab arrived back at the scene, they took additional photos of the basement, including the wine cellar. The photos did show the imprint of a Hi-Tec boot print on the concrete basement floor, near where JonBenét's body had been found. Lou Smit's notes document how the Ramsey home was thoroughly searched, and no Hi-Tec footwear were found. Further, his notes indicate that none of the responding officers or crime lab personnel were wearing Hi-Tec boots. Lou also described how the ridge patterns of the boot print were very crisp and sharp, suggesting, perhaps, they were recent.

Therefore, Lou Smit believed the killer may have been wearing Hi-Tec boots when he murdered JonBenet in the basement of the Ramsey home. Lou would later document how the reddish colored rectangular burn marks, photographed on her back and the right side of her face, appeared consistent with burn marks from a stun gun. This, he believed, was vitally important for it went to prove the intent of the attacker; to immobilize the victim and remove her from the home, until the ransom demand was paid.

Within days of the murder, most Boulder detectives came to believe Patsy had killed her six-year-old daughter, wrote the ransom note, and then staged the crime scene to look like a kidnapping. Despite there not being any prior domestic violence calls at that address or reports of child abuse, other Boulder detectives would conclude it was JonBenét's father, John Ramsey, who murdered his daughter and Patsy wrote the three-page ransom note, to cover up the murder. Another Boulder area detective claimed 9-year-old Burke had killed his sister, after jabbing her in the face and back with the model train track. The details documented in the autopsy report clearly suggest this violent sexual assault was not the work of a 9-year-old boy and the ransom note was most definitely not written by a 9-year-old.

The ransom note reads:

Mr. Ramsey,

Listen carefully! We are a group of individuals that represent a small foreign faction. We respect your business but not the country that it serves. At this time (sic) we have your daughter in our possession. She is safe and unharmed and if you want her to see 1997, you must follow our instructions to the letter.

You will withdraw $118,000.00 from your account. $100,000 will be in $100 bills and the remaining $18,000 in $20 bills. Make sure that you bring an adequate size attaché to the bank. When you get home (sic) you will put the money in a brown paper bag. I will call you between 8 and 10 a.m. tomorrow to instruct you on delivery. The delivery will be exhausting so I advise you to be rested. If we monitor you getting the money early, we might call you early to arrange an earlier delivery of the money and hence a (sic) earlier pick-up of your daughter.

Any deviation of my instructions will result in the immediate execution of your daughter. You will also be denied her remains for proper burial. The two gentlemen watching over your daughter do not particularly like you so I advise you not to provoke them. Speaking to anyone about your situation, such as the Police, FBI, etc. will result in your daughter being beheaded. If we catch you talking to a stray dog, she dies. If you alert bank authorities, she dies. If the money is in any way marked or tampered with, she dies. You will be scanned for electronic devices and if any are found, she dies. You can try to deceive us but be warned that we are familiar with Law (sic) enforcement countermeasures and tactics. You stand a 99% chance of killing your daughter if you try to out smart (sic) us. Follow our instructions and you stand a 100% chance of getting her back. You and your family are under constant scrutiny as well as the authorities. Don't try to grow a brain (sic) John. You are not the only fat cat around so don't think that killing will be difficult. Don't underestimate us (sic) John.

Use that good southern common sense of yours. It is up to you now John!

Victory!
S.B.T.C.

Lou Smit would later write, "Past experience has shown me that normally the crime is what it seems to be," and he will conclude there is undeniable physical evidence to substantiate this case, "Is a kidnapping and murder." Dave Spencer, Lou's long-time homicide partner, often quoted Ockham's Razor Theory, which implies, "the simplest solution is almost always the best." The theory is named after William of Ockham, a 14th-century logician and theologian, and used by many of the great thinkers for centuries. Unlike a few of the detectives at the Boulder PD, when it came to homicide investigations, Lou Smit and Dave Spencer were "great thinkers."

The first uniformed Boulder police officer to arrive on scene at the Ramsey residence was Rick French. He was shown the note and searched the house. In fairness, this was a big house, with four levels: three above ground and a partial basement. However, the basement contained only five small rooms: a laundry room (with a half bath off to one side), a storage room with a large closet, a train room (with a broken window standing wide open), boiler room, wine cellar (where JonBenét's body would later be found), and three small crawl spaces.

As a rookie patrol officer, I was taught to clear a building following a search pattern, usually from the ground level up, and then we'd search any levels below ground. Each floor would be searched in a clockwise or counterclockwise pattern. We paid particular attention to rooms with closed doors because there might be a bad guy hiding in that room and you never wanted to turn your back on a possible threat to you or your partner.

Common sense should dictate that if you are looking for a missing child you search anywhere that child could be—closets, clothes hampers, under the bed. Maybe the child is scared and hiding. As homicide detectives, we documented the scene with the lab personnel. We searched and measured every room, closets, or any spaces large enough to conceal a body to make sure we weren't overlooking anything important.

When Officer French searched the basement, he overlooked a window standing wide open in the train room, with a long black scuff mark on the white wall below the window. Standing upright beneath this open window was a large suitcase which Lou Smit theorized was used by the killer to stand on while exiting the home after JonBenét had been murdered. Officer French later admitted he stood in front of that closed door in the basement, behind which JonBenét's body lay dead on the floor; however, he failed to open the door to look inside the small room. JonBenét's body would not be found for another seven hours.

Other Boulder Police uniformed police officers, supervisors, detectives, and crime lab personnel also responded to the reported kidnapping at the Ramsey home. They too failed to notice the open window in the basement and not one person opened the door to the room where the murder had occurred. The crime lab photographed the residence and dusted for fingerprints, all while overlooking the body behind the closed basement door. Friends of the Ramsey's were admitted into the crime scene, as was Father Rol Hoverstock, a priest from St. John's Episcopal Church. Undeniably, the biggest single mistake made from the onset of the investigation was not properly securing the crime scene. That initial mistake was compounded when the police failed to conduct a comprehensive search for JonBenét and ignored physical evidence of an intruder.

In the book *Death of Innocence*, authored by John and Patsy Ramsey, JonBenét's parents gave a detailed first-hand account of that horrible morning, including how the Boulder police eventually moved their marked police cars down the street while waiting for instructions on how to deliver the ransom money. The parents questioned the Boulder police as to why the FBI was not there to help find whoever had kidnapped their daughter. They would later learn the Boulder police blocked the FBI from entering the residence. Among the detectives who would respond to the crime scene were Steve Thomas and Linda Arndt. Neither had ever worked a homicide case.

Boulder Detective Linda Arndt arrived at the Ramsey home around 8 a.m. Her role was to wait inside the residence, with the Ramseys, for instructions from the kidnapper(s). John Ramsey got on the phone and made arrangements to obtain the $118,000 ransom demand in cash while awaiting instructions from the kidnapper(s). No instructions or efforts to collect the ransom would be forthcoming. Around 1 p.m., Detective Arndt asked John Ramsey to search the house again. In his book, *Death of Innocence*, John Ramsey writes, "Morning drifts into afternoon, and still no phone call. The frustration of waiting for the kidnapper to contact us becomes unbearable. Finally, Detective Linda Arndt asks me to take one person, go through the entire house, and look for anything unusual or out of place."

John Ramsey explained, "I want to do anything I can to help, so I agree. I don't stop to think that we should not be allowed to roam around the house without a police officer present–much less search the entire house by ourselves. After all, it's my home. I live here. And I assume a police detective knows how to professionally handle this kind of situation. Fleet White is standing next to me, so I ask him to go with me. Fleet is my friend and a father himself... We head downstairs, and I take Fleet over to the broken windowpane and explain my breaking in there last summer. I tell him that I had found this window open earlier."

Fortunately, the Boulder crime lab had taken photographs of this open basement window. Lou Smit would later use this photo to conclude this broken basement window was likely the point of entry (POE) used by the suspect(s) to enter the Ramsey home in an attempt to kidnap their daughter. John Ramsey continues to write of his horrific experience in finding JonBenét's body, "We continued our search, and a few minutes later I'm at the door by the furnace. I open it and see JonBenét lying on the floor with a white blanket around her. Black tape covers her mouth. That's my baby, lying there like that. Her hands are above her head, tied together with a shoestring-like cord."

JonBenét's father shares the emotions he felt in finding her body, ripping the tape off her mouth, seeing her "delicate eyelids are closed and her skin is cool to the touch." He tries untying her, but the knots are too tight. He grabbed her up in his arms and stumbles out of the room. He screams as he carries her up the stairs, runs into the living room, where Linda Arndt is standing, and lays the body of his daughter on the floor in front the Christmas tree. He hugs his daughter and kisses her, trying to comfort her, as any parent would do for their child.

Detective Arndt knelt down, over JonBenét's body and checked for vital signs. She finds none. Linda Arndt was the lone police officer in the Ramsey home. She later describes, "I see John Ramsey carrying JonBenét up the last three steps, from the basement." As Detective Arndt was leaning over the little girl's body, searching for signs of life, she describes looking up into John Ramsey's eyes. "His face was just inches from mine," and in a "non-verbal exchange" she suddenly comes to the conclusion she is looking into the eyes of the killer and began "counting the bullets" in her gun in fear John Ramsey would kill everyone else in the Ramsey's home.

In their book, *Death of Innocence*, John Ramsey writes what he is thinking and happens next, "Patsy will be coming into the room, I think. Her friends have kept her in the TV room at the back of the house. She must not see JonBenét like this. I push myself off the floor and get a blanket to cover JonBenét. I lay the blanket over her as I have done many times when she falls asleep." This act of compassion likely contaminated the crime scene even more, but is certainly understandable. John Ramsey described how Patsy was "fighting to get into the room to see her baby. She rushes past me and falls onto JonBenét's body."

Once the body is found, more police rush back to the Ramsey home. John Ramsey explains, "A person comes up and says he's Detective Mason. I assume he is with the FBI. Finally, the police will get help, I think. Later I will learn that Mason is another Boulder PD detective and that the police, in fact, have kept the FBI at bay, not letting them inside the house." The FBI had been notified and did set up a phone trap on the Ramsey's home phone in case the kidnapper, now a confirmed killer, calls. Finally, the police secure the crime scene. John, Patsy, and their 9-year-old son, Burke Ramsey, are escorted by the police to a neighbor's home.

As they are leaving, John Ramsey recalls, "I see a taxi pull up to the curb. John Andrew, Melinda, and Stewart get out. They have arrived from Minneapolis after frantically arranging to take the first flight they could get. Mobilizing everything I have left in me, I go over to the kids and tell them JonBenét is gone." John Andrew and Melinda are John Ramsey's children from his first marriage; Stewart is Melinda's boyfriend. The three of them were planning to meet John, Patsy, JonBenét, and Burke, later that day, on the 26th, for a second family Christmas at their vacation home in Charlevoix, Michigan.

On the evening of December 26, 1996, the TV news broadcast footage shows the front of the Ramsey home in Boulder, decorated for Christmas with large red and white striped ornamental candy canes lining the walkway leading up to the large Tudor home. For the next several days and eventually weeks, the national news and tabloids alike continued to report no footprints were found in the snow and there was no evidence of forced entry into the home. But what Lou Smit would later point out was there was no snow on the south side of the house where a basement window, with a previously broken window, was found standing open.

In the days following JonBenét's death, the public's perception that someone within the Ramsey family was responsible for her murder grew as the Boulder Police released false and misleading information. In Paula Woodward's book, *Unsolved: The JonBenét Ramsey Murder 25 Years Later*, she writes, "Monday, December 30, 1996 Boulder Police News Conference. No Danger from a Killer on the Loose. Patsy Ramsey did not give DNA. Boulder police had a news conference to update media and the public on the case. The Boulder public information office said, 'DNA was taken from the Ramseys, but not from Patsy Ramsey. I assume it's because she is still extremely grief-stricken…'"

As Paula Woodward's book points out, "That's wrong. Look at the police report from two days earlier on Saturday December 28, 1996…4:37 p.m. Patricia "Patsy" Ramsey (along with other Ramsey family members) gives her DNA." Her book continues on the following page to identify the source, a report submitted by Boulder detective Steve Thomas, which read, "At approximately 4:57 p.m., Detective Gosage and I met with Patricia "Patsy" Ramsey, dob/12-29-56 (the mother of JonBenét, (sic) in the BCSO Records Section fingerprint/photo room. Patricia Ramsey was cooperative in our requests, but was crying/sobbing, withdrawn, and nonspeaking, and unsteady on her feet. A photo was taken, and some basic personal information was obtained.

"Patricia Ramsey had present John F. Stavely, attorney… who observed the proceedings. 4:37 p.m. blood draw. 4:42 p.m. hair samples. 4:50 p.m. fingerprints. During this processing, Patricia Ramsey sobbed/cried, and during fingerprints asked Detective Gosage, 'Will this help find who killed my baby?', and made the statement, 'I did not murder my baby."

As a former police spokesperson, the information released by the Boulder police spokeswoman, at the December 30, 1996 news conference, is disconcerting for two reasons: first, the statement is false and secondly, it included an assumption. Patsy Ramsey had given a DNA sample. When the police spokeswoman said, "DNA was taken from the Ramseys, but not from Patsy Ramsey. I assume it's because she is still extremely grief-stricken..." When the police hold a news conference, to release a statement, the public and the media have an inherent right to believe the information is true and free of any speculations or assumptions.

When the police spokeswoman said that, "DNA was taken from the Ramseys, but not from Patsy Ramsey" the spotlight was either intentionally or inadvertently cast upon her as the more likely Ramsey family member responsible for the murder. The likelihood of this false information being made public by the Boulder police inadvertently remains doubtful when viewed in light of Colorado Bureau of Investigation (CBI) Laboratory Report being prepared by Detective Thomas Trujillo on the same day the news conference was being held.

This CBI Laboratory Report requested: "DNA Testing" pertaining to "Offense: 0902 – Homicide – Willful Kill-Family" submitted by "Det. Thomas Trujillo" was dated "123096" and names "Suspect (s): Ramsey, Patsy" and "Ramsey, John" and identifies "Victim (s): Ramsey, JonBenet (sic)." Items being submitted for DNA testing included: "Bloodstains from Shirt. Bloodstains from Panties. Bloodstain Standard from JonBenet (sic) Ramsey. Swab with Saliva. Right and Left Hand Fingernails from JonBenet (sic) Ramsey. Samples from Tape. Bloodstain from White Blanket. Bloodstains from Nightgown. Semen Stains from Black Blanket."

The 123096 CBI Lab request submitted by Detective Trujillo also included "Bloodstain Standard" from ten individuals; including: "John Andrew Ramsey. Melinda Ramsey. John B. Ramsey. Patricia Ramsey. Burke Ramsey. Jeff Ramsey (sic)" along with four other individuals connected to the Ramsey family. The CBI Lab Report states the evidence was "Examined by/ Kathren M. Brown Dressel, Laboratory Agent/Criminalist." Two weeks later, on January 15, 1997, CBI notified the Boulder police that none of the names submitted matched the DNA collected from JonBenét's body or her clothing. According to Lou Smit's notes, this CBI Lab report was not shared with the Boulder DA's Office until months later.

Despite being confronted with undeniable DNA evidence, which cleared all the Ramsey family members, the Boulder police never publicly disclosed the results of the DNA testing and remained fixated on the false assumption the murder was committed by someone within the Ramsey family. By the first week of March 1997, it was apparent the Boulder police suspected the ransom note had been written by Patsy, and JonBenét's body had been staged by one or both of her parents to cover up the murder.

Paula Woodward, an investigative reporter in the Denver metro area at the time, who 25 years after the murder, authored the book *Unsolved: The JonBenét Ramsey Murder 25 Years Later*, highlights other false or misleading news headlines being flashed around the world days after the murder. "The public is not in any danger. CBS News December 31, 1996. Wednesday, January 1, 1997 John Ramsey Pilots His Plane to Funeral. John Ramsey is a pilot and flew the family to Georgia in his Plane. *Rocky Mountain News* January 1, 1997. 'We don't think there should be cause for undue concern' – (sic) Boulder Public Information Officer, NBC News January 2, 1997."

The Boulder mayor even got involved in making public statements, based on false or misleading information she was being fed by the Boulder police. According to Paula Woodward's book, *Unsolved*, "Boulder Mayor Leslie Durgin blasted her opinion to the *Boulder Daily Camera*, the *Rocky Mountain News*, CNN, and others while continuing and reinforcing the statements from the Monday news conference. She stated, 'It's not like there's someone walking around the streets of Boulder prepared to strangle young children.' She was responding to a CNN interview Patsy and John Ramsey had done the night before, Wednesday night, January 1, 1997. In the interview, the Ramseys warned 'There's a killer on the loose.' The mayor was reiterating, emphasizing, and speculating with bias."

Paula Woodward's book is appropriately critical of how the Boulder Mayor was wrong about there being "No signs of forced entry into the home. No killer on the loose... Mayor Durgin also elaborated on the Ramsey case with a stunning remark about evidence. Boulder police reports prove she was wrong. 'There were 'no visible signs (sic) of forced entry in the house' where JonBenet was found dead,' declared Durgin. Actually, eight areas of possible and questionable entry were found in the Ramsey home and written about in police reports."

One of these eight possible areas of entry was the "Metal Grate Disturbance Area: below the broken basement window." This was the most likely point of entry (POE) Lou Smit had identified and pointed to the large suitcase which had been positioned beneath the broken window. The suitcase, which did not belong to JonBenét, contained a toy and clothing belonging to the little girl. Lou theorized the suspect may have intended to put the little girl inside the suitcase to kidnap her from the home. When Lou pointed to this evidence of a possible "intruder," the Boulder police dismissed his assertion and claimed no one could have used this window to enter the home. Even after Lou had himself videotaped climbing in and out of the broken window, the Boulder police continued to dismiss this evidence of "forced entry into the house," right along with the unknown DNA found on JonBenét's body and clothing.

In the first days immediately following the murder, the Ramseys had begun to make funeral arrangements for JonBenét while reports from friends trickled in that the police were focusing on them as being responsible for the death of their daughter. In their book, John and Patsy Ramsey shared how the "Boulder County Coroner in a letter confirmed the police had considered withholding the body from proper burial, to force the parents to cooperate." John Ramsey called this an unimaginable and "barbaric" act of cruelty and served to "widen the chasm between us."

John Ramsey wrote how he understood the police needed to question the parents, but "Don't stop there!" After burying their daughter in Georgia, and making arrangements for the protection of their son, Burke, the Ramseys waited and waited to be updated by the police on the progress being made to catch the killer. They decided they needed to return to Colorado and submit to whatever the Boulder detectives asked them to do so they could get beyond the notion that they were responsible for JonBenét's death, and concentrate on catching her killer instead.

Neither Lou Smit nor I could have ever imagined the Ramsey homicide case would soon draw him out of retirement. The previous year, Lou had retired as my Captain of Detectives to spend time with his wife, Barb, who was undergoing cancer treatment. By Christmas 1996, I had moved into my new house and was halfway into my first term as El Paso County Sheriff. First impressions of me as "the new Sheriff in town" had been greatly enhanced when Lou and his team of detectives solved the high-profile kidnap-murder of Heather Dawn Church. I knew the community was safer—because of Lou Smit.

When I was first sworn in as Sheriff, I worked 10- to 14-hour days, seven days a week, for three and a half straight months. After Heather's case was solved, I started taking most Sundays off and eventually started working only half days on Saturdays. I was also rebuilding my personal life and planning to be remarried. I asked Lou to be my best man at my wedding, scheduled for March 7, 1997, in Las Vegas, Nevada. He agreed and offered to fly out a day or two early and made arrangements to meet us at the airport in a stretch limousine. My mother, Margie, and sister, Vicki, were there at our wedding. Since this was my second marriage, we opted for a small wedding at the chapel in the New York New York Hotel Casino, and planned for a large wedding reception at the Glen Eyrie Castle in Colorado Springs after we returned from our honeymoon.

As always, Lou added to the excitement when he showed up at the airport in a long black stretch limo, with a bottle of champagne in a silver ice bucket. On the way to get our marriage license at the Clark County Courthouse, Lou and I stood up through the opening in the roof of the limo to take in the lights along the Strip. As we were standing alongside one another, he told me I might be getting a call from Alex Hunter, the District Attorney in Boulder. He explained the DA had asked him to come out of retirement to help with the JonBenét Ramsey case and he had given my name and cellphone number to the DA as a reference.

While we were in Vegas, I received a phone call from Alex Hunter who asked me if I would recommend that he hire Lou Smit to be part of the DA's JonBenét Ramsey Task Force. I told him absolutely and shared how as a newly elected public official, the best thing I did was hire Lou to be my Captain of Detectives. I shared how Lou had solved the Heather Dawn Church kidnap-murder in a matter of eleven weeks, while the former Sheriff's detectives had failed to solve the case in four years. I encouraged the DA to do what

I had done in giving Lou the lead on the case and supporting him with anything he needed to bring the killer to justice.

When Lou and I first talked in Vegas about the Ramsey case, like nearly everyone who had been following the case in the news, we assumed one of the parents had likely committed the murder. The challenge would be figuring out which one. I knew going in Lou did not believe this would be a lengthy investigation. After our wedding ceremony, at the New York New York hotel and casino, we decided we wanted to ride the casino's rollercoaster. On March 8, 1997, my new bride and I left Vegas for Florida to catch a cruise ship headed to the Caribbean for a week and Lou returned to Colorado where he was hired by Alex Hunter to be part of the DA's team on the Ramsey Case. Neither Lou nor I could have ever imagined what a rollercoaster ride he, and later his family and I, were in for once he committed to working on the JonBenét Ramsey homicide investigation.

Alex Hunter had assembled an "A Team," consisting of two experienced prosecuting attorneys, Peter Hofstrom and Trip DeMuth, and two seasoned detectives, Steve Ainsworth, on loan from the Boulder County Sheriff's Office, and Lou Smit, who was hired as a full-time DA's special investigator. It is tragic the inexperienced detectives, including Linda Arndt and Steve Thomas, did not listen to Lou Smit, one of the most experienced homicide detectives in Colorado. The Ramseys would later write how they were confused when they first met Steve Thomas, who had been assigned the lead detective, because his business card said he was a narcotics detective. His Detective Commander was John Eller, who had also never investigated or managed a homicide case.

In the book, *Death of Innocence*, John Ramsey wrote how John Eller, "never once talked to us or sat across the table from us, yet apparently he was the one who concluded from the beginning that I killed JonBenét. Eller set the theory in motion, and his minions dutifully followed. Eller had kept the FBI out of the case and refused help from those more experienced with murder cases, such as the Denver Police Homicide Unit, who had offered their help and expertise. Apparently easily threatened, Eller took an extremely defensive attitude toward anyone outside the local police department. His refusing expert help is the most critical mistake for which I hold the Boulder police accountable."

Ron Walker, a retired supervisor with the FBI, would later confirm that he had offered the Boulder Police all the resources the FBI had to bring the investigation to a successful conclusion. But his offer would be refused. Other than setting up the phone trap on the Ramsey's home phone, while they waited for the call that would never come from the kidnapper(s), the FBI and experienced homicide detectives were shut completely out of the case.

John Ramsey wrote about their first meeting with Lou in his and Patsy's book, *Death of Innocence*; "While staying with the Stines, Patsy and I learned that every morning, Lou Smit drove by our house on Fifteenth Street and sat out front for a few minutes to gather his thoughts. We discovered that during this time of quiet, Lou prayed for guidance and spent time thinking about JonBenét's case. The thought that a detective asked for God's guidance was reassuring to us and solidified our confidence that a wise man was, in fact, working on the case. We knew that in some way, we had to let Lou know how much we appreciated his dedication to find the killer of our daughter."

In their book, John Ramsey continued to write, "A few days later, Patsy and I drove over to our old house early one morning, and, sure enough, Lou Smit's van was parked out front. We waited a moment and then got out of our car, went over to his van, and asked if we could speak to him. Much to our relief, Lou smiled at us and his big blue eyes sparkled. 'I'm happy to see you,' he said. 'Thank you, I'm

John Ramsey.' I extended my hand. 'This is my wife, Patsy.' 'Glad to meet you.' He shook our hands."

John Ramsey shared how he told Lou, "We hoped to talk with you for a few minutes. Patsy and I wanted you to know we thank God every day that you're here. We're willing to do anything we can to help this investigation and find the killer. You can call on us any time." Lou thanked them and replied, "I deeply appreciate your offer. I'm sure we will be calling." Then Lou said, "Maybe we could pray together. We want God's blessing on the investigation."

John Ramsey wrote, "We held hands and Lou said a short prayer. At the end Patsy and I thanked this good man again before we got out of his van and went back to our car. Patsy and I knew we'd met an important man in our lives and wanted to do everything we could to help this investigator complete his job. Patsy said she had prayed many times that God would send someone who would help find the truth. We believe he sent Lou Smit." As Lou's former detective partner, I was present with Lou Smit when he prayed for victims and their families; I was also there when he arrested many people who professed to be Christians.

In July of 1997, Lou contacted the Ramsey's attorneys to request a meeting. At this meeting with John and Patsy Ramsey, attended by Boulder Detective Tom Wickman, Ramsey's attorney Bryan Morgan and Mike Bynum, Lou shared information that he asked to remain confidential and not leave the room. The Ramseys agreed and Lou asked if they knew anyone who owned a stun gun. They did not and had never owned a stun gun themselves. Then Lou told them he thought a stun gun was used on their daughter. In Lou's mind, and in the minds of the Ramseys, this was very compelling evidence that pointed to an intruder.

However, the Boulder detectives criticized Lou for praying with the Ramseys, accused him of interfering with their investigation and dismissed his interpretation of the stun gun marks pointing toward an intruder. The Boulder police stood firmly by their belief Patsy had written the note and the parents had staged the crime scene to look like a kidnapping to cover up the murder committed by the father, or possibly the mother. Either way, the parents, in the minds of the Boulder police, the tabloids, and mainstream media, were guilty of murdering their daughter.

Not to be outdone or miss an opportunity to improve viewer ratings, the print media and TV news joined with the tabloids and continued to spread "misinformation" or "disinformation" about there being no footprints in the snow and no signs of forced entry into the home. Headlines in bold print repeated how John and Patsy Ramsey, "remain under an umbrella of suspicion." Tabloids and newspapers continued to write stories that began with "unnamed sources say…"

As a former CSPD Public Information Officer, two red flags always go up in my mind whenever I hear or read the catchphrase, "The person spoke on condition of anonymity because he wasn't authorized to speak publicly." Both red flags should be thrown against whoever is using this nebulous statement. The first red flag to me begs the question; A. "Why is this person speaking?" And B, "Why are you printing this?" Wouldn't it be helpful to know, "Is this anonymous source being paid and if so, by whom?"

John Ramsey wrote in his book, "Laurie Lounsbury, editor of the weekly *Charlevoix Courier*, said that she had refused multiple offers of payment for pictures she'd taken in previous years of us and JonBenét. 'I just said no, good-bye,' Lounsbury said. Lanie, one of Jon Benet's very special friends and baby-sitters, who was fourteen when JonBenét was killed, was called directly by the television program *Extra* and offered seven hundred and fifty dollars each for any photos of JonBenét. Lanie told them she would not part with her photos of JonBenét for any amount of money. Her dad, Carlos, later told the callers to leave his daughter alone, or else."

Chapter 25 of the Ramsey's book is titled "Cooperating with the Police." It begins: "As the story of JonBenét's murder and investigation exploded across the world, a common theme energizing the media was that Patsy and I were not cooperating with the Boulder police and were doing everything we could to avoid being interrogated. None of this could have been further from the truth…The fact is that on December 26 and 27, 1996, I was interviewed for several hours by Linda Arndt and other police officers. Patsy was with me most of the time on the twenty-seventh. Patsy and I were more than willing, and anxious, to talk as long as the police wanted–(sic) and told them so."

As parents, John Ramsey explained their focus, "immediately after JonBenét's murder, was mostly on laying our daughter to rest. Believe me, at that point, this is pretty much all you can or want to do. Following our return from JonBenét's burial in Georgia, we became aware of the law enforcement bias toward us. Nevertheless, we wanted to help, and the police were told that Patsy and I were available for a joint interview." The police chose January 18, 1997, at 10 a.m. Over concerns for Patsy's health, the Ramseys asked to be interviewed together in their attorney's office with a doctor present and they requested that Detective Arndt be involved.

The police cancelled the meeting advising the Ramsey's attorneys, in writing, "the time for interviewing John and Patsy as witnesses who could provide critical information that would be helpful in the initial stages of our investigation has passed." The Ramseys believed, "the police continued leaking the spin that we were uncooperative, as if they were fighting a publicity battle to posture Patsy and me into a corner, so we would look guilty to the public. These actions only deepened our mistrust and lack of respect for the police. Never under the watch of Police Chief Tom Koby and Detective Commander John Eller were we treated as parents of a child who was murdered, only as murderers."

Three weeks after Lou joined the Boulder DA's staff, John and Patsy Ramsey met at the DA's Office with Peter Hofstrom and Tom Wickman, of the Boulder Police Department. This meeting, on Friday, April 11, 1997, was at the request of law enforcement officials and Lou Smit was not asked to participate. Follow-up audiotaped interviews were scheduled for Wednesday, April 23, 1997. John Ramsey was to be interviewed first, at 9:30 a.m., followed by Patsy's interview at 1:30 p.m. On Tuesday, April 10, the Boulder police cancelled the meetings. Arranging a meeting, then cancelling at the last minute, is another tactic used by some police detectives to put pressure on a person of interest, especially when they have a weak case (if the police have a strong case, they don't have to play psychological games).

The Ramsey's attorneys protested with a letter delivered to the DA's Office requesting the interviews proceed as scheduled. The police answered with a press release explaining they had cancelled the meeting based on information from the FBI's Child Abduction and Serial Killer Unit, which claimed, "under the conditions to which they had already agreed," these interviews would not be productive. After several days of negotiations between the Ramsey's attorneys, the DA's Office and the Police, interrogations were rescheduled for April 30, 1997, from 8 a.m. to 5 p.m. at the Boulder County Justice Center.

Both sides agreed to limit the interrogations to eight hours. I have conducted hundreds of interviews and interrogations; four-hour interrogations are a long time and eight hours is an eternity and a real test of endurance and willpower—for both sides. Detectives Steve Thomas and Tom Trujillo conducted the interviews and began with Patsy. She was interviewed for six and a half hours. Her attorney, Pat Burke, was present and at one point, when Patsy broke down and started crying, asked for a short break while Patsy tried to compose herself. John was interviewed next. Both agreed the police did not ask them anything that wasn't previously discussed on December 26 or 27, and they remained convinced the police were trying to indict them for murder.

In the weeks and months after Lou joined the Boulder District Attorney's staff, animosity between the DA's Office and the Boulder Police Department intensified as discontent within the Boulder Police Department festered and finally reached a boiling point. On May 14, 1997, a newspaper article in the *Boulder Daily Camera* reported that both Linda Arndt and Melissa Hickman had been removed from the Ramsey homicide investigation. The Ramseys believed Linda Arndt "was being treated like the fall guy for the entire mess at the Boulder Police Department, when the real problem was in the leadership."

The Ramseys later learned, "...that Linda Arndt's attorney had asked Police Chief Tom Koby to stand publicly behind her and clarify the falsehoods from the truth, but Koby refused. The truth was Linda Arndt was involved in a number of serious mistakes that made it harder to solve JonBenét's murder, but from our perspective she did the best she could that morning and simply didn't get any help from her supervisors." Two years after the murder of JonBenét, an article written by a staff reporter appeared in the *Denver Post*, which stated, "Eleven years to the day after she joined, a 'saddened' Detective Linda Arndt wrote that she felt 'forced to leave' the Boulder Police Department in the wake of the JonBenét Ramsey case."

The *Denver Post* article quoted Linda Arndt's resignation letter which stated, "I am sad to say that I have felt a lack of support and increasing pressure from the department." Her letter continued, "I believe there are people with great strengths within the department and those people have brought and will continue to invite a sense of trust and faith in the department." The article concluded by recapping how, in May of 1998, Linda Arndt had filed a lawsuit against Chief Koby, claiming he had "violated her privacy when he didn't refute statements made about her work on the Ramsey case that he knew were false, and that he violated her First Amendment right to free speech when he wouldn't allow her to refute the statements in public."

In an A&E television documentary, retired FBI supervisor, Ron Walker, shared what he referred to as an "awkward triangle," that had emerged between the Boulder DA's Office, the Police, and the Ramseys. While the police and the media continued to claim the Ramseys were not cooperative and refused to be interviewed, the Ramseys continually pointed out that they had talked with police on the 26th and the 27th and voluntarily gave hair samples on the 28th. In retrospect, everyone agrees the Ramseys should have been immediately taken to police headquarters on the 26th and interviewed separately, if for nothing else than for their own protection.

In this A&E special, Alex Hunter told Bill Kurtis he didn't blame the Ramseys for hiring an attorney; in fact, if he had been asked by friends facing similar circumstances, he would have advised them to hire an attorney as well. Alex Hunter also shared how John Eller had come into his office accusing him or his administrative assistant of hacking into their computers. The DA was astonished by Eller's preposterous allegations. Hunter told how friends advised him to file the case against the parents, lose it, and then he could write a book and make millions of dollars.

On October 10, 1997, the lead story in the *Boulder Daily Camera* reported Police Chief Tom Koby had removed Commander John Eller from the Ramsey investigation. He was replaced by Mark Beckner, who had been with the Boulder Police Department for several years; however, he too had never been in charge of a murder investigation. In an effort to "put past mistrust aside," and get "this new investigation off on the right foot," the Ramseys extended an invitation, through Father Rol, to Mark Beckner to meet with them in their home in Atlanta.

The Ramseys later wrote in their book, "Rather than contacting us personally, Beckner chose to respond publicly: No, he would not meet with the Ramseys, as that would be to their advantage. It appeared we had been right: the investigation train was still traveling the same tracks…Their destination? Get John and Patsy Ramsey." As detective partners, Lou and I always welcomed any opportunity to meet suspects, witnesses, or victim's families in their home because it would give you a much more insightful look at how they lived, their values, their priorities.

On October 13, 1997, John Ramsey received a phone call from a senior executive with the Lockheed Martin Corporation. This company had recently acquired , the business John and Patsy started in their basement. The purpose of the call was to let John know Lockheed was selling off Access Graphics and he should expect a "severance package." John would later write, "There was no question in my mind that I had been asked to leave" because, "Patsy and I had been painted guilty by the cops, city government, the media, and the public."

In January 1998, Police Chief Tom Koby announced he would be resigning at the end of the year, after receiving a vote of no confidence from the City's police organization. Chief Koby would not make it until the end of the year; a few months before his retirement date he was put on "special assignment" in the city manager's office and Mark Beckner was promoted to Chief.

Now fifteen months into the investigation, the only public announcements being made by anyone in an official capacity was, "The parents are under an umbrella of suspicion." JonBenét's parents would accurately describe that this suspicion felt more like "a parasol of persecution." As the rift between the Boulder police and the DA's Office continued to play out in public view the "awkward triangle" became a nearly unsurmountable obstacle in the Ramsey investigation. The heat from the media spotlight intensified as the investigation continued to languish. One year to the day after the first all-day interrogations by Detectives Steve Thomas and Tom Trujillo, out of frustration, John Ramsey wrote a letter to the Boulder DA, dated April 11, 1998:

Dear Mr. Hunter,

I am writing this letter because it seems difficult at times for us to communicate through attorneys who are focused on protecting my rights as a citizen. I want to be very clear on our family's position. 1) We have no trust or confidence in the Boulder Police. They have tried, from the moment they walked in to our home on December 26, 1996, to convince others that Patsy or I or Burke killed JonBenét...2) We (myself, Patsy, Burke, John Andrew, Melinda) will meet anytime, anywhere, for as long as you want, with investigators from your office. If the purpose of a Grand Jury is to be able to talk with us, that is not necessary. We want to find the killer of our daughter and sister and will work with you twenty-four hours/day to find "it". 3) If we are subpoenaed by a Grand Jury, we will testify, regardless of any previous meeting with your investigators. I am living my life for two purposes, now. To find the killer of JonBenét and bring "it" to the maximum justice our society can impose....

It is time to rise above all this pettiness and politics and get down to the most important mission – finding JonBenét's killer. That's all we care about. The police cannot do it.... Finally, I am willing and able to put up a substantial reward ($1 million) through the help of friends if this would help drive information....Sincerely, John Ramsey.

On the evening of Saturday, May 30, 1998, John Ramsey followed up his letter to the Boulder DA, Alex Hunter, with a personal phone call to his home. Although the DA told John Ramsey it would be unethical for him to speak with the Ramseys without their attorneys present, John Ramsey stressed that both he and Patsy were available for another interrogation. He felt this conversation ended positively and would break the logjam blocking the investigation. Lou Smit would play an important role in this second round of interrogations with JonBenét's parents.

On Tuesday, June 23, 1998, John and Patsy Ramsey flew to Broomfield, Colorado. They landed at the Jefferson County Airport, not far from the Broomfield Justice Center, where the videotaped interviews were scheduled to be conducted. The DA's Office had decided on a two-team approach; Lou Smit and Grand Jury Specialist Michael Kane, would conduct the interview of John Ramsey, while Homicide Investigations Supervisor, Thomas Haney, on loan from the Denver Police Department, and Trip DeMuth, from the Boulder DA's Office, would conduct the interview with Patsy Ramsey. John Ramsey's attorney, Bryan Morgan, would be present in the interview room, while Patsy's attorney, Pat Burke, would be with Patsy during her interview.

While they were not in custody, the Ramseys knew they would be in for a long and difficult interrogation. Patsy's health was a definite consideration as she struggled to recover from stage four cancer. Videotapes were changed at two-hour intervals and sent back to the Boulder Police Department. The videos were reviewed by the seven detectives who had participated in the case, over the past eighteen months. This allowed the police to submit additional questions. Months later, John Ramsey viewed the videotapes of Patsy's interrogation and wrote, "I realized that Patsy's interviewer was far more brutal and accusatory than what I had experienced."

In his book, John Ramsey would write, "Of the interrogators, I found Lou Smit to be the most professional and skilled. He often allowed long pregnant pauses to pull more information out of me than I even knew was there. In turn, he put information before me that I didn't know existed…I learned during this interrogation that there was unidentified DNA evidence. I was encouraged. This could be the clue we hoped for. The investigators had found samples of DNA material on JonBenét's underwear and under her fingernails…At the conclusion of the three-day interrogation, I was excited. Maybe the killer could be captured after all."

In May of 1998, Lou had an opportunity to present his investigative findings to members of the Boulder Police Department and DA's Office. This information established an intruder had entered the Ramsey home in an attempted kidnapping which ended with the murder of JonBenét. Lou pointed to the strongest evidence, the DNA found on JonBenét's underwear and under her fingernails, which was that of an unknown male and excluded the DNA of each of the Ramseys. The DNA was run through the FBI's Combined DNA Index System (CODIS), a database containing more than one and a half million DNA profiles—no match was found in the system.

In a letter written on August 6, 1998, which would have been JonBenét's eighth birthday, Steve Thomas, a lead police detective for the Ramsey murder, resigned from the Boulder Police Department. The resignation letter was sent to Police Chief Mark Beckner, who had replaced Tom Koby, and a copy of the letter was sent to ABC News and Colorado Governor Roy Romer. Steve Thomas gave up his law enforcement career in protest over how he felt the DA's Office had become a hindrance to solving the Ramsey case. Steve Thomas moved out of Colorado and wrote the book, *JonBenét, Inside the Ramsey Murder Investigation*, with coauthor Don Davis. John and Patsy Ramsey sued Steve Thomas because of claims he made in his book. That suit was eventually settled against Thomas, Davis, and their publisher.

Despite Lou's efforts to show evidence that the Ramseys did not murder JonBenét, animosity between the Boulder

Police and DA's Office continued as political pressures mounted to gain a conviction against the parents. From experience, I have come to realize that when you hear a politician say, "Well, we have to do something"—you know you are in real trouble! Roy Romer, Governor of Colorado, interceded by initiating a grand jury and appointed Michael Kane as a special prosecutor. Two more special prosecutors; Bruce Levin, the Adams County Chief Trial Deputy; and Mitch Morrissey, the Denver County DA, were also added as special grand jury prosecutors while the two DA's Investigators, Smit and Ainsworth were sidelined.

Despite the fact the unknown male DNA on the victim's body and clothing had excluded all Ramsey family members, on September 15, 1998, a grand jury was convened to consider indicting the Ramseys for the murder of their daughter. It is not known if this DNA evidence was withheld or presented to members of the grand jury by prosecutors. Five days after the grand jury was impaneled, Lou Smit quietly submitted his letter of resignation to Alex Hunter. Lou showed me his resignation letter prior to turning it in to the DA. Lou explained to me that he just couldn't be part of a judicial process that was set out to convict two innocent people. Lou's resignation letter, dated September 20, 1998, was addressed to District Attorney Alex Hunter. It read:

It is with great reluctance and regret that I submit this letter of resignation. Even though I want to continue to participate in the official investigation and assist in finding the killer of JonBenét, I find that I cannot in good conscience be part of the persecution of innocent people. It would be highly improper and unethical for me to stay when I so strongly believe this.

It has been almost 19 months since we talked that day in your office and you asked me to assist you in this investigation. It has turned out to be more of a challenge than either of us anticipated. When we first met (sic) I told you that my style of approaching an investigation is from the concept of not working a particular theory, but working on the case. Detectives collect and record information from many sources, analyze it, couple that with their experience and training and let "the case" tell them where to go. This process may take days, weeks (sic) or years, depending on the direction the case tells you to go. Sometimes you must investigate "many paths" in order to find the killer. It is not a political speed contest where expediency should outweigh justice, where "resolving" the case is solving the case.

Alex, even though I have been unable to actively investigate, I have been in a position to collect, record (sic) and analyze every piece of information given to your office in the course of this investigation. I believe that I know this case better than anyone does. I know what has been investigated and what hasn't, what evidence exists and what doesn't, what information has been leaked and what hasn't. I am a detective with a proven record of successful investigations. I have looked at the murder of JonBenét Ramsey through the eyes of age and experience and a thorough knowledge of the case.

At this point in the investigation "the case" tells me that John and Patsy Ramsey did not kill their daughter, that a very dangerous killer is still out there and no one is actively looking for him. There are still many areas of investigation which must be explored before life and death decisions are made.

When I was hired (sic) I had no agenda one way or the other, my allegiance was to the case, not the Police Department nor John and Patsy Ramsey. My agenda has not changed. I only desire to be able to investigate the case and find the killer of JonBenét and will continue to do so as long as I am able. The chances of catching him working from the "outside looking in" are very slim, but I have a great "Partner" who I am sure will lead the way. There is no doubt that I will be facing a great deal of opposition and ridicule in the future, because I intend to stand with this family and somehow help them through this and find the killer of their daughter. Perhaps others who believe this will help also.

The Boulder Police Department has many fine and dedicated men and women who also want justice for JonBenét. They are just going in the wrong direction and have been since day one of the investigation. Instead of letting the case tell them where to go, they have elected to follow a theory and let their theory direct them rather than allowing the evidence to direct them. The case tells me there is substantial, credible evidence of an intruder and lack of evidence that the parents are involved. If this is true, they too are tragic victims whose misery has been compounded by a misdirected and flawed investigation, unsubstantiated leaks, rumors (sic) and accusations.

I have worked in this profession for the past 32 years and have always been loyal to it, the men and women in it, and what it represents, because I believed that justice has always prevailed. In this case, however, I believe that justice is not being served, that innocent people are being targeted and could be charged with a murder they did not commit.

The law enforcement Code of Ethics states it very well. My fundamental duty is to "serve mankind; to safeguard lives and property; to protect the innocent against deception, the weak against oppression or intimidation, the peaceful against violence or disorder. To respect the constitutional rights of all men to liberty, equality (sic) and justice." This applies to not only JonBenét but to her mother and father as well.

I want to thank you and the others in the office for the wonderful support and treatment I have received. You have a great DA's Office and the men and women who work with you are some of the most honest and dedicated people I have ever met. My life has been enriched because of this memorable time together. I have especially enjoyed working closely with Peter Hofstrom and Trip DeMuth, who also have dedicated so much of their lives to this case. I have never met two more fair, honest (sic) and dedicated defenders of our system.

Alex, you are in a difficult position. The media and peer pressure are incredible. You are inundated with conflicting facts and information, and "expert" opinions. And now you have an old detective telling you that the Ramseys did not do it and to wait and investigate this case more thoroughly before a very tragic mistake would be made. What a double travesty it could be: an innocent person indicted, and a vicious killer on the loose to prey on another innocent child and no one to stop him.

History will be the judge as to how we conducted ourselves and how we handled our responsibilities.

Shoes, shoes, the victim's shoes, who will stand in the victim's shoes?...

Slides From Lou Smit's Presentation

CONTENT WARNING
The following materials contain graphic images
of violence and abuse against a child and are
intended for a mature audience. They are being
made available with the knowledge and consent of
JonBenét Ramsey's family in the hopes of bringing
her killer to justice. Please view with care.

View additional slides in color at
http://wbp.bz/smitgallery

755 15th Street, Boulder, CO

Ramsey Family

John Ramsey

- John Bennett Ramsey
- DOB 12/7/43
- Born Omaha, Neb.
- BS in electrical engineering
- MBA
- U.S. Navy 1966-1988
- Member St. Johns' Episcopal Church
- Interests – sailing and flying

Patsy Ramsey

- Patricia Paugh Ramse
- DOB 12/29/56
- BA University of W. Virginia
- Home Maker
- Treated for stage 4 ovarian cancer
- Activities at children' schools and church

.. ._.. ._

BRUTAL

She was taken from her bed on
Christmas Night

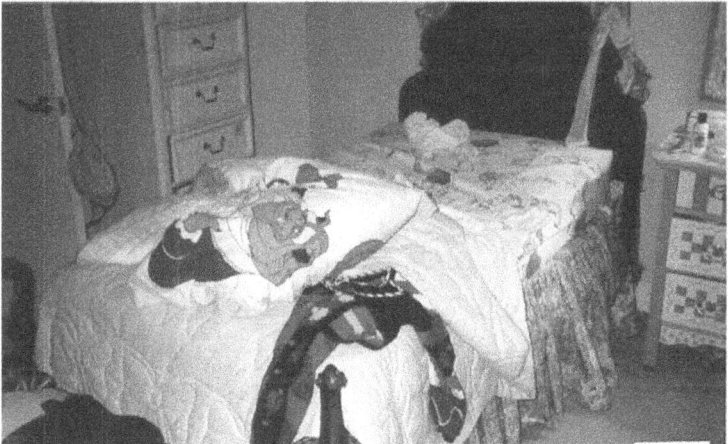

._.. ._

BRUTAL

Duct tape was placed on her mouth

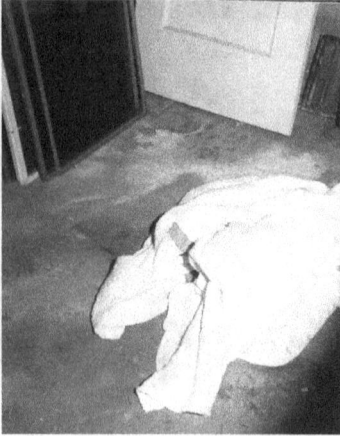

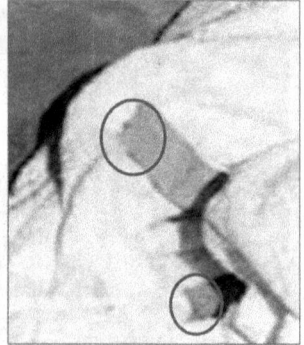

First Floor Diagram

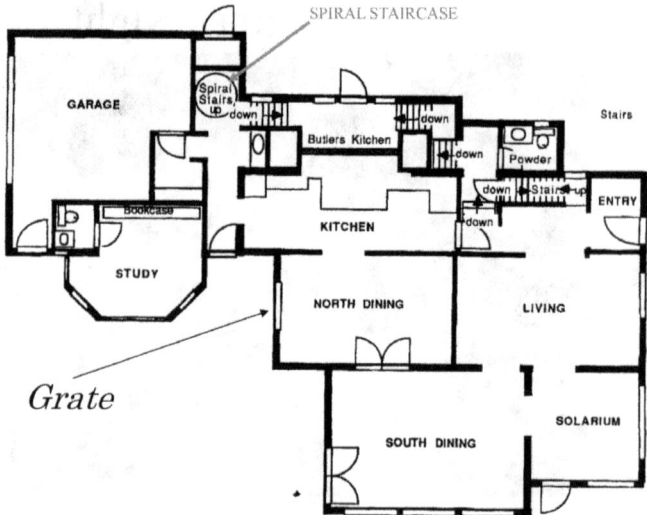

SPIRAL STAIRCASE

GARAGE

Spiral Stairs UP / down

Butlers Kitchen

Stairs

down

Powder

down Stairs up

Bookcase

KITCHEN

ENTRY

down

down

STUDY

NORTH DINING

LIVING

Grate

SOUTH DINING

SOLARIUM

Second Floor Diagram

Spiral Staircase

Guest Bedroom

N

JonBenet's
Bedroom

Second
Floor

Burke's Bedroom

DOLL HOUSE

COMPUTER DESK

COVERED DECK

TREE

'83)–" "–

Third Floor Diagram

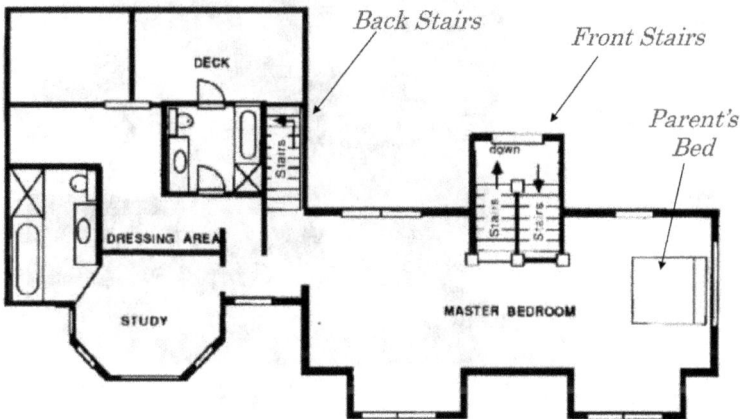

Back Stairs

Front Stairs

Parent's
Bed

DECK

Stairs

down

Stairs

Stairs

DRESSING AREA

STUDY

MASTER BEDROOM

.. ._.. ".–

Basement Diagram

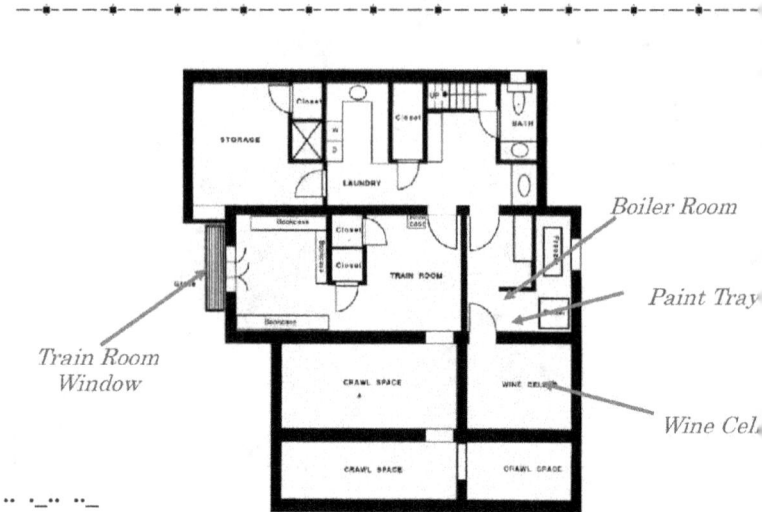

Boiler Room

Paint Tray

Train Room
Window

Wine Cel...

LOCATION OF RANSOM NOTE PAD

Where Ransom Note was found

**PHOTO OF ACTUAL RANSOM NOTE PAD TAKEN
BY JOHN RAMSEY ...EARLY AM 12/26/96..   (Whe...
unloading his camera for police)**

RANSOM NOTE

Mr. Ramsey,

Listen carefully! We are a group of individuals that represent a small foreign faction. We do respect your bussiness but not the country that it serves. At this time we have your daughter in our posession. She is safe and unharmed and if you want her to see 1997, you must follow our instructions to the letter.

You will withdraw $118,000.00 from your account. $100,000 will be in $100 bills and the remaining $18,000 in $20 bills. Make sure that you bring an adequate size attache to the bank. When you get home you will put the money in a brown paper bag. I will call you between 8 and 10 am tomorrow to instruct you on delivery. The delivery will be exhausting so I advise you to be rested. If we monitor you getting the money early, we might call you early to arrange an earlier delivery of the money and hence a earlier delivery pick-up of your daughter.

Any deviation of my instructions will result in the immediate execution of your daughter. You will also be denied her remains for proper burial. The two gentlemen watching over your daughter do not particularly like you so I advise you not to provoke them. Speaking to anyone about your situation, such as Police, F.B.I., etc., will result in your daughter being beheaded. If we catch you talking to a stray dog, she dies. If you alert bank authorities, she dies. If the money is in any way marked or tampered with, she dies. You will be scanned for electronic devices and if any are found, she dies. You can try to deceive us but be warned that we are familiar with law enforcement countermeasures and tactics. You stand a 99% chance of killing your daughter if you try to out smart us.

and you stand a 100% chance of getting her back. You and your family are under constant scrutiny as well as the authorities. Don't try to grow a brain John. You are not the only fat cat around so don't think that killing will be difficult. Don't underestimate us John. Use that good southern common sense of yours. It is up to you now John!

Victory!
S.B.T.C

AREA OF BROKEN WINDOW

THE WINDOW WELL IS IN AN AREA HIDDEN FROM VIEW

AREA OF BROKEN WINDOW

.. .-.. ..-

MARK ON WALL

.. .-.. ..-

.. ._.. ._

STUN GUN

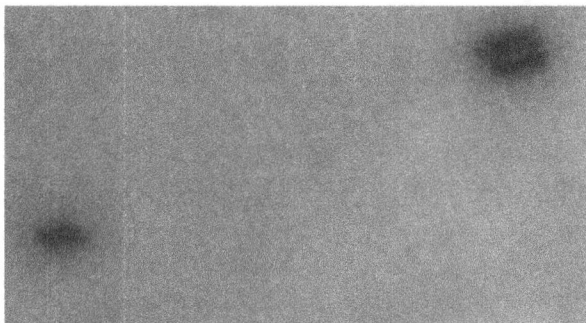

**DETECTIVE TRUJILLO IN HIS
REPORT OF THE AUTOPSY
DESCRIBES MARKS ON BACK AS
RECTANGULAR IN SHAPE**

.. ._.. ._

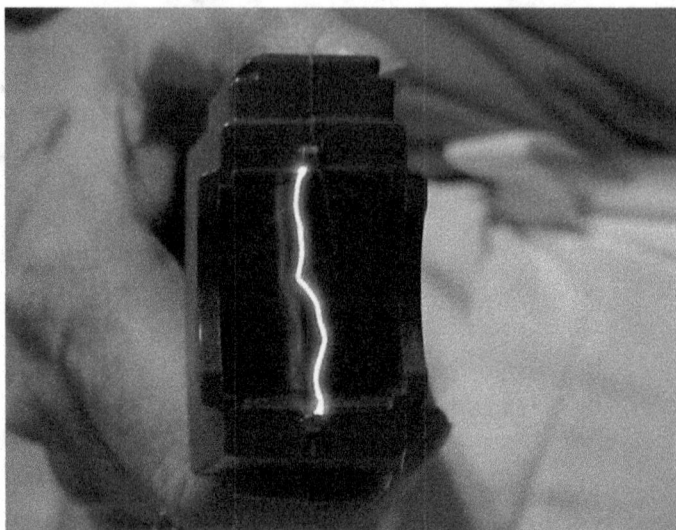

NOTE THE SIZE AND SHAPE OF THE
CONTACTS AND THE SIZE AND SHAPE OF
THE MARKS

STUN GUN

COMPARISON

AIR TAZER STUN GUN AND MARKS ON BACK

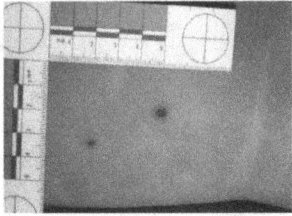

JonBenet
Ramsey's
Back

Scales are not aligned.

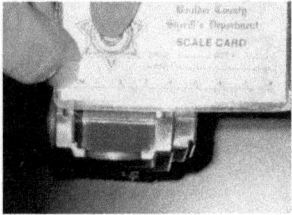

Air
Tazer:
Cartridge
removed.

MEASUREMENTS

**DISTANCE BETWEEN
THE MARKS**

AND

**DISTANCE BETWEEN
THE CONTACTS IS
VERY CLOSE**

APPROXIMATELY

3.5 cm

THE HI-TEC PRINT

DOOR TO THE WINE CELLAR

(JonBenet was behind this door when this picture was taken)

".-" "_

THE SCREAM

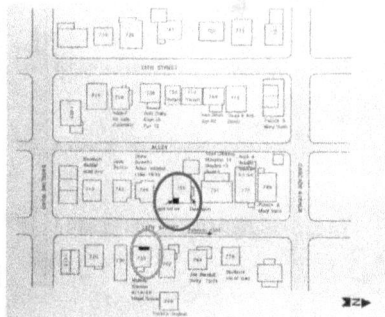

Melanie Stanton

"It was the most terrifying Child's scream I've ever heard"

".-" "_

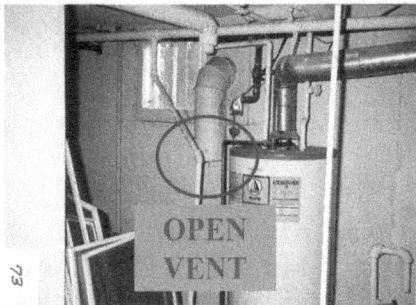

OPEN
VENT

DOOR TO
WINE CELLAR

PAINT TRAY

.. ._.. ._

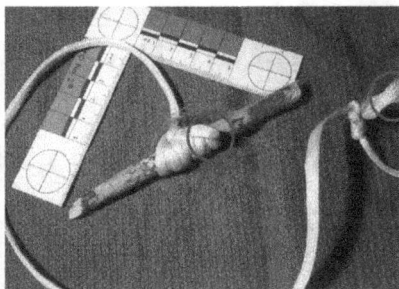

BURNED

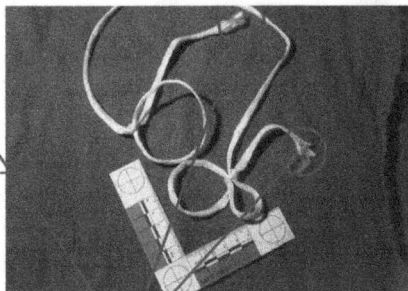

FRAYED

ONE BURNED END IS FOUND IN THE GARROTTE

THE OTHER ENDS ARE ALL FRAYED

WHERE IS THE CORD OR A PRIOR APPLICATION WITH
THE OTHER "BURNED END" OF THE CORD?

NOT FOUND

.. ._.. ._

DNA..Fingernail Clippings

※ CBI..#14, #7

※ Examiner: Kathryn Dressel

※ Date:1/15/97

※ 47-40

#14-L…Right Hand Fingernail Clippings
#14-M..Left Hand Fingernail Clippings
#7..Panties

※ **In all of the above, the DNA has a major component matching JonBenet and a minor component, if left by a single individual, would eliminate the Ramsey's as the source.**

DNA PROFILE CHART..CBI..Dressel

Panties (7)
Fingernail clippings right hand (14L)
Fingernail clippings Left Hand (14M)

7	Panties	1.2,2	BB	AB	BB	AA	AC WB	24,26
14L	Rt. Fingernails	1.2,2	BB	AB	BB	AA WB	AC WB	24,26
14M	Left. Fingernails	1.2,2	BB	AB	BB WA	AA WB	AC WB	24,26 W18

INC = INCONCLUSIVE
W = WEAK

Secondary Source

DNA...Blood in crotch of Panties

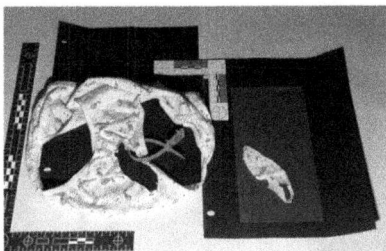

* From Crotch of victim's Panties: two spots of blood contained a mixture of DNA.
* In one blood spot (CBI 7), the primary source was from the victim and also a weak secondary source
* In the other blood spot (CBI 7-2), there was a stronger mixture. The victim being one source and the other a male

MASTER BEDROOM

BEDDING IS DISTURBED

GUEST BEDROOM

SEEN FROM GUEST BEDROOM

.. ._.. .._

THE WINDOW OF THIS BEDROOM
OVERLOOKS THE GARAGE,

.. ._.. .._

BUTLER DOOR

THE BUTLER DOOR IS LOCATED WITHIN 25' OF THE SPIRAL STAIRCASE

WHERE THE RANSOM
NOTE WAS FOUND

RANSOM NOTE

EXPERTS

Six competent examiners evaluated the note.

- CHET UBOWSKI .... **CURRENT CBI EXAMINER**

- LEONARD SPECKIN .... **PRIVATE EXAMINER**

- EDWIN ALFORD .... **PRIVATE EXAMINER**

- LLOYD CUNNINGHAM ..... **CERTIFIED CHET UBOWSKI**

- RICHARD DUSICK .... **SECRET SERVICE EXAMINER**

- HOWARD RYLE ....**FORMER CBI EXAMINER**

--•--—-•----—-•--—-•--—•--—•--—-•--—-•--—-•--—-•--—-•--—-•--—•---

•Richard Dusak – Police Expert – Document analyst for the United States Secret Service

Lack of Indications

A study and comparison of the questioned and specimen writing submitted has resulted in the conclusion that there is

no evidence to indicate that Patsy Ramsey, executed any of the questioned material appearing on the ransom note.

·· ·_·· ··_

Cemetery

--•--—-•----—-•--—-•--—•--—•--—-•--—-•--—-•--—-•--—-•--—-•--—•---

·· ·_·· ··_

Chapter 5 – Scene

The former home of John and Patsy Ramsey, 755 15th Street, in Boulder, Colorado, looks nothing like it did 26 years ago, the night JonBenét was murdered. Today the one-hundred-year-old home is crowded in by foliage and surrounded by a tall privacy fence. Inside the fence is a huge brown dog, resembling a lion, guarding the property. The actual street address has been changed, perhaps to stem the tide of curious onlookers stopping to take photographs. Built in the 1920's in an upscale neighborhood of Boulder called University Hill, the 6,500 square foot Tudor Style home was the scene of one of the most infamous crimes in American history.

Video taken from the street on December 26, 1996, showing the front of the Ramsey's large Tudor style home decorated for Christmas, was transmitted across the nation and around the world by television news crews. Photos, published in daily newspapers, made this home one of the most recognizable in America. The Ramseys had bought the house in 1991 and completely renovated it, adding a large addition to the back. The elevator was taken out and upper floors were made accessible by adding a spiral staircase. Soundproofing was also added during the remodel.

Tudor style homes, often referred to as English Tudors or English Manors, became popular in the mid-to-late-19th century and remained so until WWII. They were ideal for colder climates. Because they were expensive to build, and appeared mainly in wealthier neighborhoods, they were nicknamed, "Stockbroker's Tudors." Tudors are distinguishable by a steeply pitched roof which often comes with overlapping front-facing gables. The majority of Tudor home exteriors, including the Ramseys, are brick and accented with thin boards and stucco or stone in between the boards. Most Tudors feature tall brick chimneys with a metal or stone extension on top.

When I look at photos taken from the front of the Ramsey's home showing the tall brick chimney, I am reminded of a story Lou's daughter, Cindy, shared with me the first time she talked with her dad about his joining the Boulder DA's Ramsey investigation team. Cindy said Lou told her, "If someone did get in that house, it must've been Santa Claus coming down the chimney." But once Lou had access to the crime scene, and photos taken by the crime lab within hours of JonBenét's murder, showing an open window in the basement and no snow around the window, he began to realize many details stated about the Ramsey case were untrue.

The reason John and Patsy Ramsey wanted such a large home was they loved to entertain friends and to bring their extended family together to celebrate holidays. John had three children from his first marriage: Beth, John Andrew, and Melinda. He had two more children with Patsy: Burke and JonBenét. Unfortunately, the only holiday the entire Ramsey family would share in the newly remodeled Tudor home was Thanksgiving of 1991. Tragically, John's oldest daughter, Elizabeth "Beth" Ramsey, was killed in an automobile accident in January 1992, in Illinois. Beth was just 22 years old. She is buried in the Saint James Episcopal Cemetery in Marietta, Georgia. As a father, I cannot imagine the heartache of losing a daughter, let alone two.

In his investigative notes, Lou Smit identifies the four members of the Ramsey family who were in their home in

Boulder on Christmas Day, 1996. First was John Bennett Ramsey, born December 7, 1943, in Omaha, Nebraska. He had earned a BS degree in electrical engineering and an MBA. John had served in the U.S. Navy from 1966-1988 (including 8 years active duty followed by 14 years in the Naval Reserves in Atlanta). He and his family were members of St. John's Episcopal Church in Boulder. John's interests were sailing and flying.

Next was Patricia "Patsy" Paugh Ramsey, born December 29, 1956. She had earned a BA degree from the University of West Virginia. Patsy was a homemaker who had been treated for stage 4 ovarian cancer. Lou noted she was involved with activities at her children's schools and church. Patsy had gained public exposure by winning the Miss West Virginia beauty contest and by being a Miss America contestant in 1977. Their home had also been included in the 1995 Historic Homes Tour, a charitable fundraiser in Boulder, where hundreds of people toured their home when it was decorated for Christmas the year prior to JonBenét's murder.

Lou identified the two Ramsey children: Burke Hamilton Ramsey, age 9, born January 27, 1987, in the 4th grade at High Peaks Elementary School and JonBenét Patricia Ramsey, age 6, born August 6, 1990, who was in kindergarten at High Peaks Elementary School. Her first name, JonBenét, is a combination of her father's first and middle names, John Bennett. Her middle name was Patricia, after her mother's first name. JonBenét loved riding her bike, playing with other kids her age and participating in child beauty pageants.

The Ramseys' home was located four blocks south of the University of Colorado's Student Center and four blocks east of Chautauqua Park. Many college students live in the neighborhood and there's always a lot of foot traffic. JonBenét and her 9-year-old brother, Burke, had large bedrooms on the second level. The parent's master suite was located on the third level. The home also had a full basement, used primarily for storage. Lou Smit concluded the killer had entered the home through a basement window, abducted JonBenét from her bedroom on the second floor, and then took her to the basement where she was brutally murdered.

There is a third bedroom on the second level, which overlooks the garage area. John Andrew Ramsey, JonBenét's older half-brother, once used this bedroom, but had gone off to college. In 1996, this bedroom was used primarily as a guest room. Lou Smit would later come to believe the killer waited in this guest bedroom for the family to return on the evening of December 25, possibly hiding under the bed.

The strongest evidence to support this conclusion, in Lou's mind, was a cloth bag sitting on a chair in the guest bedroom, containing a long rope. The Ramseys were adamant this bag and the rope did not belong to them and had not been in this bedroom prior to the murder. They also pointed to drawers in the adjoining bathroom that were left open and the dust ruffle around the bed had been disturbed. Lou documented how the dust ruffle on the left and right sides of the bed had been neatly tucked under the bed, while the dust ruffle at the foot of the bed, closest to the cloth bag containing the rope, was found to be extending out away from the bed.

The only reason an intruder would bring a rope into the Ramsey's home, Lou believed, was to tie someone up; however, when the experienced detective pointed this additional evidence of an intruder out to the police, they dismissed the possibility. The alternative theory that several Boulder detectives had already bought into was the mother, Patsy, in a fit of rage over JonBenét wetting her bed, had inadvertently killed her daughter upstairs and then carried the dead body of her little girl down two flights of stairs. Lou did not believe the parents had staged the crime scene to look like a kidnapping—he believed this was the scene of a kidnapping gone awry.

This theory of Patsy killing JonBenét in a fit of rage and then staging the crime scene as a kidnapping was not supported by the physical evidence in this case. Lou documented how the family had enjoyed a wonderful Christmas Day and had planned to fly in John's private airplane, on the morning of the 26th, to meet the older children in Charlevoix, Michigan, where the Ramseys owned a vacation home. In his notes, Lou wrote, "They were planning to return to Boulder on Saturday, December 28, so that they could leave on Sunday, December 29, 1996, to fly to Florida on a commercial flight, where they had reservations for a cruise on Disney World's Big Red Boat." Lou noted that neither of the Ramseys had any prior arrests, mental illness, no domestic violence calls, or even any allegations of child abuse or sexual assault on children.

In fact, Lou established the opposite was true; John and Patsy were a highly successful couple with a loving, church-going family. They had holiday travel plans to visit family and were looking forward to sharing an exciting vacation centered on the two younger children. Lou asked, "Why would one of the parents kill their daughter and then both parents collaborate to stage a sexually violent crime scene to look like a kidnapping?" If the mother had killed her daughter, in a fit of rage over a bedwetting incident, how could anyone sit down and write a 3-page ransom note? To Lou, this made no sense—especially after reading the autopsy report.

The autopsy report, supported by the physical evidence, proved JonBenét was strangled with the garrote, which Lou believed was constructed in the basement, using a paintbrush handle. The wooden paintbrush had been located in a tray in the basement. The handle was broken into three pieces; one piece was in the tray, one piece attached to the garrote, and the third piece was missing. Lou pointed out

JonBenét's fingernail marks are visible above the ligature around her neck, proving she was alive and struggling to breathe. Fingernail marks were confirmed, by the Coroner, to be those of JonBenét—made as she was fighting for her life. DNA recovered from underneath the right and left fingernails was male and consistent with the unknown male DNA on the crotch of her panties. This DNA evidence eliminated all Ramsey family members as contributors.

From studying photographs of the two rectangular red marks left on JonBenét's back and those on her right cheek, Lou concluded the intruder brought a stun gun into the Ramsey home and used it on JonBenét. The first use of the stun gun was likely while she was still asleep in her bed. The location where the stun gun was placed, on her jaw and upper throat area, may have prevented JonBenét from screaming when she was taken from her bedroom. The second use of the stun gun was likely in the basement, to her back as she was struggling. Lou thought the second stun gun use may have accounted for the scream heard by Melody Stanton, the neighbor who sleeps with her window open, 150 feet across the street, at around 2 a.m. on December 26th.

Melody Stanton thought the scream was that of a little girl and described it as, "The most terrifying child scream I've ever heard." What Lou was curious about is how the scream could be heard across the street but not upstairs by the parents? This was a question Lou set out to resolve. The soundproofing materials the Ramseys added during the remodel could account for sound of the scream not carrying up three stories to the master bedroom. Then Lou observed in the boiler room in the basement, next to where JonBenét's body was found, a large vent pipe open on both ends extending through the exterior basement wall to the outside. Lou believed this pipe could serve like a megaphone to amplify the sound to the outside of the home toward the neighbors.

Other evidence of an intruder that Lou pointed to in the crime scene photos of the room where JonBenét was found, were small pieces of white "peanut" packing material and brown leaves similar to those found in the bottom of the window well. Lou believed the intruder inadvertently transferred this debris into the basement when he crawled through the basement window. Lou pointed to the suitcase positioned upright under the open window. He thought the killer placed the suitcase there to step on to exit the home after the sexual assault and murder of JonBenét. John Ramsey explained the suitcase had been stored elsewhere in the basement.

Lou also pointed to the Hi-Tec boot print found in the mold on the floor near JonBenét's body. The Ramseys didn't own any Hi-Tec footwear. Furthermore, this footprint did not match any of the boots worn by the police. Lou also pointed out that much of the physical evidence the parents had allegedly "staged" was actually found by the parents, not the police. In fact, when John Ramsey found JonBenét's body he "unstaged" the crime scene. The first thing John Ramsey did after finding her was to remove the duct tape from her mouth and picked her up. Lou asked, "If John Ramsey had gone to all the trouble of staging things, wouldn't he have wanted the police to see her in the condition she had been staged?"

The two-and-a-half-page ransom note, to Lou's thinking, also pointed away from the parents. Lou questioned how any parent, after supposedly accidently murdering their child in a fit of rage, staged a violent sexual crime scene and then had the presence of mind to sit down to write this ransom note using verbiage from different abduction-themed movies. Also, the duct tape had been torn off a roll and put over the little girl's mouth so she couldn't scream. Since the parents didn't own any duct tape or a stun gun, the killer had to have brought these items with him into the home and then carried them out of the home after the kidnap attempt ended in a murder.

On his computer, Lou drew four crime scene diagrams, one for each level of the house. The diagrams are carefully drawn to scale. The basement level shows the window where Lou believed the intruder entered the home. On the first level, he shows where the spiral staircase leads to the upper floors where JonBenét and Burke were asleep on the second level and where the parents were asleep on the third level. The ransom note had been written on paper from a white legal pad belonging to Patsy Ramsey, and was found by Patsy on the first step leading up from the kitchen to the second level, where JonBenét had been abducted from her bedroom.

The evidence led Lou to believe the suspect's intent was a kidnapping for ransom and something went wrong in the basement, which led the kidnapper to alter his plans. The suspect then sexually assaulted JonBenét and strangled her with the garrote constructed with the white parachute cord and the broken paintbrush handle. The same parachute cord was tied, using slip knots around JonBenét's wrists; the more she would have struggled, the tighter the knots would have constricted. Since the Ramseys didn't own any parachute cord, the suspect would have had to also bring the cord with him when he entered the home, along with the stun gun and duct tape.

The evidence led Lou to believe JonBenét struggled to free herself. The autopsy confirmed she was violently sexually assaulted and died due to strangulation; plus, she had suffered a severe blow to the top of the head delivered with such force it crushed her skull. An expert later described the degree of force as being consistent with falling on your head from a three-story building. Lou was not certain what had caused this skull fracture; but in his notes, he did mention an aluminum baseball bat that was found lying on the ground to the north side of the house.

John Andrew Ramsey believes that the baseball bat did not belong to anyone in the Ramsey family.

The closest door to where that baseball bat was found on the north side of the house, leads from the butler's kitchen outside to the back yard. A police officer later noted in his report that the door was open; however, there was some question if it had been locked throughout the night and a neighbor or another police officer might have used that door on the morning of the 26th and simply left the butler kitchen door open. In fact, knowing what doors were locked and who had keys to the Ramsey home became problematic.

John Ramsey would later say there may have been a many as 23 keys to their home in Boulder. When the home was being remodeled, the carpenters had to have access to the home when the Ramseys were away. The Ramseys had also given keys to their housekeeper and to Joe and Betty Barnhill, who lived across the street, so they could keep an eye on their home when they were away on their frequent travels. When the Barnhills lost their key to the Ramsey home, the Ramseys gave them another key.

Both John and Patsy Ramsey completely trusted their neighbors across the street, Joe and Betty Barnhill. John Ramsey had even asked Joe Barnhill to hide JonBenét's bicycle in his garage so she wouldn't see it until Christmas morning. Detective Steve Thomas had interviewed Betty and Joseph Barnhill, Sr., extensively and had also interviewed their son, Joseph Barnhill, Jr., later at police headquarters. Detective Thomas found both Joseph Barnhill Sr. and Jr. to be cooperative and collected handwriting and hair samples from both men. Besides, Detective Steve Thomas was convinced one of the Ramseys had murdered JonBenét and would come to rely heavily on the opinion of a CBI handwriting expert, Chet Ubowski, who had concluded Patsy could not be excluded as the author of the ransom note.

On October 16, 1998, *The Daily Camera* newspaper in Boulder ran this headline, "CBI expert seen with prosecutor. Handwriting analysts apparently testified before Ramsey panel." The first paragraph read, "The grand jury considering evidence in the JonBenét Ramsey murder investigation apparently heard testimony Thursday from a handwriting expert who has concluded that the child's mother could have written the ransom note." The article continued, "Colorado Bureau of Investigations handwriting analyst Chet Ubowski arrived early in the afternoon at the Boulder County Justice Center, where he was met by grand jury prosecutor Michael Kane."

Reporters were not allowed into the courtroom; however, the newspaper article stated, "According to search warrants previously unsealed in the case, Ubowski said Patsy Ramsey could not be excluded as author of the 2½-page ransom note she said she found early Dec. 26, 1996. Ubowski also determined that the note was written on paper from a white legal pad that belonged to the Ramsey's. Ubowski's analysis excluded 6-year-old JonBenét's father, John Ramsey, as a possible author of the note. It was Ubowski's analysis that triggered a second search of the Ramsey's vacation home in Charlevoix, Mich., more than two months after JonBenét's death, seeking unrehearsed samples of Patsy Ramsey's writing."

The newspaper article continued, "District Attorney Alex Hunter has characterized the ransom note as one of the most important pieces of physical evidence that investigators have to work with." Herein lies the problem, there should have been two huge red flags attached to "one the most important pieces of physical evidence that investigators have to work with." First, this ransom note was written with a felt tip pen—an unreliable writing instrument for handwriting comparison (handwriting exemplars are usually taken using a ballpoint pen; however, in this case the known handwriting should be taken using a felt tip pen—investigators, in the

Ramsey case, would have to compare unreliable known handwriting against an unreliable questioned document).

Secondly, the handwriting on the ransom note was printed. Entry-level Questioned-Document Examination-Analysts are all taught to compare cursive handwriting against cursive handwriting. Cursive, also known as script, is a style of penmanship where the characters are written joined together in a flowing manner, in contrast to block letters in printing. Printing is a very unreliable form of handwriting comparison. Furthermore, from the time the first images of this ransom note were shown to the public, questions emerged from forensic experts and amateur sleuths alike, speculating whether the note could have been written "off-hand" (meaning it was written by a right-handed person using their left hand) to disguise their handwriting.

One other little-known wrinkle in the handwriting analysis of the Ramsey ransom note was Chet Ubowski was not the first CBI forensic expert to examine the note. The first expert was a newly hired lab analyst with CBI who submitted her results to her supervisor, Chet Ubowski, who evidently testified before the grand jury that Patsy Ramsey "could have written" or "could not be excluded" as having written the ransom note.

Lou Smit's investigative notes documented opinions from five other questioned document examiners—two of whom may have been hired by the Ramsey's attorneys—later examined the two-and-a-half-page ransom note and rendered their expert opinions. All six examiners eliminated John or Burke Ramsey as being the author of the ransom note. Three examiners claimed there was a "lack of indications" suggesting Patsy had authored the note, while a fourth agreed there was a lack of indicators she wrote the note, but he too was unable to eliminate Patsy as the author.

A fifth examiner, Howard Rile, a former questioned document examiner with CBI, concluded Patsy was "probably not" the author; however, he could not eliminate her as the author. However, there was a sixth examiner, Richard Dusick, a forensic expert with the U.S. Secret Service, who rendered his opinion, after a "study and comparison of the questioned and specimen writing submitted has resulted in the conclusion that there is no evidence to indicate that Patsy Ramsey executed any of the questioned material appearing on the ransom note."

Inexperienced investigators or prosecutors can make the mistake, when "shopping" around for forensic experts, is finding one willing to tell you what it is you want to hear. When it comes to handwriting as a forensic science, in my experience, handwriting is very "subjective" and should be accepted as more of an art than a science. But until you have sat in a courtroom and listened to forensics experts for the prosecution give their expert opinions on a piece of forensic evidence, and then listened to defense experts give their opinions, which completely contradicted the first expert, it is far too easy to accept expert opinions that are in agreement with what we might want to hear and dismiss those opinions that don't support our theories or assumptions.

The objective review of the ransom note handwriting analysis is critical to understanding the underlying injustice the Ramsey family has endured for more than a quarter century. Since John or Patsy Ramsey were not charged with a crime, they have not had their "day in court." Neither Ramsey were allowed inside the grand jury nor were their attorneys. There was no voir dire process, where the qualifications of the expert witnesses could be examined, and there was no cross-examination of these experts. John and Patsy Ramsey lost their constitutional right to "face their accuser" along with their "presumption of innocence"— being innocent until proven guilty.

One of the other early mistakes frequently pointed out in the Ramsey investigation was the fact that the Ramsey home was not properly secured once the crime was reported. What is often overlooked is the Ramsey home was not very secure before Christmas of '96. But before we get too critical of the Ramseys for not taking the security of their home more seriously, perhaps we should ask ourselves how many of us have gone through the time, trouble, and expense to have every lock on every door in every house we ever lived in changed? It's an unsettling thought, but just because we lock our doors at night, how safe are we when we go to bed every night?

One year after JonBenét's murder, December 21, 1997, Susannah Chase, a 23-year-old University of Colorado college student, was walking home from a pizza parlor in Boulder when she was violently beaten with a baseball bat, dragged to a car, raped, and then dumped in an alley just north of Pearl Street in Boulder. Susannah Chase had four skull fractures. She died the next day. That murder was also investigated by the Boulder Police. It too went unsolved—for years. Twelve years later, DNA found on Susannah's body was matched to Diego Olmos Alcalde.

Alcalde had been arrested in Wyoming, in 2000, for kidnapping and raping another woman. His DNA was submitted to the FBI's Combined DNA Index System (CODIS) which matched the seminal fluid from Susannah's body and finally, in 2008, Alcalde was arrested for the murder of Susannah Chase. He had been living in Boulder at the time of the murder. He claimed the sex was consensual and someone else had evidently murdered Susannah after they had sex. The jury didn't buy his story. On June 26, 2009, the *Boulder Daily Camera* newspaper printed the story reporting how Alcalde had been convicted by a jury and was given a life sentence.

Lou had to accept the fact that CODIS had matched Alcalde to the Susannah Chase kidnap-murder and the DNA from the JonBenét murder was also in CODIS. Despite the similar MO (Modus Operandi), since there was no DNA match to link Alcalde to the Ramsey case, he had to be excluded as a possible suspect. Lou accepted that Alcalde was probably not responsible for the murder of JonBenét and he moved on to the next person of interest. In the next chapter, we will take a closer look at the physical evidence from the crime scene, including the DNA that Lou believed would be instrumental in catching and convicting the killer of JonBenét.

Chapter 6 – Evidence

The investigative principle, known as the Transfer Theory, is generally attributed to Dr. Edmond Locard (1877-1966), a pioneer in forensic science. He was known as the Sherlock Holmes of Lyon, France. If there ever was a Sherlock Holmes of Colorado Springs, Colorado, it was Detective Lou Smit. When it came to the application of the Transfer Theory at a crime scene, Lou Smit was as good as they come, and when he took the witness stand in a court of law, juries listened.

Before a forensic expert is permitted to offer their expert opinion in a court of law, they must first undergo an examination on the witness stand, where the judge determines if their qualifications are to be accepted by the court. This judicial process originated in France in the 17th Century and is known as "voir dire." In addition to being court qualified as an expert in Bloodstain Pattern Interpretation, I have also been court qualified as an expert in crime scene reconstruction. Crime scene reconstruction takes into consideration all of the forensic sciences, allowing the expert to render an opinion on the witness stand relating to a criminal investigation, including the sequence of harmful events.

Prior to being called as a witness the forensic expert must submit their curriculum vitae (C.V.). The C.V. is an extensive resume providing a detailed account of an expert's experience, educational background, training, list of publications, and professional affiliations. Depending on the circumstances of the trial, my C.V. was typically 12-15 pages in length. Because I had every confidence in my credentials as a forensic expert, I anxiously looked forward to being cross-examined during the voir dire process. I felt it was both a compliment and a sense of relief, although a bit of a disappointment, when a defense attorney looked at my C.V. and announced to the judge that they would waive the voir dire process and accept me as an expert witness.

As confident as I felt in crime scene reconstruction, including the sequence of harmful events, I knew Lou Smit was even better. While a member of the DA's staff, Lou Smit had access to the crime scene and autopsy reports and personally experienced the defensive attitude the Boulder police held against outsiders. He continually met with resistance as he tried to offer his expertise as part of the DA's Task Force. About a week after returning from our honeymoon, I met with Lou and I asked how it was going in Boulder. His immediate reply was, "Johnny, there's something wrong with this case." He went on to explain that while the police remained focused on the Ramseys, they denied any evidence of forced entry into the home.

Lou described how the first crime scene photos taken by the crime lab in the basement clearly showed a window, with a broken windowpane, standing wide open. Furthermore, he told how a black scuff mark was visible on the wall beneath the window and a large suitcase had been positioned under the window which hadn't been there before the murder. Lou was perplexed how this factual piece of evidence, proving someone had entered the Ramsey home, was totally overlooked. When he brought it to the attention of the police detectives, they dismissed the premise by pointing to the heavy metal grate on the exterior window well. They suggested that this would have prevented anyone from entering the home.

Then Lou pointed to another photo of the window well, shot just hours after the murder, depicting how vegetation was visible underneath the grate. It also showed dirt had been brushed clean on the window frame of the open window that the Boulder detectives claimed no one could have climbed through into the basement. When Lou had himself videotaped climbing through the basement window, the same window John Ramsey climbed through when he was locked out of the home the previous summer, BPD detectives pointed to a cobweb in a corner of the window that had not been disturbed, suggesting someone in the home had committed the murder.

When Lou pointed out there was no snow on the ground around the basement window, which explained why there were no footprints in the snow, Boulder detectives continued to dismiss any possibility a killer had entered the home intent on kidnapping the Ramsey's daughter–despite the ransom note! A few months after my first discussion with Lou, where he told me something was wrong with the case in Boulder, he shared how he had a chance to meet John and Patsy Ramsey and he was skeptical that either parent had murdered their daughter.

I have been completely perplexed how anyone could outright dismiss Lou's opinion that JonBenét was not killed upstairs by one of her parents and then her body carried to the basement to stage the scene to resemble a kidnapping. To give equal weight to Detective Steve Thomas' opinion that Patsy killed JonBenét upstairs in a fit of rage over a bedwetting incident, carried her body down to the basement, and then wrote the fake ransom note is just as ridiculous as accepting Linda Arndt's opinion that she looked into the eyes of John Ramsey and knew she was looking into the eyes of the person who killed JonBenét and she feared he would kill everyone else in the house!

Wound pattern interpretation is a critical component of harmful event sequencing in a homicide investigation, as is the process of inclusion and exclusion of possible suspects. The Boulder PD continued to make public statements that the parents were not cooperating, giving the illusion the Ramseys had something to hide. Not only had John, Patsy, and Burke Ramsey been interviewed multiple times, including on December 26 and 27, 1996, the parents also voluntarily gave handwriting, blood, and hair samples, including pubic hair samples.

The Ramseys signed search waivers to allow Boulder detectives to search their home, cars, airplane hangar, and John's office in downtown Boulder. They also signed waivers for credit card receipts for movie rentals. These extensive searches produced no incriminating evidence against any Ramsey family member. They had not purchased a stun gun, duct tape, or parachute cord. The Boulder police, including Detectives Steve Thomas, Linda Arndt, and their boss, Detective Commander John Eller, continued to dismiss evidence that should have excluded the Ramseys as suspects, and they ignored the evidence proving Lou Smit was right about an intruder.

First, let's take a close look through the magnifying lens of Detective Lou Smit, at what he believed to be the most critical physical evidence taken away from the crime scene by the killer:

1. Parachute Cord: White nylon parachute cord was used to construct the garrote and tie the ligature around JonBenét's wrists. Parachute cord, referred to as type-III paracord or 550 cord, is lightweight braided nylon originally used for the suspension lines on parachutes. For the past fifty years, it has been used as a general purpose utility cord. Since the Ramseys did not own any parachute cord, Lou believed the suspect brought the cord into the home, cut a piece off to construct the garrote and used a second piece to make the ligature tied around JonBenét's wrists, and took the remaining parachute cord with him when he left the crime scene.

2. Roll of Duct Tape: When JonBenét's father found his daughter's body in the basement, he removed a six-inch piece of black duct tape from her mouth. Lou noted how both ends of the duct tape had been torn from a roll, rather than being cut. Therefore, if the roll of duct tape could be found, one of the two ends of the piece of tape removed from the victim's mouth could conceivably be matched to that particular roll of tape. However, no roll of duct tape was ever found in the Ramsey's home and the parents denied ever owning any black duct tape. Furthermore, the Ramsey home was thoroughly searched for any duct tape that might have been used anywhere in the home prior to the murder. A different color of duct tape was found to have been used on the back of a picture frame, to hold the photo in place. This picture frame with the duct tape was submitted to CBI for comparison purposes and was found not to match the black duct tape placed over the victim's mouth. Therefore, Lou concluded the suspect had to have brought the roll of black duct tape with him and took the remaining roll with him when he left the crime scene.

3. Stun Gun: Lou believed the two rectangular-shaped red marks on the right side of JonBenét's face and on her back were made by a stun gun. Lou determined the distance between the rectangular marks was approximately 3.5 cm, consistent with an Air Taser stun gun. Between the two red marks on JonBenét's back, Lou noticed a faint light blue line visible just below the surface of the skin resembled the irregular electrical arc which runs between the two metal rectangular probes when activated. This might be a contusion, an injury just below the surface of the skin caused when the blood capillaries have been ruptured. Human blood below the surface of the skin appears more bluish in color; blood does not take on a red color until it is exposed to the air. Since there was no stun gun found at the crime scene, and the Ramseys deny ever owning a stun gun, Lou believed the suspect had to have brought the stun gun into the home and then he took it with him when he exited the crime scene. If true, this is the strongest piece of evidence to prove the intent of the suspect—kidnapping, exactly what the ransom note indicated.

4. Hi-Tec Boots: The fresh footprint impression left in the mold on the floor of the basement, next to the body of JonBenét, read Hi-Tec. Since the Ramseys did not own any Hi-Tec footwear, and none of the police officers who walked through the crime scene were known to have worn this type of boot, Lou believed the killer may have been wearing Hi-Tec boots when he committed the murder.

5. Paintbrush Handle: The end piece of the paintbrush handle used to construct the improvised garrote was missing from the crime scene. The middle piece of the paintbrush handle was found at the scene, wrapped with the white parachute cord, and the broken bristled end was found in a plastic tray containing other paintbrushes in the basement. However, the upper end of the paintbrush handle, measuring 6-8 inches, was missing. Lou believed this broken paintbrush handle was possibly used to penetrate the vagina since small pieces of wood material were found inside the victim's body. Some rapists have been known to keep an item as a trophy, such as a pair of the victim's panties, to reenact their sexual crime. This led Lou to conclude there is a possibility the missing end of the paintbrush was taken by the suspect.

6. Practice Note: There were five pages missing from the front of the notepad found in the Ramsey home. The ransom note was written on a note pad confirmed to have belonged to Patsy Ramsey. There were three pages torn out of the note pad and left on the first step of the spiral staircase leading from the kitchen up to the second level where JonBenét's bedroom was located. However, the first five pages have never been located. This led to the speculation the suspect may have started writing the note, then for some reason started over again, perhaps more than once, using the same notepad. However, the first five pages were not located in the house, suggesting the suspect may have taken those pages with him from the scene.

7. DNA: While the above-listed items could have been easily destroyed or thrown away in the last quarter century, undeniably, the single most critical physical evidence the killer took with him from the crime scene—was himself. The one thing the killer can never throw away or destroy is his DNA. Lou Smit believed the DNA left behind at the crime scene by the suspect is what will eventually lead to identifying the killer and solving the murder of JonBenét Ramsey.

Now, let's closely examine the physical evidence Detective Lou Smit documented that he believed was left at the crime scene by the suspect/s:

1. Garrote: While homicide deaths caused by strangulation are not uncommon, a stick being used to tighten an improvised garrote is very uncommon. In fact, in my nearly half-century experience with homicide investigations, the Ramsey murder is the only murder I am personally familiar with that was committed with a stick being used in the construction of an improvised garrote. A garrote can be made out of various materials, including rope, cloth, guitar strings, or piano wire. Many elite military special forces units around the world have been trained how to make and use improvised garrotes as a weapon to loop over a sentry's head and pulled tight from behind. In the murder of JonBenét, the garrote was constructed by wrapping white parachute cord around a piece of a paintbrush handle and pulled tight from behind. Lou noted how the same white parachute cord was used to construct the ligature tied around JonBenét's wrists. Lou pointed to the two reddish abrasions on the front of JonBenét's neck, caused by the garrote, and the fingernail marks above the garrote, proving the device was applied prior to her death. The reddish color in the skin is blood and could only have been made when the heart is pumping blood throughout the body. The FBI adopted a term, referred to as the "familiarity with the fatal agency," which suggests the person who uses a weapon to cause a death usually has some familiarity with the weapon. Whoever constructed the improvised garrote used in the murder of JonBenét would have had some prior training or experience in constructing the weapon. Lou Smit was right; this highly unusual, improvised garrote was not constructed by a parent trying to stage a kidnapping to cover up an accidental death. This device was constructed by a methodical killer who had practiced constructing this type of lethal weapon.

2. Ligature: A ligature is defined as, "Anything that binds or ties." In the Ramsey case, the killer brought parachute cord into the home as part of his "Kidnapping Kit." The same white parachute cord used to construct the garrote was also used as the ligature tied around JonBenét's wrists. Lou pointed out how the two ends of the parachute cord used as the ligature were frayed. He further noted that only one end of the cord used to construct the garrote was frayed, while the other end had been burnt to keep it from unraveling. Since the Ramseys didn't own any parachute cord, and other than these two pieces, there wasn't any parachute cord in the home, Lou determined the killer brought the parachute cord into the house, cut a length of it to make the garrote and then cut another length off of the same cord to fashion the ligature. The killer took the remaining cord with him when he left the crime scene. Lou also pointed out how these ligatures were not hastily tied as simple square knots, but were slip knots intended to constrict tighter the more the victim struggled. As with the garrote, Lou believed the ligature was intended to control the victim and she was alive at the time they were tied around her wrists.

3. Duct Tape: A piece of black duct tape had been placed over JonBenét's mouth, presumably to prevent her from screaming. The duct tape, measuring approximately six inches in length, was removed from the victim's mouth by her father when her body was found. The Ramseys claim they never owned any black duct tape and a search of the entire household failed to produce the roll of duct tape this piece had been torn from; therefore, as Lou Smit pointed out, the suspect had to have also brought a roll of duct tape into the crime scene and taken it with him when he left the house. If the roll of tape is ever found, one end of the duct tape found at the crime scene could theoretically be matched to the end on the roll or to the previous piece of tape last used by the suspect on an item in his possession.

4. Ransom Note: In his investigative notes, Lou documented how the three-page ransom note was… "Planned and carefully constructed. Brutal. Not written in haste or panic." He also documented how the note contained lines from several movies that involved kidnapping for ransom. The movie *Ransom* was playing in Boulder in November and December 1996. Lou's notes read how the plot of this movie involved "a high profile (sic) executive of a prominent company…recently in the media…very similar phraseology…3 people watching over the victim…the victim is bound and a small piece of duct tape used." The ransom note also contained specific instructions on how much money was to be paid in $100 bills with the remaining paid in smaller denominations. In the movie *Ruthless People*, Lou pointed out how both ransom notes start out with "Listen carefully" or "Listen very carefully." And in the movie *Nick* *of Time*, which was playing on TV in Boulder the night of the murder, the ransom note also makes reference to "Listen Carefully" and "We are a group of individuals that represent a small foreign faction." In the movie *Seven*, Lou notes, the "psychopathic killer has a line in it about proper burial" and references the victim being "beheaded." And in the movie *Speed*, the note also reads, "Don't try to grow a brain (sic) John. You are not the only fat cat around so don't think killing will be difficult." In Lou's mind, there was no doubt the intruder had studied these movies and wrote the ransom note using lines from several kidnap-themed movies, that the parents of JonBenét claim they had never watched. The ransom note left for JonBenét's parents was oddly signed, "Victory! S.B.T.C." which had no meaning to either parent. The handwritten note was also printed, rather than being written in cursive handwriting, which makes handwriting comparisons by experts less reliable. Lou's investigation revealed the ransom note was examined by "Six competent examiners who evaluated the note: Chet Ubowski, current CBI examiner; Leonard Speckin, private examiner; Edwin Alford, private examiner; Lloyd Cunningham, Richard Dusick, Secret Service examiner, and Howard Ryle, former CBI examiner." Lou's notes went into great detail on the results and findings of each of the six handwriting experts. Chet Ubowski was the only examiner who stated there were "indications" that Patsy *may* have written the note; "but the evidence falls short of that necessary to support a definite conclusion." Lou concluded, the general consensus of the examiners is that "Patsy did not write the note and none of them say John Ramsey or Burke Ramsey wrote the note."

5. Stun Gun Marks: On the left side of JonBenét's back and below her ear lobe on the right side of her right cheek, Lou observed what he believed were two pairs of two rectangular reddish-colored burn marks made by a stun gun. From studying the autopsy photos of JonBenét's face, Lou came to believe the stun gun may have been deployed through the duct tape, suggesting the duct tape was applied before the stun gun was used on her cheek. If this is the case, then the application of the duct tape to her mouth may have been one of the first "harmful events" intended to muffle any screams when she was taken from her bed located on the second level of the home. The Boulder Police dismissed Lou's assertion these marks were made by a stun gun; however, in his autopsy report, Detective Tom Trujillo did describe the two marks on her back as being "rectangular in shape." Lou noted the marks were reddish in color, which means they were caused prior to JonBenét's death. After Lou had resigned from the Boulder DA's Task Force, he spent years pursuing his belief the intruder entered the Ramsey's home armed with a stun gun and took the weapon with him after killing JonBenét. No stun gun was ever found at the crime scene and the Ramseys denied ever owning a stun gun. In his research, Lou found, "Different manufacturers of stun guns have different voltages and measurements between contacts. Note: The contacts of the Air Tazer stun gun compare the closest to matching the injuries on JonBenét that we have found so far." The distance between the two rectangular shaped probes on the Air Tazer stun gun is 3.5 cm, approximately the same distance between the two sets of red rectangular marks on the victim's body. He also studied other homicide cases where a stun gun was confirmed to have been used on the victim. One of the cases Lou studied was the Gerald Boggs case, where the stun gun was deployed to the right side of the victim's cheek, below the ear lobe, which left a very similar pattern as the marks on JonBenét.

6. Hi-Tec Boot Print: An unidentified boot print, brand name "Hi-Tec," was observed in the mold on the floor in the basement next to the body of JonBenét. The Hi-Tec Corporation was founded in 1974 and by 1996 the boots had become very popular with people who enjoyed the outdoors and first responders.

7. Rope & Bag: A cloth bag containing a long piece of rope was found sitting on a chair in the guest bedroom just down the hall from JonBenét's bedroom. Neither this bag nor the rope belonged to the Ramseys and suggested to Lou that the intruder brought the rope with him with the intent of tying someone up inside the home. Both ends of the rope had been burnt, to keep from fraying, similar to the one end of white parachute cord used to construct the garrote. The guest bedroom is the closest one to JonBenét's bedroom. In addition to the "Dust Ruffle (being) Disturbed," at the end of the bed in the "Guest Bedroom," as opposed to it being "Tucked In" on the two sides of the bed, Lou's notes pointed to three drawers in the adjoining bathroom that were left open. Lou's notes also pointed to the window in the guest bedroom which overlooks the garage area, the perfect location for someone to wait and watch out the window for the Ramseys to return home.

8. Pubic Hair: An unidentified pubic hair was found on the white blanket wrapped around JonBenét's body when she was found in the basement wine cellar. This pubic hair was not a match to either of JonBenét's parents.

9. Palmprint: An unidentified palmprint was discovered on the door leading into the wine cellar where JonBenét's body was found. It did not match either of JonBenét's parents. There is a small wooden latch, at the top of the door frame, which was used to secure the door leading into the wine cellar. This door was closed and the latch was in the locked position when it was first photographed by Boulder police personnel.

10. Flashlight: An aluminum 3-cell Maglite flashlight was found on the kitchen table the morning JonBenét's body was found. The Ramseys said the flashlight did not belong to them and none of the police who were in the crime scene claimed to have left a flashlight behind at the crime scene. Lou believed the flashlight may have belonged to the intruder who entered the home at night and did not want to turn on any lights as he moved throughout the house after dark.

11. Baseball Bat: A black aluminum baseball bat was found on the north side of the house, lying on the ground below a window. John Ramsey did not believe the bat belonged to anyone in his family. Lou's notes also mention, "A fiber from the basement carpet is found on the bat located near the north window." Note—This baseball bat may have been used to cause the 8" skull fracture to JonBenét's head.

12. DNA: On January 15, 1997, three weeks after the murder of JonBenét, Lou Smit's investigative notes indicate that a DNA expert with the Colorado Bureau of Investigation (CBI), conducted forensic testing of JonBenét's fingernails and underwear. In addition to JonBenét's DNA, she also found foreign (unknown) male DNA. Lou's notes read, "It is foreign. It is male. It is not John or Patsy…Ten (10) identifyable (sic) foreign markers have been found. This information has been entered into CODIS." Why this information was not leaked to the media is not a mystery— it did not advance the Boulder detectives' theory that "The Ramseys did it." In fact, the opposite is true; the presence of unknown male DNA remains as the strongest evidence to support Lou's "Intruder Theory." Foreign male DNA proves the innocence of the Ramseys and remains the best forensic tool to identify the killer. My last conversations with Lou, as he lay dying on his hospital bed in hospice, were his undying belief that the unknown male DNA found under the victim's fingernails, and on her panties and long johns, will one day solve the murder of JonBenét.

Lastly, let's examine the physical evidence gained through the autopsy of JonBenét, as seen through the experienced eyes of Lou Smit and the medically-trained pathologist who conducted the autopsy. The doctor who conducted the autopsy on JonBenét's body was John E. Meyer, M.D., the Boulder County Coroner who was elected in 1986. Dr. John Meyer was the first physician to be elected coroner in Boulder County, Colorado. Prior to 1986, the Coroner's Office had been held by morticians, a common practice in smaller counties in Colorado. The autopsy report, signed by Dr. John E. Meyer, is dated 12/27/96, and declares the manner and cause of death was asphyxia due to strangulation.

Lou noted two distinct parallel abrasions around the front of JonBenét's neck caused by the garrote. His notes read, "The lower first placement of the ligature" and then a second abrasion about an inch above where the lower abrasion can be seen in the autopsy photos. Lou points out the white parachute cord was "caught" in a gold necklace, along with several strands of JonBenét's long blonde hair. Lou's notes also point to several, "Fingernail marks above ligature." These small reddish crescent-shaped abrasions were confirmed by the coroner to be fingernail marks, which could only have been made when the little girl was still alive and fighting for her life.

Lou also made a specific reference to "Vaginal Injuries," which included, "A tear of the hymen at the 7 o'clock position," and noted there was "Bleeding from the vagina." Bleeding requires a beating heart. JonBenét was alive when these injuries occurred. Lou also noted the skull fracture, which ran from the front to the back of the head, measuring approximately eight inches in length, was caused by a terrific crushing blow. A further reference Lou made indicated "Material...similar to the wooden shards (from the paintbrush handle) are found in the vagina."

Perhaps the most compelling evidence that JonBenét was alive when the garrote was placed around her neck—and not tied around her neck while trying to stage a kidnapping scene as alleged by Boulder detectives—comes from the Boulder detectives themselves. Detective Tom Trujillo attended JonBenét's autopsy and his report reads, "I observed what appeared to be petechiae (sic) hemorrhage on JonBenét's lower left eyelid. Petechiae (sic) hemorrhages were present on JonBenét's upper left eyelid. Petechiae (sic) hemorrhage was also seen on JonBenét's upper and lower right eyelid."

Petechial hemorrhages can occur as a result of strangulation when blood is pumped from the heart to the head, through the carotid arteries, above the ligature device. Blood circulating throughout the body is returned to the heart through veins. Blood pumped by the heart is under pressure; however, blood returning back to the heart is not under pressure. Therefore, during strangulation, there can occur a buildup of blood beyond the ligature device. This blood cannot return to the heart, resulting in tiny ruptures or hemorrhages of the blood vessels closest to the surface to the skin. Petechia cannot occur postmortem—it requires a beating heart. JonBenét was definitely alive when the garrote was applied.

Detective Trujillo's police report, documenting his observations during the autopsy, continued, "Dr. Meyer had to cut JonBenét's hair so that the ligature could be removed. There was a four inch (sic) length of white cord extending from this knot. The end of this length of cord was frayed. On the far end of the neck ligature was a stick. The stick was attached to the ligature by a series of loops and a knot. The end of this length of cord was singed to keep it from fraying. This stick was broken on both ends, and had exposed rough edges. The stick was approximately 4 'i2 (sic) inches long and had the word 'Korea" printed on it. The total length of the neck ligature was approximately 17 inches long."

Detective Trujillo's police report continued, "Upon examination of the skull of JonBenét, a skull fracture with associated bleeding was seen. The fracture was located along the entire length of the upper right side of JonBenét's head. I observed what was described as fresh hemorrhage on the brain directly underneath this fracture. There was a rectangular shaped area of displaced skull at the rear of this fracture line."

From having personally attended dozens of autopsies with blunt force trauma to the head, and studying the autopsy photos with Lou Smit, I concurred with his findings; this skull fracture required significant force and was almost certainly not "accidental." The autopsy findings concluded the "Cause of death of this six year old (sic) female is asphyxia by strangulation associated with craniocerebral trauma." Lou concluded this crime had definitely not been committed by a parent trying to cover up the accidental death of their child. As a court-qualified expert in crime scene reconstruction, after a comprehensive review of the autopsy report and crime scene and evidence photos over the past decade, I concur with Lou Smit's findings. This crime was the act of a sexually-violent pedophile who had attempted a kidnapping for ransom and in the end brutally murdered this innocent six-year-old little girl.

Part III

Chapter 7 – Jury

Lou Smit had to fight his way in to testify before the grand jury in Boulder. When Michael Kane was appointed special prosecutor for the grand jury by the Governor of Colorado, Roy Romer, Lou feared the grand jury was being manipulated to indict JonBenét's parents. Lou insisted he had information the grand jury needed to hear, but was told by the grand jury chief prosecutor that he would not be allowed to testify. Lou then wrote a letter to the grand jury foreperson, which was published in Paula Woodward's book, *Unsolved, The JonBenet Ramsey Murder, 25 Years Later*.

Lou's letter to the Grand Jury Foreperson, dated January 21, 1999, read, "Dear Mr. Plese, My name is Lou Smit, a retired detective previously assigned to the JonBenet (sic) Ramsey case who resigned from the case in September 1998. I was hired by Alex Hunter in March 1997 to assist his office in organizing and analyzing the case materials presented to his office by the Boulder Police Department. During the 19 months spent in Boulder, I worked very closely with D.A.s Trip DeMuth and Peter Hofstrom. Together we examined all aspects of this case.

"I have been in law enforcement for 32 years, have been involved in over 200 homicide investigations and have worked many high-profile cases in Colorado. I was hired because of my experience and background. I take my work very seriously and truly desire to seek justice not only for JonBenet (sic) but her parents as well.

"I resigned because I do not agree with others in authority, that John and Patsy Ramsey killed their daughter. I see evidence in the case of an intruder, and I cannot in good conscience assist in the prosecution of people I believe to be innocent.

"That is why I am writing you this letter. I would respectfully request that I be called to give testimony before the Grand Jury to provide an "intruder" side of the story. Please take the time to consider what I have to say while evaluating the evidence and making such difficult decisions regarding an indictment in this case.

"I have prepared a presentation which would take about eight hours of the Grand Jury's time. Respectfully submitted, Lou Smit, Retired Detective 719-633-5178.

Within a month, the chief prosecutor wrote Lou a letter advising him he could not tell anyone about his letter to the grand jury. Instead of being intimidated, Lou met with Bob Russel, former 4th Judicial District DA, and Greg Walta, former head of the State's Public Defender's Office, who both agreed to represent Lou pro bono.

When Greg Walta called Michael Kane, he explained that his client, Lou Smit, had prepared a slide presentation with information about the murder the grand jury needed to see. The special prosecutor said no, Lou wasn't going to testify, and they wanted to take away his slide presentation. The prosecutors didn't need his presentation, they just didn't want him to have it and there was some concern they just wanted to destroy his slide presentation. Lou's attorneys argued that his slides reflected his investigative notes and were his work product provided to him with the consent of the Boulder DA. Besides, the Boulder law enforcement authorities already had all the original documents, photos, and lab reports.

Lou's attorneys explained that if Lou was not allowed to testify before the grand jury, he would have to go public. After some discussion, the attorneys finally stipulated that Lou would be allowed to testify and show his slide presentation to the grand jury, as long as he did not go public until after the grand jury had returned a True Bill. After the grand jury was concluded, Lou would be allowed to show his slide presentation to anyone he wanted. He asked for eight hours to present his intruder theory—he was reluctantly given two hours.

While it is not known for certain which slides Lou was able to present to the grand jury during his two-hour testimony, he did have several slides which showed the DNA under JonBenét's fingernails and on her panties was "not John or Patsy" but "is foreign" and "male." This DNA analysis was conducted by an examiner with CBI. A lab report was sent to Boulder law enforcement authorities, dated January 15, 1997—three weeks after the murder of JonBenét—excluding as suspects: John Andrew Ramsey, Melinda Ramsey, John B. Ramsey, Patricia Ramsey, Burke Ramsey, John Fernie, Priscilla White, and Mervin Pugh.

The grand jury was empanelled late in 1998 and returned their findings to Alex Hunter in 1999 asking for an indictment against John and Patsy Ramsey. How any criminal prosecutor, police detective, or grand jury member could dismiss this vital piece of DNA evidence is unbelievable. Were the grand jury members not told about this evidence? Lou could not understand how people couldn't realize the DNA under JonBenét's fingernails got there when she clawed the suspect while fighting for her life? And the foreign male DNA was obviously deposited on her panties as she was being sexually assaulted. Why wasn't this information leaked to the media? In fact, the Boulder police withheld this DNA information from the DA's Office for months and has never shared the CBI lab report with the Ramsey family or the public.

Although Lou could not discuss the grand jury proceedings until the jury was dismissed, he later told me he had never been more mistreated, by both the prosecutors and members of the grand jury, in his 32 years in law enforcement. The grand juries that Lou and I had experienced in the 4th Judicial District were always secret proceedings and held at night. As sworn grand jury investigators, we didn't even know the names of the grand jury members; they were always referred to as numbers. In Boulder, the proceedings were conducted during the day and the grand jury members had to navigate through a swarm of paparazzi just to get inside the courthouse.

In 1999, the new Colorado Governor, Bill Owens, spoke out publicly telling the Ramseys to, "quit hiding behind their attorneys, quit hiding behind their PR firm." But the Boulder DA, Alex Hunter, found himself on the horns of a dilemma. The grand jury had returned a True Bill indicting both John and Patsy Ramsey on charges of placing their child at risk in a way that led to her death and obstructing an investigation of murder. Alex Hunter called a press conference where he announced the grand jury had been concluded and there was not sufficient proof beyond a reasonable doubt to convict anyone with the murder of JonBenét Ramsey.

Innocent people are always the hardest ones to convict.

One of the grand jury members, Jonathan Webb, later told 20/20 that, "Smit's intruder theory didn't make sense. For someone to get through a small window like that and not disturb the cobwebs would be remarkable." Lou said the little cobweb was only in one corner of the window, but the grand jury wasn't interested in facts and like the Boulder police, they dismissed his contention a stun gun had been used on JonBenét and either didn't know or chose to ignore the foreign male DNA found on the body did not match any Ramsey family member. In the court of public opinion, the Ramseys were still guilty of murdering their child and the grand jury prosecutors had accomplished exactly what they had set out to do—indict the Ramseys.

Alex Hunter retired in 2001; however, the grand jury indictments against the Ramseys would not be made public until long after the True Bill was returned. I never spoke to Alex Hunter about his decision not to charge the Ramseys; however, I believe he faced two insurmountable problems. First, he knew the Ramseys were represented by Haddon, Morgan & Foreman, one of the best criminal defense firms in Colorado. This law firm, founded in 1976 by former public defenders Hal Haddon, Bryan Morgan, and Lee Foreman, is still recognized for their aggressive defense of their clients and representation of them in civil rights litigation cases, including wrongful arrest or malicious prosecution. Secondly, it would not have been lost on Alex Hunter that the star witness for the criminal defense team would be his former DA special investigator—Lou Smit.

On February 23, 2000, *Perfect Murder Perfect Town*, a television miniseries directed by Lawrence Schiller, was broadcast by CBS. The miniseries was based on the book of Lawrence Schiller by the same name, *Perfect Murder Perfect Town*. The book and miniseries went into detail about the botched investigation and the feud between the Boulder DA and the Boulder Police over how the case should be investigated. Alex Hunter was played by Ken Howard, Steve Thomas was played by Scott Cohen, and Lou Smit was played by Kris Kristofferson.

I had gotten a call from Lou and he told me about the film being shot in Boulder, and he asked me to go with him to meet Kris Kristofferson. Lou explained that Kristofferson would be coming to Colorado Springs the day before he was needed in Boulder and would be staying at the exclusive Broadmoor Hotel. I told him, "Absolutely!"—I wasn't about to miss a chance to meet Kris Kristofferson!

When it came time for us to meet, I arrived early at the plush 5-star hotel and spotted Kris Kristofferson standing where he said he'd be, lakeside at the top of the escalators. I introduced myself and got to shake hands with one of my favorite country-western singers and songwriters (to me, country music just doesn't get any better than *Sunday Mornin Comin' Down*, *Me* and *Bobby McGee*, etc.!). His musical performance with Johnny Cash, Willie Nelson, and Waylon Jennings, as one of the four Highwaymen (1985-1995), is still legendary today. Lou arrived right on time and the two of them hit it off immediately.

Kris explained that as an actor he had played many different roles, but had never played the role of someone who was still living. He said he just wanted to spend some time with Lou, get to know him and try to pick up any mannerisms that may help him stay more true to the character of the person he was portraying. Lou suggested that I drive the three of us around Colorado Springs while he and Kris sat in the back seat to talk; we'd show Kris some of the local sights. I drove us through the majestic Garden of the Gods and downtown past the Sheriff's Office, while Lou and Kris visited in the back seat, mostly about the Ramsey case.

From reading Schiller's movie script, Kris already had a good understanding of Lou's participation in the Ramsey homicide investigation; but hearing Lou's account of why he agreed to be part of the DA's Task Force, his interpretation of the evidence and why he felt compelled to resign when the grand jury was convened, gave Kris a much better understanding of Lou's moral character and his unending devotion to the case.

After an hour or so, I asked if Kris had any plans for dinner. He replied no, he was not expected in Boulder until the next day and had no plans for dinner, but wanted to spend as much time with Lou as possible. Lou said he and Barb didn't have any plans for dinner either, so I called home to ask my wife if she would mind if I brought three people home for dinner. She was pretty excited to get the call and replied, "No, as long as one of them is Kris Kristofferson!"

This was in November of 1999 and my wife fixed a wonderful turkey dinner, with mashed potatoes, dressing, gravy, and all the trimmings. Kris laughed and commented, "Hey, you fixed Thanksgiving dinner!" Lou, Barb, Kris, my wife, and our two-year-old daughter, and I sat around our dining room table and enjoyed a delightful conversation over a wonderful turkey dinner. Kris and Lou were about the same age (Lou was 64 and Kris was 63). I hadn't known this, but before Kris had become a famous singer and songwriter, he had attended Oxford University as a Rhodes Scholar and joined the U.S. Army where he served as a helicopter pilot.

We had a large doll house set up in the living room for our daughter to play in and we watched as Kris got down on the floor to look through the windows as our two-year-old crawled inside to show him all her toys. He told us that he had eight children of his own and how he loved kids and it showed. After dinner, Kris held our daughter on his lap, just the way John Ramsey had held JonBenét. When the miniseries aired a few months later, tucked into the corner of Kris Kristofferson's mouth was Lou Smit's quintessential trademark—a wooden toothpick.

There is a fine line between how TV shows are produced and how books or newspaper articles are written; are they meant for entertainment or to disseminate information? People will pay for entertainment and there can be a lot of drama within certain groups, especially cops, firefighters, or people in the medical field, which explains why these kinds of TV shows are so popular. People like Joe Kenda have become hugely successful by telling dramatic stories about homicide cases. I was paid to appear on five of Lieutenant Joe Kenda's *Homicide Hunter* TV shows. In the highly competitive and rapidly evolving industry of news reporting, the lines often blur between tabloids, written primarily for entertainment purposes, and traditional newspapers, meant to inform the public of newsworthy people, places or events. But it is important to keep in mind that these are businesses, not charities, and ratings drive advertising dollars.

It's only human nature for people to be interested in seeing someone who holds a position of high status—a TV or sports celebrity, a member of the British Royal Family, or perhaps someone like the Ramseys who had achieved a high level of success—"fall from grace." On Christmas 1996, John Ramsey's company, Access Graphics, a company he and Patsy had started in their basement, had just passed the $1 billion mark in sales and had recently been acquired by Lockheed Martin. One of the lessons I learned in being a candidate and serving in public office is, "Whenever you stick your head up above the crowd someone is going to throw a rock at you."

The Ramseys were "living the American dream," when they went to sleep on Christmas Day 1996. They would awake the next morning to a parent's worst nightmare. I have met and talked with John Ramsey, along with his oldest son, John Andrew Ramsey, many times since that horrible day, over twenty-five years ago. While I met Patsy Ramsey just one time, she left a lasting memory in my mind, not of a murderer, but of a loving mother who was overwhelmed by the grief of losing a child. Like Lou, in my career that also spanned over three decades, I have met many loving parents and violent killers. Patsy definitely belonged in the first category.

In August 2000, Bill Kurtis, a respected journalist and news anchor with CBS, who also holds a law degree, served as the host for an A&E television special on the Ramsey case. To try to get to the truth, Bill Kurtis spoke to a number of reporters, including Charlie Brennan, who had written an article published in the *Rocky Mountain News*, suggesting that only a family member could have murdered JonBenét. Brennan defended his actions and explained, "I had a trusted law enforcement source tell me …When the first officers arrived, at least one officer thought it was worth noting in his report, 'strange—no footprints'."

Bill Kurtis spoke with another reporter, Julie Hayden, of Denver's Channel 7 News, about the issue of whether or not there were "no footprints in the snow." After reviewing all the video footage available to her, Julie Hayden concluded, "…one of the things I observed was, there did not seem to be snow going to all the doors. So in my opinion, this no-footprints in the snow issue has all been much ado about nothing. It seemed clear to me that people have gotten into the house, whether they did or not, without traipsing through the snow."

When Bill Kurtis asked Charlie Brennan about another story that he had also covered, reporting "There had been no break-in," Brennan again defended himself by saying, "That was coming from law enforcement sources, and you know, I know that you know this is a story that was heavily reported through unnamed sources, and I'm not going to name that source now. But law enforcement was telling us from December that they saw no signs of forced entry." When crime scene photos were leaked to a tabloid newspaper, a DA's investigation revealed a former Boulder County Sheriff's Deputy was being paid $50 an hour for any information on the case.

Kurtis asked Charlie Brennan, "Would it be reasonable to assume that the information about 'no forced entry' was false information that was being leaked by the authorities?" Brennan answered, "Yes, that would be fair to say. Particularly in light of where you can start at least from the broken window in the basement. In January '97, February '97, March '97, we didn't know that there was a broken window in the basement." Kurtis concluded, "The reality of the situation is that an intruder could easily have gotten in, and once in, moved around undetected and unheard." Despite this A&E special being watched by over 4 million viewers, an urban myth had been born and continues to live a quarter of a century later.

John or Patsy Ramsey were not allowed to testify before the grand jury—in the court of public opinion, they had already been found guilty of murdering their daughter. Melinda Ramsey tried to explain, "I'm John Ramsey's daughter. I grew up with him, he raised me and I saw him raise JonBenét and I don't understand why they don't believe me. That he is the most caring father in the world. He has never, ever, ever abused us in any way. I just wish I could say something to convince them." Burke Ramsey, who was nine years old at the time of the murder, was interviewed by the police three times and would confirm, "We didn't get spanked, nothing of the sort, nothing close, nothing near laying a finger on us, let alone killing your child."

Lou courageously faced was what he called a "Lynch Mob Mentality" and "Guilt by Innuendo." His intention was to help solve the murder of JonBenét; his biggest obstacle was the Boulder PD. Lou pointed out in his notes the police and others repeated publicly there were, "No footprints in the snow. No evidence of entry or exit. No stun gun was used. Pasty wrote the note. The Ramseys are not cooperating." The Boulder Mayor appeared on television and said, "There is no threat to the public. Your children are safe." Lou and I spoke often about the challenges of him trying to investigate a homicide "from the outside looking in" to get to the truth.

After leaving the DA's Office, Lou set up an office in a spare bedroom in his home and continued working the case on his own. He also stayed in touch with the Ramsey family, but refused to accept any payment for his investigative services after leaving the DA's Office. John Ramsey later shared a memory of trying to buy Lou Smit an ice cream cone and Lou refused, explaining he never wanted anyone to ever say he accepted one cent for his work on the case. Lou always said he, "Wasn't working for John or Patsy Ramsey, he was working for JonBenét."

When the Ramseys explained they wanted to hire additional private investigators in Colorado Springs, Lou introduced them to Ollie Gray and John San Agustin. Both Ollie and John had worked for me at the Sheriff's Office and Lou kept in touch with them after they were hired by the Ramseys. Lou would often compare notes with other private citizens working to find justice for JonBenét. He also stayed in contact with the Boulder PD and sent frequent tips, which he called "darts," to the detectives hoping they might follow up on these unresolved leads. It does not appear that the Boulder PD ever acknowledged any of Lou's darts.

Then, between May 6th and May 17th, 2000, John and Patsy Ramsey voluntarily took polygraph tests in Atlanta, Georgia, and Los Angeles, California. Their tests were administered by Edward I. Gelb, Ph.D., of Los Angeles, California, who had conducted over 30,000 polygraph tests in his career. At the time, Dr. Gelb was administering polygraph tests for five police agencies in California and teaching FBI polygraph operators. Because the Ramseys felt they were being targeted by the Boulder police for JonBenét's murder, they were not comfortable in submitting to a polygraph given by anyone involved with the Boulder police, including the FBI.

However, the Ramseys were anxious to do anything they could to prove they were not responsible for the murder of their daughter and to shift the focus of the homicide investigation away from them and onto the real killer. Against the advice of their attorney, Lin Wood, the Ramseys agreed to lie detector tests. According to Lou's research, supported by Charlie Hess, who had been an FBI polygraph operator, Dr. Gelb was considered one of the top polygraph experts in the country. His test results were confirmed by Cleve Baxter, another nationally recognized polygraph operator, who stated, "After careful review…without any reservation whatsoever, I agree with the conclusions that have been reached by the original examiner."

While it is well understood that the results of polygraph tests are not admissible in court, there can be little doubt that if the Ramseys had failed their polygraphs, most people, including the Boulder police detectives, would have said, "See, that proves they are guilty of murdering their daughter." If they had passed their polygraphs, most people, most especially the Boulder police detectives, would say, "See, that's why polygraphs are not admissible in court."

On May 24, 2000, at 1:01 p.m., Lou's notes reflect that Dr. Gelb publicly released the results stating that both John and Patsy Ramsey had passed their polygraph examinations. Dr. Gelb's conclusion read, "Based on the numerical scoring of the examination in this series, John Ramsey was telling the truth when he denied inflicting the injuries that caused the death of his daughter, JonBenét. Based on the numerical scoring of the examinations in this series, John Ramsey was telling the truth when he denied knowing who killed JonBenét."

The test results for Patsy Ramsey read, "Based on the numerical scoring of the examinations in this series, Patsy Ramsey was telling the truth when she denied inflicting the injuries that caused the death of her daughter, JonBenét. Based on the numerical scoring of the examinations in this series, Patsy Ramsey was telling the truth when she denied writing the JonBenét ransom note." Dr. Gelb's final written conclusion read, "Based on extensive polygraph examinations, neither John nor Patsy Ramsey were attempting deception when they gave the indicated answers to the relative questions."

Not surprisingly, the Boulder Police dismissed the polygraph results since the tests were not administered by the FBI. Ironically, one of the tabloids had offered $1 million if the Ramseys would take a polygraph administered by Dr. Gelb, but their offer expired at the end of '97. None of the tabloids or mainstream news media ran the headlines, "The Ramseys Pass Polygraphs." No doubt, had the results been reversed, nearly every news outlet worldwide would have led with the story, "The Ramseys Fail Polygraphs!" John and Patsy Ramsey knew there was too much at risk for them to submit to another series of tests given by a polygraph examiner chosen by the Boulder Police. In the court of public opinion, the Ramseys were still guilty of murder.

To further prove his belief a stun gun was used to make the two rectangular marks on JonBenét's back and cheek, Lou Smit bought a fully grown pig. On September 1, 2000, Lou had the pig euthanized and conducted a series of experiments using an Air Tazer stun gun with Dr. Michael Doberson, the Arapahoe County Coroner. The results of the stun gun experiment showed the marks left on the pig were consistent with the marks on JonBenét's body. Lou's notes state there were, "No cuts. No swelling. No blisters. No scrapes. No bruising." Lou noted that the marks appeared to be, "Electrical type burns reddish in color."

On November 7, 2002, Court TV "The Elite" aired an interview with Lou Smit and Dr. Michael Doberson titled, "JonBenet A Second Look." A verbatim transcript for part of the interview reads as follows:

"NARRATOR - Smit looked for other murder cases where a stun gun had been used and found Gerald Boggs. These photos show the injuries made by the weapon in the Boggs case.

LOU SMIT - They compared very closely with the same marks on JonBenét. In fact, the marks were on the same side of the face and it was a large mark and a small mark. The reason that happens that way is because if contact of the stun gun is placed directly against the skin, it leaves a smaller mark. But if the other contact is left off the skin just a little bit, the arc of electricity dances around on the skin causing the larger mark.

NARRATOR - Smit also identified the particular weapon which he believed caused these injuries.

LOU - The stun gun that we came up with is this one and it's the Air Taser stun gun. If a stun gun is used on a little girl, I'm sure it would have knocked her flat and it would have allowed the killer to take her from her bed without her struggling.

NARRATOR - The Boulder police rejected Smit's evidence about a stun gun. They spoke to Colorado's leading expert, pathologist Mike Dobersen, and claimed he discounted the possibility.

MIKE DOBERSEN - That's right—and that was something of a mistatement (sic) since my real conclusion was that I couldn't, at that time, say whether this was a stun gun injury or not because we had to have a weapon to compare it to.

NARRATOR - When Smit showed him the Air Tazer stun gun, Doberson took a different position.

MIKE DOBERSEN - Lou had found a weapon with characteristics which fit, as exactly as you could expect, the injuries on JonBenét's body.

NARRATOR - Since then, Mike Dobersen (sic) has conducted experiments on anaesthetized pigs. The Tazer stun gun exactly replicated the injuries on JonBenét and the distance, 3.5 centimeters, between those injuries.

MIKE DOBERSEN - "My experiments, and the observations that we made and all the work that's been done, I feel that I can testify to a reasonably degree of medical certainty that these are stun gun injuries."

Lou Smit spent the rest of his life trying to convince others that a stun gun was used on JonBenét, proving the intent of the killer was in fact a kidnap for ransom—a theory supported by the ransom note. Doubters of Lou's stun gun theory, including Boulder area law enforcement, pointed to a model train set in the basement and suggested JonBenét's brother Burke may have poked her with the end of the train tracks. Lou countered by pointing out these marks were not visible on her face in any of the Christmas photos taken of JonBenét that morning and the parents had not noticed the marks when they put her to bed on Christmas night.

The distance between the two outer rails on a Model O train track is 3.5 cm, consistent with the distance Lou measured between the two rectangular probes on an Air Taser stun gun. However, the Model O track does have a middle track and there are only two abrasions on JonBenét's back and right cheek. After comparing photos of the marks on JonBenét's body, with those on the pig, I do concur with Lou's wound pattern conclusion—a stun gun was used on JonBenét. Lou also had an additional advantage over most other investigators with the Boulder police or DA's investigators; he had spent considerable time with John and Patsy Ramsey.

I am not sure why Lou wanted me to meet John and Patsy Ramsey, but I remain grateful that he invited me to meet them shortly after he had left the Boulder DA's Office. We met at the law office of Elvin Gentry, one of the most prominent defense attorneys in Colorado Springs. I know they were still worried about being arrested for the murder of their daughter. Lou was more focused on getting another killer off the streets so he could not kill again. This was the only time I met Patsy; she passed away on June 24, 2006, in Atlanta, Georgia. She was only 49. Patsy is buried in the St. James Episcopal Cemetery in Marietta, Georgia, next to JonBenét.

Shortly before Patsy passed away, Lou traveled to Georgia to talk with her one last time. As police officers, we were taught that hearsay, statements made out of court, are not admissible in a court of law. However, we were also taught one very important exception to the hearsay rule—a dying declaration. A dying declaration is a statement made by a person who is unavailable to testify in court. For a dying declaration to be admissible two requirements must be met: 1) the person must believe they are about to die and 2) they must, in fact, die.

This rule of law dates back to the medieval English courts, to a case in 1202. The rationale was and remains today, that when a person is close to death, they have less incentive to fabricate a lie; therefore, hearsay statements carry some credibility. With this in mind, Lou visited Patsy, in Marietta, Georgia, as she lay dying from cancer. I know Lou did not expect her to confess to murdering her daughter, but Lou was such a thorough investigator, he simply could not leave this one stone unturned. Lou told me later how he had gone to Georgia and met with John and prayed at Patsy's bedside. Her last words to him were, "Lou, catch this guy." Lou Smit dedicated the rest of his life trying to fulfill Patsy's last wish of him—to catch the killer of JonBenét.

Another investigative principle Lou understood was the significance of "other bad acts" which typically escalate in severity. For example, a pattern that manifests itself at a young age with serial killers, often includes, "late bedwetting, fire setting (sic) and cruelty to animals." If child abuse or spousal abuse results in a death, there is almost always a pattern of abuse that escalates in the severity of violent behavior. In the homicide of JonBenét, there was no prior physical or sexual abuse with JonBenét or any of the other Ramsey children. In fact, Burke, John Andrew, and Melinda Ramsey repeatedly told the police what loving parents they had. Even John Ramsey's ex-wife told authorities what a loving, caring parent John was to his children.

JonBenét's pediatrician, Dr. Beuf, released a statement that he had seen her 27 times between March 1993 and November 1996, the month before the murder. That's an average of 9 doctor's visit every year; which might seem excessive to many parents. But with JonBenét, anytime she had an ailment Patsy would take her to see the pediatrician. If there had been any prior indications of child abuse, JonBenét's mother or pediatrician certainly would have noticed. In his written statement, Dr. Beuf wrote that he had never once seen any signs that JonBenét had been sexually molested or had any unusual marks or injuries. There was no evidence of prior sexual abuse. After JonBenét's death, John and Patsy Ramsey continued to be loving, caring parents for the other Ramsey children. To this day, John Ramsey remains a loving, caring father to his three surviving children and shows the same love and affection for his grandchildren.

The Boulder District Attorney who followed Alex Hunter was Mary Lacy. On July 9, 2008, she announced that based on newly developed touch or trace DNA analysis, the Ramseys were excluded as possible suspects in the case. This new DNA testing technology was developed to detect small amounts of "touch" or "trace" DNA left behind on objects touched by the criminal. The test had been run on JonBenét's long johns, which she had been wearing as pajama bottoms when she went to bed on December 25, 1996. The DNA results tested positive for the presence of at least one unknown male DNA, which was consistent with the DNA found under JonBenét's fingernails and on her panties. The new DNA analysis suggested the possibly of even two unknown males; however, the samples were comingled with JonBenét's DNA.

I do know Lou was in contact with Mary Lacy at that time and he was familiar with this new touch DNA evidence, which may have produced four more genetic markers than was produced by the DNA in the underwear. In reviewing Lou's investigative notes, I don't see where he mentions the possibly of there now being fourteen genetic DNA markers. However, after reviewing Lou's investigative notes and his slide presentation, it appears he was aware that the new long johns DNA analysis was consistent with the ten unknown male genetic DNA markers that had been found on JonBenét's panties and under her fingernails.

Lou had hoped this new DNA analysis would help establish that John and Patsy Ramsey were innocent and shift the Boulder detectives' investigation from the Ramseys to pursuing an intruder. Lou believed that over time, DNA analysis technology would continue to improve and would one day identify the killer of JonBenét. I do not know how much influence Lou Smit may have had on Mary Lacy, but it became widely known that she had written John Ramsey a letter telling him that, based on this new DNA analysis, her office does not consider him, Patsy, or anyone in their immediate family to be under suspicion for the death of JonBenét.

Chief Mark Beckner adamantly disagreed with exonerating the Ramseys and stated, "Exonerating anyone based on a small piece of evidence that has not yet been proved to even be connected to the crime is absurd." Steven Pitt, a forensic psychiatrist on the payroll of the Boulder PD, said, "Lacy's public exoneration of the Ramseys was a big slap in the face to Chief Beckner and the core group of detectives who had been working on the case for years."

John Ramsey wrote in his and Patsy's book, that "America has lost the presumption of innocence." In Lou Smit's mind, the Ramseys weren't presumed innocent— they were innocent! Lou Smit would devote the rest of his life in search of justice for JonBenét.

Chapter 8 – Legacy

On January 14, 2003, after serving eight years as the El Paso County Sheriff, I was term-limited in office and retired from a 30-year law enforcement career. Looking back on my two terms as Sheriff, I am proud of what we as a team had accomplished. My proudest moments in leading over five hundred dedicated law enforcement professionals, includes the capture of the Texas Seven, the Columbine High School shooting reinvestigation, and Lou Smit and his team catching the killer responsible for the kidnap-murder of 13-year-old Heather Dawn Church.

The Columbine High School shooting reinvestigation had come about at the request of the Jefferson County Sheriff, John Stone, who called me to request our detectives conduct an independent investigation of their shooting on April 20, 1999, that left 12 students and one teacher dead. Twenty-one others were injured and there had been an exchange of gunfire with the police before the two suspects, both high school students, turned the guns on themselves and committed suicide. Before Columbine, Lou Smit had retired from the Sheriff's Office to spend more time with Barb, but he had reorganized and trained almost everyone in our detective bureau.

What prompted an independent investigation was an allegation from one of the parents who claimed their son was accidently shot in the back by a Denver Police SWAT sergeant during the exchange of heavy gunfire. The SWAT sergeant had fired multiple rounds in what he claimed was "suppression fire," intended to distract a gunman, so wounded students lying on the ground outside of the school could be rescued. Our investigation proved beyond any reasonable doubt that their son was not accidently shot by the SWAT sergeant, but that he had been shot and killed by one of the student gunmen. This complex case was one of our finest investigations.

The Columbine High School massacre was also transformational in the way police respond to what became known as "active shooter" calls. In the multiagency response to Columbine High School, the police did exactly what they had been trained to do; establish containment, call in a SWAT team, and buy time by initiating negotiations with the suspects to find out what they wanted. That didn't work at Columbine; the two suspects weren't going anywhere, time wasn't on our side, and what the suspects wanted was to stay there to kill more innocent victims.

In the wake of Columbine, I had made the decision, as the Sheriff of El Paso County, to radically change how we would train for and respond to active shooter calls. Instead of setting up containment, the first three officers on scene would form into a small 3-person mobile assault team and engage the shooters. In addition to a handgun and shotgun, patrol officers were also issued assault rifles. Specialized training was provided for these new tactics, firearms and tactical procedures. Initially I did get some pushback by a few deputies, but I wasn't asking my deputies to do anything I wasn't prepared to do myself. Other police agencies adopted similar policies.

When Lou Smit was hired, CSPD didn't have a SWAT team; they didn't exist. SWAT teams came along in the early 1970's during the post-Vietnam era. LAPD was the first police department in the U.S. to field a SWAT team and a TV program called SWAT helped popularize the concept around the country. Over the next quarter century SWAT teams became an integral part of law enforcement in the U.S. and abroad. In the capture of the Texas 7, three SWAT teams were mobilized; the El Paso County and Teller County Sheriffs' SWAT teams, along with the FBI's Colorado-Wyoming SWAT team. A quarter of a century after JonBenét's death, Boulder PD responded to an active shooter 911 call at the King Soopers on Table Mesa Drive.

The first three Boulder police officers to arrive on scene formed themselves into a small 3-person SWAT team and heroically entered the store to engage the active shooter clad in body armor. Nine people were killed before the officers entered the store, but once they got inside, no more innocent civilians would die. Tragically, there would be one more victim that day; Boulder Police Officer Eric Talley was shot and killed by the suspect, who was then shot by one of the other two officers. The suspect was handcuffed and taken into custody, using Officer Talley's handcuffs. I didn't know Officer Eric Talley, but I do know this—you always lose your best.

Throughout this book I have been critical of several Boulder police officers, detectives, command officers and police chiefs. Their lack of investigative experience, failed leadership and in some cases, arrogance, led to the public persecution of an innocent family of a murdered child. As individual police officers, their actions are inexcusable and they should be held accountable. That said, I have always believed the Boulder Police Department was a good department, with many dedicated police professionals. On March 22, 2021, Officer Talley, and the other officers who responded to the active shooter call on Table Mesa Drive, proved this point.

My purpose in writing this book, and taking an unpopular stand, in the shoes of my friend Lou Smit, in being critical of the poor behavior, inactions, and failed leadership of the Boulder police in the Ramsey homicide investigation, is to point out lessons learned and best practices that can be adopted by professional law enforcement agencies in the future. Let me be clear, I have made my fair share of mistakes, but I learned from my mistakes and always tried to surround myself with people who were smarter and more capable than me—one of those people was Lou Smit.

After Lou retired as my Captain of Detectives, he returned as a volunteer to start a homicide cold case unit at the Sheriff's Office. He recruited two other volunteers, Charlie Hess and Scott Fischer, to work unsolved cases. The other detectives named Lou's team the Apple Dumpling Gang, after a 1975 American comedy-western movie starring Bill Bixby, Don Knotts, and Tim Conway. The plot was about a gambler who was duped into taking care of a group of orphans who eventually strikes gold. Lou's Apple Dumpling Gang struck gold almost instantly by solving another cold homicide case in Colorado Springs, resulting with a second life sentence on Robert Browne, the serial killer who had kidnapped and murdered Heather Dawn Church.

In my life, I have had the privilege of meeting many extraordinary people whom I would not have otherwise met had I not been elected Sheriff. As Sheriff, the one duty I never delegated to anyone was the swearing in of newly appointed deputies. I shook each of their hands after they took their oath to serve and protect the citizens of El Paso County and the State of Colorado. I also shook hands with three U.S. Presidents and served on their executive protection details. I have gotten to know many U.S. Senators and Congressmen, including Senators Ben Nighthorse Campbell and Ken Salazar.

By the time I retired as Sheriff, we had grown the office to 533 fulltime employees, including 404 sworn deputies, and I had over a dozen honorary deputies. One of my honorary deputies was Bob Norris, the original Marlboro man; another was retired CSPD Sergeant Jerry Busemeyer. I attended both their funerals and remain forever grateful they were a part of my life. While serving as Sheriff we attained the coveted national Triple Crown of Accreditation and implemented the first 5-year strategic plan in county history. I served on The Hundred Club, brought back a Mounted Unit, enacted an El Paso County Model Traffic Code and started our first ever full-time Traffic Unit, which, of course, included motorcycles.

The morning after I retired as Sheriff, I started a new position with the Lockheed Martin Corporation. With 9/11 in mind, I focused on homeland and corporate security. I enjoyed many exciting assignments in exotic places, including a combat zone on the Horn of Africa and worked with the Abu Dhabi Police in the United Arab Emirates (UAE). Although I travelled extensively, I remained in close contact with my friend, Lou Smit. He visited me for a few days when I was on a six-month assignment at the Lockheed Martin Center for Innovation, in Tidewater, Virginia. We went to Virginia Beach, swam in the ocean and talked long into the night about what leads he was following to solve the murder of JonBenét. I was proud my partner was still on the case.

While I was employed by Lockheed Martin I introduced my boss, Al Sarno, to Lou Smit and CSPD Detective Captain Harry Killa. Al and I had met while I was still in office and I knew he had an intense interest in criminal investigations. Al was a retired U.S. Army Colonel who had experienced combat in Vietnam. He had been with the CIA before coming to work for GE Aerospace, which had been acquired by Lockheed Martin. When the CSPD was awarded a grant to work cold cases using DNA, Al was hired part-time, along with Charlie Hess and another of my CSPD friends, Bill Lidh, who had recently retired from the Department.

On February 29, 2004, Lou's beloved wife, Barb, lost her battle with cancer and died at the age of 67. I rode with Lou in the limo the funeral home provided, as we escorted Barb from their church in Colorado Springs to her final resting place in the Chapel Hill Memorial Gardens in Littleton, Colorado. Six years later I made that long trip one more time with Lou's family and friends, when Lou succumbed to cancer. He died August 11, 2010, at age 75. Lou left behind four loving children, nine grandchildren, thousands of friends and a long list of persons of interest who were associated with the JonBenét Ramsey case.

Lou had been on a trip to Iowa when he started to have abdominal pain. He endured the pain until he got back home to schedule a doctor's appointment. In April 2010 Lou was seen by the doctors. At first, they thought there might be a problem with his gallbladder, but it was later determined to be a mass in his abdomen that required exploratory surgery to investigate. During the surgery, they found he had inoperable cancer. Lou was allowed to go home from the hospital, but he knew time was running out. I was one of many of Lou's friends who stopped by his house where he showed us his spreadsheet and slide presentation he was working on to document his investigative notes on the Ramsey homicide. We talked many more times about the case after Lou was in hospice, and he continued to share his thoughts on JonBenét's case with his family.

John Ramsey came to visit Lou in the hospital and prayed at his bedside, just as Lou had done at Patsy's bedside. A few months before Lou was admitted to hospice, my mother had been in hospice. Mom had been in declining health for some time, but I got to visit her one last time before I was sent on a corporate security assignment back to the Horn of Africa. My mother, Margie Lou Conry Davis, died on March 15, 2010, while I was returning on an international United Airlines flight from Frankfurt, Germany, to the Denver International Airport. Saying goodbye to a loved one is always hard to do and all too soon, I would be saying goodbye to Lou.

Three months after mom died, Lou was admitted to hospice. For me, personally, 2010 was a rough year. For someone who has not lost a loved one in hospice care, it might be hard to understand how anyone can start out praying for their loved ones to get better, then to simply stop praying altogether, only to start up again, but this time praying their loved one will just be allowed to die. But it can happen. It happened to me twice in six months, with my mother and my best friend—both of whom I loved dearly. My mom and Lou always cheered the loudest at my successes, overlooked my failures, and always assured me things would get better with time.

I was having lunch with Kurt Pillard when Lou's daughter, Cindy Smit Marra, called to let me know hospice thought Lou had only a few hours to live. The family was inviting me to be at Lou's side when he died. I drove over to Saint Francis hospital, parked in the same parking lot where I had parked to visit Sergeant Jerry Busemeyer, after he had been shot in the summer of 1972. But Jerry had lived another 43 years; Lou would not live through the night. When I got off the hospital elevator upstairs, I found Lou's room overflowing with his four loving children and their children, but they graciously made room for me and another of Lou's personal friends.

Lou had slipped into a coma days before and was not in any pain. He was ready to go. I had visited Lou many times while he was in hospice and there was almost always family or friends in his room. But whenever it was just the two of us, I would hold his hand and we'd talk. Naturally, we talked about the many adventures we had shared and discussed his final thoughts about his list of suspects on the Ramsey case. During one of our last conversations, Lou whispered, "Soon, I'm going to know who killed JonBenét and I will tell you, Johnny, if I can." A few days later he slipped into a coma and our conversations became one sided. I'd like to think he heard my voice; occasionally he'd squeeze my hand. I just didn't want Lou to die alone.

In the last hours before he died, Cindy pulled me aside and said the family wanted me to give a eulogy for Lou at his funeral service. I knew Lou's funeral would be one of the most difficult I would ever attend and confided to Cindy that I wasn't sure I'd be able to talk, let alone deliver a eulogy fitting of her father. She asked me to think about it and let her know, and then we returned to Lou's hospital room.

When Cindy and I walked into Lou's room I noticed Lou's son, Mark, was sitting in the chair beside Lou's bed. Lou had been unresponsive for two days. Hospice told us the end was near. Mark was holding Lou's hand and tapping his index finger on Lou's hand. Mark was tapping, "dot, dot, space, dot, dash, dot, dot, space, dot, dot dash."—Morse code for, "I love you." Lou had taught his children how to say "I love you" in many ways, including in Morse code. Six years earlier, when their mother was unresponsive in hospice, Lou had held her hand and in the same way used Morse code to tell her, "I love you" until the moment she slipped away.

I was at Lou's side when he died. Cindy must have noticed something, as she suddenly leaned over Lou and said, "He's gone." The medical staff at hospice came in and confirmed Lou had just passed away. The hospital notified the funeral home to come take possession of his body. I waited with Mark as all of Lou's family said their goodbyes and left the hospital. When the man from the funeral home arrived, he recognized Lou and me from our years together working cases involving death. I walked alongside Mark to escort Lou's body strapped to a gurney, downstairs, through the coroner's office where we, as homicide detectives, had attended countless autopsies. The black hearse was waiting outside.

After the hearse drove away, I called Dave Spencer and shared Lou's final moments, including his family's request for me to deliver a eulogy. I told Dave I didn't think I would be able to pull this off. I was embarrassed because tears would just start to overflow and a lump would form in my throat to where I couldn't speak. But Dave settled the matter, telling me, "You have to do this, John." And so I did. I knew I was being given a high honor to speak on behalf of Lou's former homicide partners. I was committed to giving the best eulogy I could at his funeral and called several of his other detective partners to ask what I should say. Dave summed it up best when he said, "We knew if we were ever half the detective Lou was, we would have achieved something special."

The "Celebration of Life" for Andrew Louis "Lou" Smit was just that—a celebration in recognition of the life of an extraordinary man. His service was held at the New Life Church in Colorado Springs, primarily because this was one of the few venues in the Pikes Peak area large enough to hold the thousands of people who wanted to say farewell to a man who had touched their lives. The funeral services began at 10 a.m. on Friday, August 20, 2010, with Lou's casket being escorted into the Church by dual honor guards from the Colorado Springs Police Department (CSPD) and the El Paso County Sheriff's Office (EPSO).

In lieu of flowers the family requested donations to be made to the Colorado Springs Police Protective Association. Still, there were hundreds of flowers there, including beautiful floral arrangements clustered around his open casket. The fabric on the inside of the coffin lid had images of the four badges Lou had carried during his law enforcement career. Some floral arrangements had been sent by famous people, such as Katie Couric, who had interviewed Lou on the JonBenét Ramsey case. For a man who tried to avoid the spotlight, Lou had also been interviewed by Barbara Walters and he appeared on *Larry King Live*, sharing his thoughts on JonBenét. If nothing else, Lou knew he had to "stir the pot" to keep her case from going cold.

One section of the church had been cordoned off and Lou's grandchildren had attached a single white rose to the back of over 200 church seats. Below each white rose was a white note card printed with the names of every one of the victims from Lou's homicide cases. The names were in alphabetical order and most were familiar to me; Heather Dawn Church, Karen Grammar and of course, JonBenét Ramsey. A few of Lou's victims I did not know, including Baby Doe. They were all there in name, if not in spirit.

Former DA Bob Russel came to Lou's funeral, even though he was on oxygen. After Bob stopped to pay his respects to Lou at the front of the church, I noticed him struggling to keep the plastic oxygen hose inserted in his nose from disconnecting from his wheeled oxygen tank. He looked for an open seat nearby, but the first two rows had been reserved for family. Finally, Bob spotted me and being accustomed to giving orders said gruffly, "Anderson, get me a seat!" And I, being accustomed to taking orders from this DA, jumped up and found him a seat at the end of a pew, to accommodate him and his wheeled metal oxygen tank.

Mark Smit spoke eloquently about his father and invited each of the homicide victim's families in attendance to please take the single white rose, representing the life of their loved one, with them when they left church that morning. Then that dreaded moment came, when I had to go up on stage to deliver the eulogy for my best friend. Dave and Ruth Spencer were seated in the pew next to me and I had given a copy of my eulogy to Dave. He promised to finish reading what I had written if I broke down before finishing (a copy of my eulogy can be found at the back of this book).

When I walked up on stage and looked into the faces of the thousands of people seated before me, I realized that other than the funeral for a police officer killed in the line of duty, I had never seen such a large gathering of law enforcement personnel assembled in one place at one time. Recognizing the faces of most of the people in the crowd, including Lou's family seated up front, along with our extended law enforcement families, gave me the strength I needed to read the eulogy I had written to honor Lou. John Ramsey and Trip DeMuth did a remarkable job delivering their eulogies, honoring a man who had a profound effect on their lives as well.

The honor guard played "Taps" and gave Lou a 21-gun salute. There are some songs that never sound as good as they do on bagpipes—*Amazing Grace* is one. The drummers and bagpipers at Lou's service played beautifully. New Life Church and Lou's family had made arrangements for light refreshments to be served at the church and we had an opportunity to hug friends we hadn't seen in a while; some we would never see again. I especially enjoyed talking with Heather's father, Michael Church, after the service. I had spotted him in the crowd, while I was on the stage. It was heartwarming to know he was there to represent Heather and her family.

All too soon, it was time to once again take that long trip to the Chapel Hill Memorial Gardens, in Littleton, Colorado. I was never more proud of being part of the law enforcement community than I was that day following the hearse carrying Lou's casket from Colorado Springs to Littleton, escorted by dozens of police motorcycles from the CSPD; the traffic unit I supervised as a sergeant; and EPSO, the traffic unit I started when I was the Sheriff. Not far from Lou and Barb's grave marker, in the Chapel Hill Memorial Gardens, is a permanent memorial to the 12 students and the one teacher killed during the Columbine High School massacre. At Lou's graveside service I spoke briefly with John Ramsey and he introduced me to his oldest son, John Andrew Ramsey. This was the first time I talked with John Andrew; it would not be the last.

A few months after Lou's funeral I received a call from Cindy, Lou's middle daughter, telling me she and their family had committed to fulfilling her father's dying wish, "I want someone to continue this case. Please don't let this die." Cindy later told how shortly before Lou had slipped into a coma, "He asked me to write down a name, and I did. I got a pen and paper and he gave me a name, and he said, 'Start with this name'." Cindy told me Dave Spencer had already agreed to be part of the Smit Family JonBenét Ramsey (JBR) Team being organized to ensure the investigation of the murder of JonBenét did not die with Lou.

I felt honored to be asked to be part of the JBR Smit family team and comforted to know Dave had already committed to continue Lou's search for the killer of JonBenét. Unfortunately, we had all come to the same conclusion that Lou had; we had no confidence the Boulder Police would ever solve the murder of JonBenét on their own. Toward the end of Dave's career with CSPD, he had transferred as a detective from Robbery to the Falcon Division. There he joined a small team of detectives, working primarily property crimes. Dick Reisler was their sergeant.

After Dave retired from the Department, he became a private investigator (PI), working primarily for a handful of attorneys he trusted. He was really good at locating people and became proficient searching for people using internet databases; many required a subscription service fee. Dave was always good at documenting critical information and writing detailed reports. When Dick Reisler retired from CSPD he also started doing some PI work, primarily for a small group of trusted Colorado-based attorneys, but like Dave he avoided most criminal cases.

Mark Smit hosted the first of our Smit Family JBR Team meetings in his home in Colorado Springs. Cindy and her husband Kent Marra were also there, along with Lou's youngest daughter Dawn. I think Dawn's husband Dan may have been there as well and each of us shared conversations we remembered having with Lou about JonBenét's case. Before Lou had gone into hospice, Dan had spent eight hours video recording Lou talking about the spreadsheet and his slide presentation he had put together on JonBenét's case.

Mark was very talented when it came to computer technology, both hardware and software. He had helped his dad create the slide presentation and spreadsheet. As executor of Lou's estate, Mark had taken possession of Lou's computers, including the digital version of his Ramsey investigation case file. In addition to Lou's presentation with 632 individual slides, Lou had developed a massive multipage spreadsheet with 882 rows. Lou had grouped these rows into four tiers. These tiers indicated descending priority of the names of people connected to the investigation and items of interest. The name Lou had asked Cindy to write down was at the top.

Although Lou had shown both Dave and me his JonBenét spreadsheet and slides on many occasions, we were both stunned at how much information he had amassed on this homicide case. Dave and I had worked many major cases, involving countless pieces of evidence, hundreds of crime scene photos and thousands of pages of police, crime lab and autopsy reports. However, what we saw before us was truly extraordinary, not only in size, depth and scope, but in organization. Lou's spreadsheet was searchable to where names of individuals connected to the case could be brought up instantly. You could scroll your cursor over most of the names and a separate window would pop up to explain how that person was connected to the case.

As you read across the multiple columns on the spreadsheet, an X occasionally appeared to indicate the person had given handwriting, DNA, or hair samples. Another column further to the right was marked to indicate if the lab results had been completed and if the forensic analysis had eliminated that person of interest. Lou had marked 134 names as cleared. Lou's slide presentation was meticulously organized into 59 searchable categories, under labels such as, Garrote, Ransom Note, Duct Tape, and an audio recording of Patsy's 911 Call. In the lower left-hand corner of each of his 632 slides was a small "dot, dot, space, dot, dash, dot, dot, space, dot, dot dash." Lou's way of still saying, "I love you."

It took Dave and me a few days at Mark's house, with Lou's family, poring over Lou's slide presentation and then searching for names on his spreadsheet, until we began to realize what he had left behind—this was Lou's legacy. The JonBenét Ramsey homicide case file was Detective Lou Smit's opus. Equally important to Lou's legacy was his loving family and friends. Exploring Lou's massive homicide case file, we realized he was still serving in his former role of a navigator; he had charted our way through this complex maze of rumor and innuendo, sorting out fact from fiction, truth from deception, to lay bare the evidence of an intruder who had attempted a kidnapping for ransom which ended with the brutal murder of a little girl.

Unlike the title of the miniseries *Perfect Murder, Perfect Town*, where Kris Kristofferson had played the role of Detective Lou Smit, the murder of JonBenét Ramsey was not a perfect murder and Boulder was not a perfect town. And the JonBenét Ramsey investigation was anything but a perfect investigation. In September 2010, the month after Lou died, the Police Executive Research Forum (PERF) published, *It's More Complex than You Think: A Chief's Guide to DNA*, by Molly E. Griswold and Gerald R. Murphy. The foreword reads, "Everyday, DNA evidence becomes more useful, not only in the identification and prosecution of criminal offenders, but also in ruling out innocent persons."

As Lou pointed out, once you look past the Ramseys, there is a world of possible suspects and DNA can solve this case. However, the Boulder detectives continued to dismiss the DNA which had ruled out the Ramsey family in the killing of JonBenét. Boulder detectives were not interested in pursuing the possibility an intruder had committed this murder. Fortunately for our team, Lou had told Cindy where to start—the name he asked her to write down. After several more team meetings, we all agreed why Lou was interested in this person's name, a family with ties to Access Graphics in Boulder, John Ramsey's former business. For thirteen years, Lou had poured his unequaled talent as a homicide detective into solving the murder of JonBenét. Now our team would be taking over where he had left off—we would stand in his shoes.

In 2010, I was still working for Lockheed Martin, but Dave volunteered to go through Lou's case file to see if he could locate information on this person and other persons of interest. Our team met almost every month to share updates and discuss ways to obtain handwriting and DNA from individuals listed at the top of Lou's list. Over time we were able to clear another 134 entries on Lou's spreadsheet, including four names of the family he asked Cindy to write down. Eventually, we gave up the notion of obtaining handwriting from suspects to compare against the ransom note. We decided handwriting was overly subjective and began to concentrate primarily on collecting and testing DNA.

Members of the Smit Family Team developed a very good understanding of DNA and a few team members even paid their own way to visit one of the leading DNA labs on the east coast. Dave joined Cindy and other team members in visiting one of the private DNA labs in Colorado. Had the latest DNA technology existed while Lou was still alive, he might have had the tools necessary to advance or solve the case years ago. Instead, he was left anticipating a day when DNA technology would evolve to the point it could identify JonBenét's killer.

Since Dave and I were the only team members with prior law enforcement experience, we volunteered our time. I enjoyed getting together with Dave for an occasional surveillance. Two of Lou's children and their spouses moved out of the area, but stayed in touch with family in Colorado Springs, and Mark was always there to provide IT support, prayers, and encouragement. Cindy and her husband, Kent, along with other family members, also helped on surveillances and we all laughed hearing stories of Kent going "dumpster diving" in search of discarded DNA.

Our Smit Family JBR Team was well aware that there were other individuals or teams working this cold case in search of the killer of JonBenét. We wished them well, and just like Lou, we stayed open to comparing a few notes or sharing limited information on our team's progress. One advantage our team had, thanks to Lou, was the DNA genetic markers from the crime scene, which had been entered into CODIS, but was not publicly accessible. As DNA technology continued to evolve, it became commonly used by individuals interested in researching their family genealogy. Private DNA labs, such as Ancestry.com and 23andMe began to flourish as databases continued to expand exponentially.

One other crucial advantage our JBR Team had was credibility with the Ramsey family. Like Lou, we let the Ramsey family know what we were doing in our efforts to collect and test DNA from persons of interest. We had frequent telephone calls, emails exchanges and occasionally meetings, attended in person or virtually with John Andrew Ramsey and his and JonBenét's father. During one of the conference calls our team had with JonBenét's father, John B. Ramsey, we discussed the $118,000 ransom demand.

John Ramsey agreed that $118,000 seemed to be an odd amount for a ransom demand. The only explanation he had ever concluded was $118,000 was approximately the amount of his bonus for 1996. This bonus was paid to him at the beginning of 1996 and the amount was printed on each of his payroll check stubs, which could be found throughout their home (note—the exact bonus amount was $118,117.50).

Even though John Ramsey and I worked for the same company, we never met—Lockheed Martin is a big company. On October 12, 2012, I retired from the Lockheed Martin Corporation to launch a small consulting firm, JW Anderson & Associates, Ltd., which allowed me the freedom to pursue my interests in history, writing and the arts. With less travel demands and more control over my schedule, I committed to driving my daughter to school and picking her up after school every day so she wouldn't have to ride the school bus. Our home was only ten minutes from the school, but I wouldn't trade those twenty minutes I got to spend with her every day for anything. I know John Ramsey would have given anything to have JonBenét back in his life, even if it was for only twenty minutes for just one more day.

I also got to spend more time with Dave on the Ramsey investigation. Like Dave and Dick Reisler, I did a little PI work for a select number of respected attorneys, but I preferred to concentrate on my writing and art. Dave was an excellent golfer, and he took me golfing a few times, but I was always lousy at it. Dave and I got together to buy one another lunch on our birthdays, or I met Dick Reisler and some of our other cop friends for coffee, but most of our time together was on surveillance trips primarily in the Boulder or Denver Metro area. We took turns driving and paid for our own gas and meals. If we were fortunate enough to collect a DNA sample from a person of interest, the Smit family chipped in to pay for the DNA analysis.

In 2014, Dave and Kurt Pillard both received subpoenas to appear in court on a murder trial. Since they had been retired for a number of years, they initially thought there had been a clerical error. But there was no mistake; 39 years after the murder of Janet Conrad, at the Antlers Hotel in downtown Colorado Springs, detectives had matched DNA evidence found on her body to Robert Wolfgang Bailie, an inmate at the Colorado State Reformatory in Buena Vista, Colorado. Robert Bailie had been incarcerated in the Colorado Department of Corrections (DOC) since 1983, while serving time for two felony rape convictions in Colorado.

In 2014, Bailie was eligible for parole and his DNA was collected and, for the first time, was run through CODIS, which connected him to the murder of Janet Conrad. CSPD Detective Jerry Schiffelbein, along with cold case investigators Al Sarno, Charlie Hess, and Bill Lidh, who had been hired part-time through a DNA grant to work cold cases, reactivated the homicide investigation. When Bailie was confronted about the murder of Janet Conrad, he denied any involvement. But DNA evidence doesn't lie; only two people's DNA was found in the victim's vaginal area—that of the victim and Robert Bailie–a 1 in 700 billion match.

On September 3, 2014, an email from former CSPD Sergeant, Dwight Haverkorn, was sent to me and a number of other CSPD retirees. It read, "Robert Wolfgang Baillie (sic), about 2 hours ago, was convicted of killing Janet Kate Conrad at the Antlers Hotel on December 3, 1976. The DA's office just called and let me know. Some times (sic) the system does work." Our JBR team celebrated the success of the CSPD cold case team and were inspired, knowing justice for Janet and her family had been found. This success gave our team encouragement to continue finding innovative ways to collect and test DNA from Lou's list of persons of interest.

On September 12, 2014 *The Gazette* newspaper carried the headline, "Robert Baillie sentenced to life in prison for 1976 murder." The article reported how Janet's three sons, Randy, Ron, and Ray French, asked 4th Judicial District Judge Schutz to make sure the life sentence would run consecutive with the two terms Bailie was already serving in the Colorado Department of Corrections on the two previous felony rape convictions. Ron and Ray said they thank God the "mystery is solved." I think you could add,

"Thank God and DNA the mystery is solved"—but that might be redundant.

I asked Kurt what that was like, testifying before a jury about a murder 39 years after it had happened. He shared that he thought his testimony went very well and the jury thought it was humorous when he explained that in 1976 he was still a rookie and was made to park the police car. Kurt also told me that when he first came on the department, he followed the advice of some of the senior officers and went to watch Detective Lou Smit testify in court. Lou was always very well prepared going into a courtroom and knew every detail of his case.

Although it had taken nearly four decades to solve the murder of Janet Conrad, Dave Spencer was proud of the work that he and his detective partner, Lou Smit, had contributed to her homicide investigation. Knowing Janet's cold case was solved through DNA gave our Smit Family JBR Team renewed confidence that JonBenét's case could also be solved. However, our team's efforts were substantially impeded by not having direct access to the physical evidence or any law enforcement databases and we had we had to pay for our own travel and DNA testing.

Until 2015, our team had been operating in the shadows, but that was about to change. We were coming up on the 20-year anniversary of JonBenét's murder and neither we nor the police had yet identified the killer. The majority of people around the world familiar with the case still believed a Ramsey family member was responsible. Lou's children decided we might be more successful in identifying JonBenét's killer if we came out publicly about what our team was doing to help solve the murder. If nothing else, as Lou would say, you have to "stir the pot" to keep the case from growing cold.

In 2016, Cindy was interviewed for an A&E 2-hour TV Special, *"The Killing of JonBenét: The Truth Uncovered"* which premiered September 5, 2016. This documentary marked the 20-year anniversary of the murder. During her interview Cindy showed viewers the DNA lab report with the 14 genetic markers from JonBenét's body which proved to be from an unknown male and not a Ramsey family member. A&E revealed details of Burke Ramsey's interview in 1998 and featured a sit-down interview with John Ramsey, intended to reveal "shocking DNA evidence" and "uncover" the truth. Despite the presence of foreign male DNA, much of the public, and the Boulder police, once again refused to accept Lou's intruder theory.

Once our team had come out publicly, new leads started pouring in on who may have killed JonBenét. Twenty years after the murder, there was still huge interest in seeing this case solved. Ironically, little to no interest was shown by the law enforcement agency charged with investigating this case—the Boulder Police. Cindy and Dave did a good job sorting through the waves of information and searching through Lou's investigative notes to see if these "people of interest" could be located and if they had any prior criminal record for similar offenses. Then we tried to devise a way to collect their DNA and pay to have it tested by a private lab.

Another benefit of us coming out publicly was it allowed Cindy to set up a GoFundMe account to solicit donations to pay for DNA testing and travel expenses (www.gofundme. com JonBenét: Lou Smit's Family Searches for Justice). Several members of our Smit Family JBR team and the Ramsey family donated to our GoFundMe account and within a few months we had collected over $40,000. We were still volunteering our time, but at least now we could be reimbursed for travel expenses and didn't have to "pass the hat" to pay for DNA testing. We also offered to pay for DNA tests from other teams or individuals who wanted to mail us DNA from their persons of interest. The process was slow, but progress was being made.

In an article titled, "Grand Juror Who Saw Original Evidence in JonBenét Ramsey Case Speaks Out" published by ABC News on December 16, 2016, written by Tom Berman, Andrew Paparella and Alexa Valiente, told of how one grand jury member told 20/20 he believed, "that there was enough evidence to indict John and Patsy Ramsey for a crime, but he doesn't think they would have been convicted." The Boulder DA who followed Alex Hunter was Mary Lacy, and she was followed by Stan Garnett, who pointed out that the statute of limitations had expired on the crimes cited on the True Bill indictments against JonBenét's parents.

On April 24, 2018, a major breakthrough in DNA analysis occurred when Sacramento County Sheriff's deputies arrested Joseph James DeAngelo, Jr., better known as the Golden State Killer. DeAngelo, a former police officer, was charged with eight counts of first degree murder and was later charged with four additional counts of first degree murder. The breakthrough happened when detectives uploaded the killer's DNA profile from a Ventura County rape kit to the personal genomics website established by GEDmatch. The website identified 10-20 people who had the same great-great-great-grandparents as the Golden State Killer.

Working with a genealogist, a team of investigators used this list to construct a family tree which identified two possible suspects. Using DNA from a relative, one possible suspect was eliminated, leaving only Joseph DeAngelo. Six days before DeAngelo was arrested, investigators surreptitiously collected a DNA sample from the door handle of his car and another sample was later collected from a tissue found in his garbage can which was set out on the curb. The DNA from both those samples positively identified DeAngelo as the Golden State Killer.

DeAngelo was suspected of at least 13 murders, 50 rapes and 120 burglaries in California between 1973 and 1986. Unfortunately, the statute of limitations had expired on the rapes and burglaries; however, he was charged with 13 counts of murder and 13 counts of kidnapping. As part of a plea bargaining agreement, DeAngelo plead guilty to the 13 counts of murder and 13 counts of kidnapping to avoid the death penalty, and he received multiple life sentences. The major takeaway for our JBR team was that we no longer had to have the DNA from our person of interest; we could also use biological samples collected from their living relatives.

As word of the Golden State Killer being identified through DNA analysis spread in law enforcement, agencies across the country began reexamining evidence in their cold cases. The headline, "Golden State Killer sentenced to life for 26 rapes, slayings," was followed with another "Cold case is solved after four decades. A nearly 45-year-old cold case involving the murder of 19-year-old Deborah Tomlinson has been solved, the Grand Junction Police Department announced Wednesday. After decades of the case going unsolved...the case was given a 'fresh look' by detectives, who later sought assistance from Parabon NanoLabs, a DNA technology company based outside of Washington, D.C." But Boulder police remained silent.

The Colorado Springs Police Department dedicated two full-time detectives to work cold cases and the results were astonishing. On June 15, 2019, headlines on the front page of the Colorado Springs Gazette newspaper read, "DNA cracks the killing of female soldier in 1987." The article shared how, "For decades, justice went unserved in the brutal rape and killing of 20-year-old Fort Carson soldier Darlene Krashoc. Two years ago, the Army put up a $10,000 reward and released a computer-generated picture of what the killer looked like in 1987 based on his DNA and what he might look like 30 years later." Investigators were "stirring the pot."

The newspaper article continued, "But it was genetic genealogy DNA analysis—the new forensic field combining DNA comparisons with family trees that helped nab the Golden State Killer—that led authorities to a suspect this year. Michael Whyte, 58, was arrested Thursday on suspicion of first-degree murder at his home in the 1500 block of East 131st Place in Thornton, police said. Whyte also was a soldier stationed at Fort Carson, said police spokesman Lt. Jim Sokolik. Krashoc's partially nude body was found by two police officers on routine patrol about 5:20 a.m. on March 17, St. Patrick's Day, behind the Korean Club Restaurant, 2710 S. Academy Blvd., police said."

Details of the murder, reported by the Gazette, said the victim, "…had been strangled with a coat hanger and leather straps after being severely beaten, bitten and sexually assaulted. She also may have been thrown from a moving car…Eventually, the case went cold. But in 2004 and 2011, it was reopened for laboratory testing (from existing items of evidence collected at the crime scene), and an unknown male DNA profile was found on several pieces of evidence, police said."

The newspaper article continued, "In 2016, agents from Army Criminal Investigations Command and Colorado Springs police officers submitted evidence to the United States Army Criminal Investigation laboratory for additional DNA testing in a collective effort to identify additional potential leads…The testing included reanalysis of previously submitted items for Y-STR and evaluation for phenotyping." Y-STR comes from the Y male chromosome and is frequently used in genealogy research or paternity and criminal cases. Phenotyping uses the DNA left at the crime scene to predict what the suspect may look like, including hair, skin and eye color, and generates a computer-drawn mug shot.

The Gazette article quoted Police Chief Vince Niski in saying, "There is a lot to be proud of today. The work done by these detectives has been nothing short of exceptional. Since 1987, CSPD Cold Case Detectives, Violent Crimes Detectives, and U.S. Army CID Investigators have worked tirelessly to bring this investigation to a conclusion.

Throughout these last 32 years, they never lost sight of what was most important: finding answers for Ms. Krashoc's family. We hope this arrest will provide those answers and some comfort."

The article then reported, "The arrest in Krashoc's killing is the second in decades-old cold cases in the past two years in Colorado Springs. Last year, police arrested James Papol in the death of Mary Lynn Vialpando in 1988. Papol, 46, was 15 when Vialpando was beaten, raped, and stabbed to death in Old Colorado City. Despite periodic appeals by police and her family, no one was ever arrested. A routine search by the Colorado Bureau of Investigation matched an updated DNA sample found on her body with Papol's profile in a law enforcement database."

On June 23, 2020, Fox News carried the story, "DNA cold case: Colorado police seek suspect identified in 1963 killing of Girl Scout." The story told how, "Nearly 57 years after a Colorado Girl Scout counselor was found raped and strangled in her tent during a camping trip (near Deckers, Colorado) authorities say that genetic genealogy has helped them identify her killer. The body of Margaret Elizabeth 'Peggy' Beck, 16, of Denver, was found inside her tent Aug. 18, 1963, at the Flying G Ranch, a Girl Scout campsite in the Pike National Forest."

Jefferson County Sheriff Jeff Shrader said, "In 2007, a John Doe DNA profile was created from evidence originally collected from the crime scene, and the profile was entered into the Combined DNA Index System (CODIS). In June of 2019, a more comprehensive profile was created and submitted for investigative genetic genealogy testing. Investigators followed up on obtained leads and were able to determine the DNA was that of James Raymond Taylor."

The Fox News story concluded that, "Taylor, who was 23 years old at the time of the murder, was last seen in 1976. If still alive, he would now be 80 years old. Taylor's last known location was in the Las Vegas area, though his family, who helped authorities definitely identify him as the source of the DNA in Peggy's death, has not seen or heard from him in more than 43 years."

Although the murder of Peggy Beck did not end with an arrest of her killer, reading about other cold cases being solved using the advancements being made in DNA technology, coupled with an understanding how ancestral genealogy databases were continuing to expand, gave our Smit Family JBR Team renewed optimism. Every day we hoped to hear that the Boulder PD used DNA to clear JonBenét's case. Certainly they too were aware of arrests being made by other law enforcement agencies using existing DNA evidence to solve their cold cases. But Boulder PD continued to remain silent and appeared to resist any opportunities to use the technological advancements being made in DNA research to solve the murder of JonBenét.

In an attempt to establish a "collective effort"—that had been proven effective in using DNA to capture the Golden State Killer—I called the Boulder DA's Office to request a meeting with DA Michael Dougherty and our JBR Smit Family Team. I couldn't even get past his administrative assistant, who lectured me about how busy her boss was and how many other people call the DA's Office wanting a meeting with him on this case. Having held public office for eight years in a county much larger than Boulder, I knew something about managing a busy work schedule—it's not just about managing your time, it's about managing your priorities.

Since Lou Smit had been an employee with the Boulder DA's Office, we saw what our team was doing as a continuation of his work as an investigator on the Ramsey case. We thought a meeting with Michael Dougherty was a priority, at least to our way of thinking. To get past his "gatekeeper" we asked around to see who we knew who had direct access to the DA, who could request a meeting for our team. One of those people was John San Agustin. He was a friend of Lou's and had worked for me at the Sheriff's Office. John and Ollie Gray, who had since passed away, had been hired by the Ramseys, following Lou's recommendation, and were on board with Lou's intruder theory.

John San Agustin was able to arrange a meeting with the Boulder DA, which was scheduled for 11 a.m. on June 26, 2019. The meeting was held in the Boulder DA's Office, 1777 Sixth Street, the same building where Lou had worked as an investigator on the Ramsey murder in 1997-98. Representing our JBR Smit Family Team were Cindy Smit Marra, Dave Spencer, John San Agustin, and me. Michael Dougherty met our team in the lobby and escorted us upstairs to a conference room where we were introduced to Detective Heather Frey and Sergeant Barry Hartkopp, from the Boulder Police Department.

Detective Frey was the lead detective assigned to the JonBenét Ramsey homicide investigation and Sergeant Hartkopp was her immediate supervisor. As near as Dave and I could determine, Heather Frey had never been assigned a homicide investigation prior to the Ramsey case. In fact, the only noteworthy investigation we could find mentioning Detective Frey was an article reported in the *Boulder Daily Camera* newspaper, dated August 4, 2010, which ran the headline "Boulder Police arrest two brothers suspected of stealing 65 bikes."

At the beginning of our meeting, we explained the purpose of our requesting this meeting was to suggest a collective effort to help identify potential suspects and leads starting with the reanalysis of previously submitted items for Y-STR testing and evaluation for phenotyping. We handed out copies of the original case DNA lab reports to make things easy as possible for the police to understand what we as a team were focused on, in collecting and testing DNA on Lou's persons of interest, and shared the next steps we intended to pursue, hopefully with their support.

One of the original lab reports identified, very specifically, some items of evidence from the 1996 crime scene that were viable candidates for first-time, or revisited, DNA analysis. Some of those items included the neck ligature, broken paint brush handle, wrist ligatures, panties, and long underwear bottoms. Interestingly, four of those items had been returned from the DNA lab to the investigators with the notation "not processed at this time."

We didn't know why these items were not tested, but clearly they should be examined. For the long underwear bottoms, there was a note: the DNA profile "contains a mixture of at least two individuals including the victim and at least one male contributor. The (DNA) profiles associated with the following individuals are excluded" as possible contributors: Burke Ramsey, Patricia Ramsey, John B. Ramsey, Melinda Ramsey, and John Andrew Ramsey. Neither of the two Boulder detectives or the DA seemed to be familiar with this lab report and did not know why these four items were returned untested; however, a different report cited budgetary concerns. Since the sample collected from the long johns was that of an unknown male, and eliminated JonBenét's immediate family, our team felt progress was being made.

The only question asked by Detective Frey during the meeting was if our team would be willing to share our Top 20 list of persons of interest. We replied absolutely; we want to share our Top 20 and our list of persons of interest that we had already eliminated through our private DNA testing. We explained what we hoped to accomplish by sharing information was to not waste our time or money on individuals where DNA had already eliminated them as suspects. We shared our GoFundMe financial target was $100K, based on testing our Top 20 persons of interest, which cost about $5,000 per individual (including travel and DNA lab analysis).

At the conclusion of the meeting, the DA did say they would be willing to tell us which individuals had already been eliminated through DNA testing. After leaving this first meeting, it seemed to our team that we had reached a consensus; the key to solving JonBenét's murder may be in identifying the unknown male DNA contributor. Since the Y-STR comes from the Y male chromosome and is commonly used for genealogy research, as well as in forensic cases, we felt progress was finally being made with Boulder area law enforcement on the Ramsey case.

If the reexamination of the DNA evidence provided sufficient samples for phenotyping or other current DNA testing opportunities and produced a computer-drawn mug shot, we offered to use our GoFundMe account to pay for the computer analysis and leverage Lou's spreadsheet to search for the names of individuals or leads generated after the mug shot was released. We also offered to return to Boulder and show Lou's slides which explained how the evidence and facts of the case led him to conclude an intruder committed this murder. Detective Frey and Sergeant Hartkopp had said very little during our meeting; however, I had no doubt they would be briefing their chain of command about our offer to collaborate with them to help solve this cold case. We never heard back from Detective Frey or Sergeant Hartkopp.

To gain a better understanding of how other law enforcement agencies were solving their cold cases through the advancements being made in DNA technology, Dave Spencer and I made an appointment to meet with CSPD Cold Case Unit detectives. Our meeting took place on October 3, 2019, in the CSPD Detective Bureau, on the 2nd floor of the Police Operations Center (POC), 705 S. Nevada Avenue, Colorado Springs, CO 80903. It had been several years since I had been in the Detective Bureau and it felt good to see so many friends that I hadn't seen since my retirement. We met in a conference room with detectives assigned to the Cold Case Unit.

These detectives had cleared the Krashoc and Vialpando murders and were intimately familiar with how DNA was used to identify the killers on these two unrelated CSPD homicide investigations. Dave and I explained our involvement with the JBR Smit Family Team in trying to help solve the murder of JonBenét. The detectives described how they had started on the Vialpando case by laying out all the physical evidence and reevaluated each piece, one at a time, asking the question "Is this piece of evidence worth retesting?" With all the advancements being made, especially with smaller amounts of trace or touch DNA being required for testing, taking a second look at evidence from a crime scene every 18 months can produce positive results.

At the time of our meeting, Detective Jim Isham was one of the two CSPD detectives working cold cases full time. Detective Isham walked us through how a specialized DNA lab, Parabon NanoLabs, had helped them leverage the DNA on their cold cases. He gave us copies of handout materials he had downloaded from the lab's website which explained the DNA services they offer law enforcement. He also gave us the name and phone number for his contact at the DNA lab and said they were wonderful to work with and if contacted, said the lab would be more than willing to help out on the Ramsey case.

The lab CSPD used had access to public genealogy databases instead of government-owned criminal databases such as CODIS. The detectives said it would be fine to give the Boulder police detectives their contact information and offered to meet with BPD detectives anytime. One of the detectives volunteered to drive to Boulder, on his own time, and spend the day with BPD detectives reevaluating the evidence on the Ramsey case.

Our Smit Family Team continued to focus on eliminating persons of interest from our Top 20 List and hoped to hear something, anything, back from the Boulder DA or PD regarding our team's offer to return to Boulder for a second meeting or Boulder PD accepting CSPD detectives' offer of assistance. Weeks turned into months without hearing anything from Boulder PD, so our team decided to take the initiative. I sent an email to DA Michael Dougherty requesting a second meeting with him and the Boulder police detectives. The DA did reply to my email request for a second meeting and cc'ed Detective Commander Tom Trujillo. DA Dougherty's email directed me to coordinate any future meeting requests with Commander Trujillo, since this was their homicide investigation.

The initial email exchanges with Commander Trujillo were very positive and the DA agreed to attend a future meeting at the Boulder Police Department, if his schedule allowed. It had been years since I had seen Tom Trujillo and had considered him a friend. I was looking forward to our meeting which was scheduled for March 18, 2020. Then the COVID-19 pandemic hit. Boulder city officials prohibited all their personnel from attending in-person meetings. Our meeting was postponed for six months, until rescheduled for September 18, 2020. In keeping with city COVID protocols, we limited our team to only two persons, Cindy and me, and we wore masks to the meeting and adhered to social distancing.

I had requested two hours for the meeting and was granted only one hour, from 4:00-5:00 p.m. on Friday, September 18, 2020. From having personally sat through countless meetings listening to people express their opinions on a case, I was determined to not waste their time and to leave Boulder PD with "actionable" items which might help them identify the killer of JonBenét. The meeting was held in a conference room on the second floor of the Boulder Police Department, 1805 33rd, Street, Boulder, CO 80301. Present during the meeting, in addition to Commander Trujillo, Cindy, and me, were Police Commander Ron Gosage and the DA, Michael Dougherty. Trujillo shared how he and

Gosage were the only two Boulder police officers left on the Department who were there when the murder of JonBenét happened in December 1996. To make best use of the one hour allowed for our meeting, Cindy and I had prepared a comprehensive two-page meeting agenda.

In following our proposed meeting agenda, we began by providing an overview of Lou's homicide case file and described both his slide presentation and spreadsheet. We explained how Lou's spreadsheet listed 887 names, descriptors, or articles prioritized into 4 tiers. Of those, Lou had marked 134 as "cleared" and, since 2010, our team had reprioritized or cleared another 163 entries. We explained our approach was limited to collecting DNA and testing DNA. We emphasized our team was focused on facts not theories and on identifying the unknown male DNA from the crime scene and remained committed to sharing our DNA testing results with BPD/DA.

We reviewed our last BPD/DA meeting at the DA's Office, with Detective Frey and Sergeant Hartkopp, and turned over copies of our current Top 20 Persons of Interest List along with our list of the eight persons of interest our team had cleared using DNA. Despite what the DA had committed to during our first meeting in his office, to tell us which names could be eliminated from our Top 20 list, Trujillo made it clear they would not be sharing any information about their open investigation; our meeting was going to be "a one-way street." As it turned out, our team's efforts to work with the Boulder police to help them solve this murder, this "one-way street" would be more like a "dead-end."

Gosage glanced at our Top 20 list, then tossed it aside as he commented this was just a list of names and didn't provide them anything that could be pursued. I explained that we would be happy to go over each of the names on the list one at a time, if they were willing to give us a second hour, which we had asked for, but they had scheduled the meeting from 4:00-5:00 p.m. on a Friday. We were the only thing standing in their way to the weekend. We strongly expressed interest in reevaluating evidence, specifically the ligature from the neck, the broken paint brush handle used to fashion the garrote and the Wednesday panties, in search of a DNA Single Source Contributor. We pointed out Lou's conclusion that a stun gun had been brought into the Ramsey home and used on JonBenét, which proved the killer's intent; however, Trujillo said he did not believe a stun gun was used to cause the red marks on JonBenét's body.

We pointed out that the long johns DNA report revealed comingled DNA, referred to as Unknown Male 1 and Unknown Male 2. We told them of a cutting-edge DNA software advancement which could be used to attempt to unravel these two DNA sources which could then be run through CODIS. We provided the name and contact information of one lab that specializes in this type of analysis and even offered to pay for any costs or fees associated with this DNA analysis. This advanced procedure might reveal a single source DNA contributor which could help identify the killer and only required a phone call from Trujillo to the lab; I watched as he made a note to himself but said nothing.

We left behind a 3-ring binder with a color printout of Lou's complete slide presentation, consisting of 632 slides, offered again to return to present the slide presentation in person. We concluded the meeting by providing the names and contact information for the detectives from the CSPD cold case unit who had offered to meet with the Boulder PD detectives to share their successes. Neither of the CSPD Cold Case detectives nor anyone at the DNA technology labs ever received an email or a phone call from the Boulder PD/DA regarding the Ramsey homicide.

After our meeting I sent an email thanking Commanders Trujillo and Gosage and DA Dougherty for meeting with our team and suggested we schedule a return date for a follow-up meeting where we could present Lou's slide presentation. After waiting over a week for an email reply I called Commander Trujillo's office phone number and left a voicemail message asking him to please return my call. After considerable effort, we had detectives with the CSPD cold case unit and DNA experts from private labs lined up to help BPD/DA with the Ramsey homicide investigation; if Boulder didn't want to work with our team, that would be okay, they could work directly with the cold case detectives from CSPD and the private DNA labs.

Three weeks after our meeting, I still had not received a reply to my email or voicemail and no one at CSPD or the DNA labs had been contacted by Boulder authorities. On the morning of October 5, 2020, I called to request a meeting with the new Boulder Police Chief Maris Harold. I identified myself as the retired El Paso County Sheriff, hoping she would extend me the professional courtesy, as a former police executive, of scheduling a meeting.

That afternoon, Commander Trujillo called to say he was returning my phone call to him and to Chief Harold. He asked if my meeting request was related to Lou's intruder theory. When I answered yes, Trujillo advised me the Boulder PD had no further interest in meeting with the Smit Family. Then Trujillo reminded me that since I was retired, I was no longer in law enforcement, a point of which I was already somewhat aware. We had worked hard to make all the preparations necessary and felt we delivered actionable leads to the Boulder authorities on silver platter. We even offered to pay for all the DNA testing. All they needed to do was make a phone call. Our efforts have been completely ignored. Now we knew how Lou Smit had felt trying to work with Boulder detectives.

As word spread about what our team was doing to help solve the murder of JonBenét, the Smit and Ramsey families were contacted by the producers of The Dr. Oz Show, 20/20, and Arrow Media, from the UK, asking if we would agree to be interviewed. Arrow Media and 20/20 were both filming two-hour documentaries and the Dr. Oz Show wanted to host a one-hour episode. The producers explained they could not pay any of us for being on their program; however, they promised to mention our GoFundMe account. Several members of the Smit and Ramsey family had appeared on a previous Dr. Oz Show and felt, if nothing else, this would be one way we could "stir the pot."

With COVID restrictions in place, filming the three documentaries proved a challenge. Arrow Media and 20/20 sent film crews to Colorado Springs, while The Dr. Oz Show was prerecorded using a virtual Zoom platform. Of the three shows, our team felt The Dr. Oz Show one-hour program, *"Will DNA Finally Expose JonBenét Ramsey's killer?"* presented twice as much useful information in half the air time. The producer of The Dr. Oz Show had come up with a brilliant idea to use their model makers to build a scale model of the Ramsey home in Boulder, to help Dr. Oz explain the crime scene and Lou's Intruder Theory to his viewers. In addition to interviewing Cindy, John San Agustin, and me, Dr. Oz also interviewed John Andrew Ramsey, who also stressed how he believed this case could be solved using DNA.

The two-hour documentary, produced by Arrow Media in the UK, was shown across Great Britain, Australia, New Zealand, the U.S., and in parts of Europe. The three shows were watched by untold millions of viewers and Cindy and I appeared afterward on several live TV and radio programs. Two of Lou's granddaughters began a podcast, sharing various aspects of the Ramsey homicide investigation. I have no doubt their grandfather would be proud of their determination to help keep this case from growing colder.

As the calendar year 2020 came to an end, leads from around the world began pouring in to members of our team. Dozens of people reached out to us expressing their opinions on who killed JonBenét. We filtered these inputs by focusing on what we knew we could do that would render the best results—collect DNA and test DNA. By searching Lou's spreadsheet, we were able to tell at a glance if these people had already been contacted by Boulder PD and might have already eliminated as possible suspects. While COVID restrictions made it difficult to meet in person, travel, and follow-up on leads, our team remained focused on Lou's undying belief that DNA will ultimately solve this case.

But our team was about to suffer a tragic loss. Dave Spencer was having trouble swallowing and had been losing weight for months. He was diagnosed with throat cancer and bravely endured a series of grueling radiation treatments. The doctors thought he was in remission, but all too soon he began losing more weight. Toward the end of 2020, Dave's doctor confirmed our worst fears, the cancer was back and this time it was untreatable. A few days later, Dave commented to me privately, "I guess we'll find out if I'm as tough as I think I am." He was.

Dave asked a few of his closest friends to get together for coffee, one last time, but all the restaurants and coffee shops were closed due to the COVID pandemic. But Dick Reisler hosted Dave and me and another of our retired cop friends in his house. The four of us sat around Dick's kitchen table and laughed as we shared war stories. None of us wanted that coffee to end—but it did. Dave never once complained, even after he was admitted to hospice care at home. Toward the very end, he asked me to drop by his house to pick up his notes on the Ramsey case. While I was there, Dave told me he was "at peace" and we talked quietly about how we both knew Lou would be there waiting for him when he passed away. As Christmas approached, Dave and I texted one another a few more times. Then his texts stopped.

Dave Spencer died on December 26, 2020, the 24-year anniversary of the death of JonBenét.

Chapter 9 – Team

Dave's funeral service was on a snowy Saturday, January 9, 2021, in Colorado Springs. The service was broadcast live, so his family in Kansas could watch. Despite COVID restrictions, the CSPD honor guard and Chief Niski did a commendable job with Dave's service, which included Taps being played and a 21-gun salute. The CSPD Honor Guard also officiated over the flag folding ceremony, which was presented to Dave's widow, Ruth Spencer, by Chief Niski. Dave's obituary, which was written by Ruth, read in part, "David R. Spencer, 3/22/1950 – 12/26/2020. David was born and raised in Goodland, Kansas, to Richard and Nina Spencer, where he found his love of golf playing on sand greens.

The obituary went on to share how, "David attended college in Tucson, AZ, then returned to Kansas to serve as a deputy on the Sherman County Sheriff's Department. On 2/14/72 he joined the Colorado Springs Police Department where he proudly and faithfully served in Patrol, Homicide, Career Criminal Unit, and Robbery until his retirement on 3/24/00. Many life long (sic) friends and many memories were made during his 28 years with the CSPD. Dave married his wife Ruth in 1979. Dave was Ruth's best friend, forever love, hero (sic) and her rock…

Dave's obituary concluded with, "In Heaven he will play the perfect round of golf with his best friend Lou Smit and his father in-law Miff...Dave lived his life with honesty, gusto and passion and died with dignity and peace. Dave often said that he was blessed to have had an extraordinary career with remarkable partners at the CSPD, a wonderful marriage and amazing children and grandchildren...In lieu of flowers charitable donations may be made to the CSPPA Fallen Officers Relief Fund..."

Three of Lou's children: Cindy, Mark, and Lori, along with their spouses, attended Dave's service. Dave's wife, Ruth, had asked Mark Smit and Dick Reisler to give Dave's eulogy. They shared stories of Dave and Lou's many adventures together as homicide partners. I was honored to have been with them on dozens of those investigations. Dave was a direct link from me to Lou, and now that chain was broken and I was heartbroken. But there was some comfort knowing Dave and Lou were together again, enjoying that perfect round of golf.

Dave had been such an integral part of our Smit Family JBR Team that his passing left a discernible void in our team. Now, I was the last remaining member of our team with any prior law enforcement experience. I wouldn't admit this out loud, but I wondered if our team could survive. Prior to Christmas 2020 we had scheduled a team meeting at Cindy's law office for after the holidays. I called Cindy in advance to discuss agenda topics. I asked what she and her family would think about me calling Dick Reisler to invite him to join our JBR Smit Family Team. She and the rest of Lou's family thought this was a great idea and Dick readily accepted.

A few days after recruiting Dick, I was on the phone with Kurt Pillard, talking about something unrelated, but when Dave's passing came up, Kurt volunteered to join our team. Kurt was the former Detective Commander for the CSPD Investigations Division with oversight over all homicides and child death investigations. He is also a graduate of the prestigious FBI National Academy and a recognized criminal investigations expert in Federal Court. I was excited to have Kurt join our JBR Smit Family Team and called Cindy to ask how she and her family felt about Kurt also joining our team. She said they'd all be delighted.

Like Dick and me, Kurt had also talked with Lou in-depth about the JonBenét Ramsey homicide investigation. At the time, Kurt was also an associate professor for Regis University and he told me how he had invited Lou to speak to his students during one of his criminology classes. Lou showed the students his slide presentation and discussed the general details of this and other homicide investigations.

When Dick and Kurt attended our next JBR Smit Family Team meeting, on January 30, 2021, amazingly, I realized that instead of our team being at risk of folding, we had grown even stronger. Our Smit Family Team had been meeting for the past ten years, with an average of ten meetings per year. With over 100 team meetings this was the only time I remember Dave not being with us. The void he left could never be filled but it felt good to welcome Dick and Kurt to our team; two pairs of fresh, and experienced, eyes would be welcomed.

What I realized going into this first meeting without Dave was just how much I had come to rely on him to capture relevant information and document the details of our investigative progress. Dave was four years older than me, and senior to me in terms of law enforcement and PI experience, so I naturally followed Dave's lead; but now it was time for me to step up. I emailed out a proposed agenda prior to our meeting, with our team's mission, "Justice for JonBenét" and highlighted our objectives, "Collect and test DNA from Persons of Interest."

Attached to my email was an updated confidential list of persons who we had eliminated through our independent DNA testing and our Top 20 persons of interest; most were named on Lou's spreadsheet in either Tier I or II. We discussed upcoming media events, the monetary balance in our GoFundMe account and reviewed our Top 20 list, along with the list of persons we had previously eliminated. Of particular interest was a new lead that had come in to Lou's granddaughters, through their podcast, which had also been communicated to Cindy through our JBR GoFundMe account.

This lead had been from a woman who believed her ex-husband had murdered JonBenét. She shared how their family lived in Boulder during Christmas 1996. She divorced her husband soon after the murder, when she found out her husband had been sexually molesting their daughter from the time she was two until she turned six years old. The woman said she had reported her husband to the Boulder Police in 1997, which we were able to confirm through Lou's investigative notes. The Boulder detectives interviewed the ex-husband in 1997 at police headquarters where he denied the allegations, and provided handwriting and head hair samples.

Lou's spreadsheet listed this person; however, he was fairly far down the list in Tier III. A Boulder PD supplemental report, written by Detective Ron Gosage, documented the interview and mentioned the collection of handwriting and hair sample; however, the detective said he would collect DNA samples later if necessary. In talking on the phone with the ex-wife and the now grown daughter, they both agreed to meet with representatives from our JBR team and the daughter agreed to provide us with a DNA sample.

The mother had moved out of Colorado shortly after her divorce to escape their abusive situation. John Andrew Ramsey joined our meeting virtually at around noon, to meet Dick and Kurt and to share information on this person of interest that had been developed, including his possible home and business address. Dick and John Andrew volunteered to go meet with the mother and daughter and collect her DNA sample. On March 4, 2021, Dick and John Andrew met at DIA, and flew to the nearest airport where the mother and daughter lived. When Dick and John Andrew landed, they rented a car and drove to meet the mother and daughter, along with their attorney, at a hotel near where they lived. When they returned Dick wrote up an excellent trip report and turned the DNA samples over to Cindy who mailed them to the DNA lab.

The following week Kurt and I drove by the ex-husband's home and business address, located in the mountains west of Denver, to get a sense of where he might be found should we get a match on our DNA analysis. Our team had not laid eyes on the ex-husband yet, but we had a general idea of what he looked like, where he worked, where he lived and what cars he drove. We had exhausted our internet searches and there wasn't much more we could do except wait for the lab results. The waiting is often the hardest part about these investigations. We had promised to share the lab results with the Ramsey family and the suspect's ex-wife and daughter.

Our JBR Smit Family team waited anxiously for two weeks to get the lab results. During the wait, you go through a rollercoaster of emotions; hoping the DNA test is positive, so an arrest can be made and finally, after 25 years, the Ramsey family will know who had killed JonBenét. The ex-wife was also waiting anxiously to confirm what she had suspected for the past 25 years; that her ex-husband, the father of her daughter, was the man who had killed JonBenét.

When the DNA test results were in, Cindy notified our team and then called John Andrew. Then Dick called the suspect's ex-wife to share the lab results—the DNA test was negative. No match. The biological father of the young woman, who grew up believing her father may have killed JonBenét, was not the killer. As much as our team and the Ramsey family wanted this man, this pedophile, to be the murderer of JonBenét, the evidence doesn't lie; his DNA was not a match.

As Lou would say, "Time to move on to the next man." Thanks to Lou's spreadsheet, there are plenty of other names of persons of interest and leads to follow. Sherlock Holmes once said, "I can discover facts, Watson, but I cannot change them." The facts of this case led us to one inescapable conclusion—the person who committed this violent murder has left behind an invaluable clue—his DNA. This DNA has eliminated the Ramsey family and allowed our Smit Family Team to eliminate more than a dozen persons of interest from our Top 20 List.

From the onset of the JonBenét Ramsey homicide investigation suspicion fell upon her parents, Patsy and John Ramsey. Had it not been for one man, retired Detective Lou Smit, both parents may very well have been arrested for a murder they didn't commit. When Lou resigned from the Boulder DA's task force, in September 1998, he resigned in protest stating "the Ramseys did not do it" and he cited "substantial, credible evidence of an intruder" including DNA and other physical evidence proving some other person was responsible for this horrible crime.

Although Lou Smit was no longer being paid to investigate the murder of JonBenét, he continued the investigation on his own time and at his own expense until 2010, when he was diagnosed with inoperable colon cancer. As a homicide detective, Lou Smit had no equal. He had worked over two hundred homicides with four different law enforcement agencies in El Paso County; including the Colorado Springs Police Department, El Paso County Coroner's Office, Fourth Judicial District Attorney's Office and the El Paso County Sheriff's Office.

Lou Smit had investigated violent deaths and crime scenes from every possible angle. The work he began on the Ramsey murder, as an investigator with the Boulder DA's Office, and continued until he was admitted into hospice in 2010, may have been his finest work. When Lou joined the Boulder DA's task force, he used his own personal computer to capture his investigative notes, which he used to create and evolve his spreadsheet, as well as his slide presentation, that he had shown, in part, to the Boulder grand jury.

Lou Smit's dying wish was that this case didn't die with him. Lou's estate, passed down to his four children, included his personal computers and investigative notes on every homicide case he had ever worked, including the JonBenét Ramsey homicide. The most important piece of evidence in the Ramsey homicide was the DNA genetic profile, which Lou told his children and former homicide partners about, was what he believed would be the key to solving the murder of JonBenét. This DNA, collected from under her fingernails, from the crotch of her panties, and waistband of her long johns, has identified an unknown male and excluded all members of the Ramsey family.

Our Smit Family Team has made several attempts to request the Boulder Police to release the electronic version of the DNA collected from JonBenét's body and clothing to private advanced DNA research labs. After several failed attempts, the Smit Family JBR Team has retained the legal services of attorney Greg Walta, who had previously served as Lou's legal counsel on this case.

Discussions were held with Colorado legislators to offer legislation which would require the automatic release of digital DNA evidence to the public no later than six months from the date the crime was reported. Declaring a specific date the DNA is to be released essential. By making electronic DNA analysis from violent crimes a public record, after a period of six months, unless an extension of time has been granted, the rapidly evolving DNA technologies, from the private, public, and academic communities, could be fully exploited as a forensic science.

As was the case in the Golden State Killer, it is important to remind ourselves that as he remained at large he continued to commit other crimes, including murder and rape. Furthermore, by the time the Golden State Killer was arrested, the statute of limitations had expired on many of his crimes, including rape and burglary. However, there is another important consideration; in addition to identifying the person responsible for the violent crime, DNA analysis has also proven beneficial in protecting innocent people who have been falsely accused—such as the family of JonBenét. Unfortunately, that proposed DNA legislation effort in Colorado failed to gather support from either political party.

In writing this book, Lou's children granted me unrestricted access to his investigative notes. I went through his massive spreadsheet and slide presentation countless times. I reviewed each of his 632 slides again and again, to carefully down-select the 36 slides included in the photo section of this book. In rereading each word Lou had typed on each of his 632 slides, over and over, it felt as if my former partner was still sitting behind me, pointing over my shoulder, to a crime scene photo on my computer monitor and whispering in my ear, "See there Johnny, there's no footprints in the snow because there's no snow on that side of the house. And there, see, that's the broken window that was found standing open and that green suitcase there, had been moved beneath the window, and there's a black scuffmark on the wall below the window. And remember, the DNA, that's the key to solving this case."

As I was writing this final chapter, and contemplating the passing of the 26-year anniversary of the death of JonBenét, I tried to reconstruct the horrific events in my mind that led up to the death of that innocent little six-year old little girl while she laid sleeping in her bed on Christmas night. Then a thought struck me to reach out to the manufacture of the Taser stun gun that Lou had believed was used on the right side of JonBenet's face and back.

A quick internet search produced the following statement: TASER STUNGUN "A Taser is an electroshock weapon sold by Axon, formerly TASER International. It fires two small barbed darts intended to puncture the skin and remain attached to the target, at 180 feet (55 m) per second. Their range extends from 15 feet (4.57 m) for non-law enforcement Tasers to 35 feet (10.67 m) for police officer Tasers. The darts are connected to the main unit by thin insulated copper wire and deliver a modulated electric current designed to disrupt voluntary control of muscles, causing "neuromuscular incapacitation". The effects of a Taser device may only be localized pain or strong involuntary long muscle contractions, based on the mode of use and connectivity of the darts. The term Taser was initially "TASER", abbreviating "Thomas A. Swift Electronic Rifle" after the 1911 novel Tom Swift and His Electric Rifle, and has been trademarked as a brand name of Axon, but has become informally used to refer generically to similar devices."

Wikipedia provided the following additional information, "Law enforcement TASER® weapons can be purchased by law enforcement only from Axon at prices ranging from $1,199.99 up to $3,600.00 on a five year (sic) lease. Quality refurbished law enforcement TASER® weapons can be legally purchased by federal, state, county, and municipal law enforcement agencies and officers, corrections officers, probation officers, reserve officers, marshals, wardens, rangers, security agencies and officers, bailiffs, bail bondsmen, fugitive recovery agents, and ordinary civilians at discount prices ranging from $399.95 to $599.00."

From my law enforcement experience I was personally familiar with how Taser stun guns can be used by detaching the upper cartridge, which shoots the two metal barbed darts, allowing the stun gun to be used as an immobilization device when coming in direct contact with the skin of an individual. I wrote an email to Axon, the manufacturer of the Taser stun gun, explaining that I was writing a book about the JonBenét murder investigation and was eventually contacted by Michael Brave, Manager/Sole Member of

LAAW International, LLC, in Scottsdale, Arizona and Legal Advisor to Axon Scientific and Medical Research and Medical Advisory Board.

On November 13, 2021, Mike Brave and I had a lengthy phone conversation about Lou Smit's theory about a Taser stun gun being used on JonBenét and we exchanged a series of emails over the next several weeks. Mike had not seen the autopsy photos but did provide me with his 97-page CV plus a stack of documents and articles on Taser stun gun wound pattern to review. One of those documents was Chapter 4 of the book *Atlas of Conducted Electrical Weapon Wounds and Forensic Analysis*, written by two medical doctors Jeffrey D. Ho and Donald M. Dawes. This book by Drs. Ho and Dawes was published in 2012, two years after the passing of Lou Smit.

Chapter 4 is titled Conducted Electrical Weapon Drive-Stun Wounds. The second paragraph explains how most conducted electrical weapons (CEW) can be used by "directly contacting the front of the device or the front of a device cartridge to a subject. The front of the CEW has two electrodes allowing for completion of a circuit. The method of direct contact application is often called a 'drive stun'." The next paragraph states in part, "In the case of the TASER M26 and X26 CEW (the most common CEWs in use today), the metal contacts are 40 mm apart on the front of the device and 45 mm apart on a diagonal on the front of the cartridge (Figs. 4.1 and 4.2)."

This paragraph concludes, "In general, the close spacing between the electrodes yields a painful stimulus when activated but minimizes capture of peripheral motor neurons. Therefore, the drive stun method of CEW application is largely considered to be a pain compliance tool and not a true incapacitation method of control." In my law enforcement training I remembered how the pain caused during the application of a stun gun may cause the person receiving the electrical discharge to occasionally lose control of their bladder and urinate. This recollection made me wonder, since JonBenét's under panties were stained with urine, but not her bed, if this may have happened when the stun gun was used on her the second time, most likely in the basement. This would also imply the first stun gun contact was while JonBenét was asleep in her bed, on the right side of her jaw, which may have rendered her incapable of screaming or calling out.

In referring to Table 4.1, labeled "Common CEWs in use and their electrode spread measurements," at the top of page 63, the distance between the two rectangular shaped electrodes for the more common models, is 40 mm. However the distance between metal probes is 35 mm (3.5 cm) on the Taser Model C2 (with a spent cartridge in place) and 35 mm with no cartridge and the Model X3 measures 30 mm/35 mm (with a spent cartridge in place) and 35 mm with no cartridge in place. Turning to Figure 4.5, at the bottom of page 64, the authors provided a color photo of the "Taser X26 CEW drive stun (wounds), (with) no cartridge" which are identical to the two rectangular burn marks shown in the autopsy photos of JonBenét's back.

Furthermore, on Page 63, the authors write, "Tissue injury is directly proportional to exposure time, so longer duration exposures may cause more thermal injury." Then on Page 67, "CEW or subject movement can also cause unique wounds or marking patterns. The blending of a single wound when the metal contact slides a small amount during the exposure creates a 'smear' sign that is more ovoid than rectangular (Fig. 4.11). Movement may also lead to a 'pivot' sign in which the CEW is rotated on one contact point during the exposure (one contact point remains in solid contact with the subject while the second contact point moves or pivots)…This is most likely to occur on unclothed skin."

The last paragraph on Page 67 states, "One of the most important principles in examining and documenting drive-stun wounds is to note if the measured distance between the wound is consistent with the measured electrode distance of the CEW in question." It is also important to measure length and width of the rectangular wounds caused by the electrodes during a drive-stun. In several of the color photos in Chapter 4 a metric scale is shown next to the red drive-stun wounds providing a measurement of 3-4 mm in length and 2-3 mm in width—identical to the measurements shown in the autopsy photos of the two rectangular red marks on JonBenét's back.

Figure 4.10, shown at the top of page 67, shows a color photo of a "Single TASER X26 CEW drive stun, moving subject, moving operator..." which shows a red rectangular shaped electrode mark while the second electrode mark is more of a jagged oval shaped wound pattern created when either the operator or subject moves. At the top of the next page, Figure 4.11 shows a photo of "A 'smear' sign from a single drive stun at 48 h post exposure." These "smear, skip or drag marks" are consistent with the marks on the right side of JonBenét's face.

Lou Smit was right—a stun gun was used on JonBenét in her attempted abduction. Since the Ramsey family did not own a stun gun, and one was not found at the crime scene, this fact further proves Lou Smit's Intruder Theory, which is supported by the ransom note. Patsy Ramsey did not write the ransom note she found on the lower step of the spiral staircase. This fact is further supported by forensic handwriting experts and corroborated by both John and Patsy Ramsey passing polygraph examinations by one of the leading polygraph operators in the nation.

There was physical evidence of unlawful entry into the home, through a broken basement window, and there were no footprints in the snow because there was no snow on the sunlit, southern-facing side of the house. The intruder brought with him black duct tape, parachute cord, a stun gun, and took those items with him when he left the crime scene.

However, the single most undeniable evidence that proves a yet unidentified man killed JonBenet, and exonerates all members of the Ramsey family, is the unknown male DNA found on the victim's clothing and under her fingernails. This attempted kidnap for ransom turned into one of the most brutal murders, and one of the worst miscarriages of criminal justice, in American history. But, after more than twenty-five years, this case is still solvable. Every year, DNA technology gets better and DNA databases are growing exponentially. All that is required to solve this case, is for the right person or team, with the knowledge, skill, and ability, to step forward and commit to finding justice for JonBenét.

One of the most inspirational slides Lou left behind is an introductory slide titled, "A New Day." The slide reads, "This is the beginning of a new day. God has given me this day to use as I will. I can waste it—or use it for good, but what I do today is important because I am exchanging a day of my life for it! I want it to be a gain, and not a loss; good, and not evil; love and not hate; success and not failure; in order that I shall not regret the price I paid for it."

When I look back on the amount of time my partner had to have dedicated to preparing his slide presentation, building his spreadsheet, and working on this case almost daily from early in 1997 until his death in 2010, I cannot help but be inspired by his dedication to a little girl he never met. I also draw motivation from the undying commitment to carry on made nearly every day by Lou's family and the other dedicated members of the JBR Smit Family Team. It has taken me over a year to write this book, along with countless hours contributed by Lou's family and my family and friends who volunteered their time reading over my draft manuscripts, to make this a better book. I do not regret the price I paid for it.

As we take one final look back at the past quarter century since the murder of JonBenét Ramsey, the family and friends of Lou Smit have independently collected and tested the DNA of more than a dozen persons of interest. We do not work for the Ramseys and have never been paid for our time. Like Lou, we believe we work for JonBenét. And while we have yet to identify the killer of JonBenét, we remain optimistic that the advances being made every year in DNA technology, coupled with the exponential growth of public and private DNA databases, that one day the killer will be identified and justice will finally be found for JonBenét and her family.

Conclusion

The undeniable facts in this case are these: At 5:52 a.m., on the morning of December 26, 1996, the Boulder Police Department received a 911 call from Patsy Ramsey reporting a kidnapping. When the first police officer arrived at the Ramsey home, he parked his marked patrol car in front of the Ramsey home and was handed a ransom note demanding $118,000 in cash for return of the Ramseys' daughter, JonBenét. The parents said they had last seen their daughter when they put her to bed in her bedroom on the second floor of the residence. The kidnapping note warned the parents not to go to the police or the FBI.

Other uniformed police officers, detectives, and crime scene technicians were called to the Ramsey home. The police searched the home; however, they failed to secure the crime scene or find the body of six-year-old JonBenét Ramsey lying on the floor in one of the rooms in the basement. Friends and neighbors of the Ramseys were allowed into the residence. The FBI was notified and did set up a phone trap on the Ramsey's home phone; however, they were denied access to the crime scene by the Boulder Police. No phone call from the kidnapper was ever received by the Ramseys.

Seven hours after the police first arrived at the Ramsey's home, Detective Linda Arndt suggested the victim's father, John Ramsey, take one of the other men in the house to search the home again. During this search, John Ramsey pointed to a broken window in the basement that was standing open, with a suitcase positioned below the window. He then opened a door to a small room in the basement where he discovered the body of his daughter laying on the floor. She had been tied up with a cord and black duct tape had been placed on her mouth. The father removed the duct tape and carried his daughter's body upstairs.

Rigor mortis had set in indicating that she had been dead for several hours. An autopsy performed by the Boulder County Coroner, concluded she had been strangled, using a garrote, constructed of white parachute cord and a broken piece of a paint brush handle. This same cord was used to bind her wrists, using a slip knot, which would tighten as she struggled. She had also been struck over the head with sufficient force to cause an eight-inch skull fracture. The coroner also concluded there was evidence in the vaginal area indicating she had been sexually assaulted.

Autopsy photos also showed two small rectangular-shaped red marks on JonBenét's back and on the right side of her face. Lou Smit rightfully concluded these injuries were burn marks caused by a stun gun. This was a significant revelation, especially when taken into consideration with the duct tape placed over the victim's mouth and white parachute cord used to bind her wrists and to construct the murder weapon, the garrote. The duct tape was torn from a roll of duct tape and the parachute cord was cut from a length of cord. As with the stun gun, the parents did not own any duct tape, parachute cord, or a stun gun and none were found at the crime scene.

The suspect or suspects had to have brought these items into the Ramsey home with the intent to immobilize someone, consistent with a kidnapping. Lou also dispelled the urban legend that there was no forced entry into the home. Lou showed how the intruder had gained entry through the broken basement window found standing wide open near where the victim's body was found. Lou also noted that there were "no footprints in the snow" because there was no snow around this southern-facing basement window. In addition to having access to the crime scene, along with the police and autopsy reports, Lou also had access to John and Patsy Ramsey. As a homicide detective, Lou was known as being a very experienced and skilled police interrogator, which is why he was selected to lead the interrogation of John Ramsey.

After spending an extraordinary amount of time, over multiple sessions, with both John and Patsy Ramsey, Lou concluded without any doubt, that the parents were not involved in any way in the death of their daughter. Lou's conclusions were validated when both parents passed polygraph examinations administered by one of the foremost polygraph operators in the nation. The results of these two lie detector tests, which established the parents were telling the truth, were independently verified by a second nationally recognized polygraph examiner.

As I conclude the writing of this book, I realize there are three likely groups of readers: 1) those who remain convinced of the Ramseys' guilt, 2) those who are convinced of the Ramseys' innocence, and 3) those who may be undecided. For those of you in this last group, ask yourself these final questions. What if the Ramseys didn't do it? Would this case not stand as one of the worst injustices in American history? Are there any lessons learned that can be adopted by law enforcement agencies and prosecutors to prevent this injustice from happening in the future? And lastly, with all the advancements that have been made in DNA technologies over the last quarter century, has there ever been a better time than now to use DNA to solve this case?

The DNA collected from fingernail clippings and from the crotch area of the victim's panties, came from the victim and a secondary source—not John, Patsy, or Burke Ramsey. This DNA was from an unknown male and is consistent with the DNA found using trace or touch DNA on the victim's long johns in 2008. This DNA is referred by the forensic lab as genetic profiles from "Unknown Male 1" and "Unknown Male 2." As his book goes to print, our team's requests to meet with Boulder law enforcement authorities and help pay for the costs associated with additional DNA testing continues to be ignored.

As of the publication date, the Smit Family JonBenét Ramsey Team has eliminated more than a dozen potential persons of interest and continues to collect and test DNA from our Top 20 list of Persons of Interest. In an interview in January 2021 with ABC News, JonBenét's older brother, John Andrew Ramsey, said, "The family has not lost the will to fight and the will … to find the killer." Inspired the undying devotion of Lou Smit, and encouraged by the technological advancements being made in DNA research, the Smit Family JBR Team has also "not lost the will to fight and to find the killer." The family and friends of Lou Smit continue to stand in the shoes of a legendary lawman and continue his quest to solve the murder of JonBenét Ramsey.

Every day brings new hope; on September 7, 2022, a story reported on Fox News, claimed, "Georgia investigators identify suspect who allegedly killed Michigan teen in 33-year-old cold case. Henry Fredrick Wise, also known as Hoss Wise, was identified as the killer through genealogy DNA." The news announcement shared that, "GBI (Georgia Bureau of Investigation) agents assigned to this investigation sought the FBI to assist with genealogy DNA," the GBI said in a press release. "FBI used Othram, a lab specializing in this advanced testing, and received positive results on June 13, 2022."

While it appears unlikely Boulder law enforcement authorities are willing to turn this case over to the FBI, or ask our Smit Family Team for help in solving the murder of JonBenét, it is encouraging to know the FBI is using genealogy DNA and advanced DNA testing capabilities developed by private labs. Lastly, if nothing else, it is hoped that this book has established that the murder of JonBenét was not by a family member and was the direct result of an attempted kidnap for ransom, which is a federal crime. This kidnap/homicide investigation should have been—and can still be—investigated by the FBI and potentially prosecuted under the Federal Kidnapping Act (commonly known as the Lindbergh Law).

Shoes

By Detective Lou Smit
Colorado Springs Police Department

It's three o'clock in the morning and we're looking down on a lifeless corpse. Many things are racing through our minds. Who is he? How was he killed? Who did it? Why? Who's going to notify the next of kin? So many questions; so few answers. We start making notes, sketches, recording information on physical description, blood, wounds, clothing.

My eyes are drawn to the man's shoes. I don't know why, but in almost every case my eyes are drawn to the victim's shoes and thoughts flash through my mind: When he put them on the last time, did he even suspect it would be the last? He won't wear them again. He'll never tie those laces again.

Shoes, shoes, the dead man's shoes. I always remember something I read long ago: "THE DETECTIVE STANDS IN THE DEAD MAN'S SHOES TO PROTECT 'HIS' INTERESTS AGAINST THOSE OF ANYONE ELSE IN THE WORLD."

I guess - - THAT'S WHAT IT'S ALL ABOUT.

So many awesome responsibilities are associated with standing in that dead man's shoes: It means: Becoming personally involved in the case and with the victim.

It means: Consoling relatives and friends. It means: Caring for the victim's personal possessions and belongings.

It means: Respecting that person's body and integrity no matter what race, creed, social upbringing and past faults or reputation, always remembering that something has been taken from him which is priceless and irreplaceable - - his life.

It means: Closing all doors and answering all unanswered questions. It means: Solving the crime, finding the right killers.

It means: Putting into the case part of yourself, not just making it a nine-to-five job.

It means: Going that extra distance, even if all of this distance is uphill. It's not "just getting by", but finding that extra piece of evidence or that extra witness, thus developing that extra "depth" to the case.

It means: Making commitments and keeping them.

It means: Squeezing as much out of the justice system as you can. Granted, sometimes it's not exactly what you want. Always strive for "everything" that the courts and the law will allow, standing your ground and fighting, even though the odds are long and the battle is tough. Get used to fighting and drawing your lines, trying not to retreat from what is right.

It means: Always "placing the CASE FIRST." Don't let your personal pride and feelings be placed in front of your real job, that is, representing the victim.

Remember, try to think of it as not working for the prosecution or the defense. YOU WORK FOR THE VICTIM.

Anyone can stand in this victim's shoes, either by working on the case directly or by supporting it verbally. Just remember: All of you can stand in his shoes and bring his case one step closer to a successful conclusion.

When the case is finished:

-- You may experience a great deal of personal satisfaction.

-- You may be thanked by the victim's family and loved ones.

I would also like to think that, someday, as we travel through eternity, that we will meet the victim, who will also say, "WELL DONE, FRIEND, WELL DONE."

Eulogy

August 20, 2010 – New Life Church, Colorado Springs, CO

Mark, Cindy, Lori, and Dawn, thank you for allowing us the privilege of gathering here today to pay tribute to your dad. I also want to say thank you for extending me the honor of being with you, at Lou's side, when he died and thank you for inviting me to speak here today to reflect on what it was like to be Lou's partner.

I feel I stand here today representing all of Lou's former partners to pay tribute to this humble, yet incredible man, who touched so many people on such a personal level and along the way became a law enforcement legend. I also want to thank Lou's former partners Dave and Dick and Boomer and all of you who have shared with me your most intimate memories of Lou over these past few weeks.

Would all of Lou's detective partners please stand and be recognized, and remain standing as I invite those of you here today that worked alongside of Lou to please stand; all the police officers, deputy sheriffs, coroners, District Attorneys, Judges, defense attorneys, PIs, deputy DAs, investigators, FBI Agents, if you've worked a case with Lou Smit on a professional level, would you to please stand and be recognized. Thank you, please be seated.

Now, if you have been a victim of a crime, or are a family member of a victim of a crime that Lou worked, would you please stand and be recognized, for Lou always

272 | JOHN WESLEY ANDERSON

reminded us, it was you who we worked for; thank you, we are honored by your presence here today. Lastly, if you are a suspect in one of Lou Smit's few remaining unsolved cases, would you please stand and be recognized, that first group who just stood up would like a word with you after Lou's services are complete. Thank you.

It was not so much that being a detective defined Lou Smit, as it was that Lou Smit defined being a detective. Those of us who were privileged to have worked with Lou Smit and came to love him, would agree, when it came to being a homicide detective, Lou Smit had no equal. Dave Spencer, another of Lou's partners, got it right when he said, "Lou taught the rest of us how to be detectives. We knew we could never be as good as he was, but if we could only become half as good as he was, we knew we would have achieved something special." As his partners we were all aware that we were in the presence of a truly remarkable man and an uncommonly unique homicide detective.

If I were forced to limit myself to only three descriptors of Lou Smit's investigative traits that separated him from the rest of us, it would be his devotion to his victim, faith in God, and attention to detail. Lou Smit's undying devotion to what he defined as his duty to represent the victims and the victim's family was a lifelong commitment, as demonstrated just last year, when at the age of 74, Lou Smit and former District Attorney Bob Russel appeared at the parole hearing to represent Karen Grammar, the victim of a homicide who had died a violent death nearly 40 years ago.

It was this devotion to his victim that drove in him a relentless pursuit of their killers, a pursuit that had no geographical or spatial boundaries. If you were a suspect of a violent crime, you did not want Lou on your tail. If you were a defense attorney representing someone who Lou had arrested for a murder, you didn't want to hear Smit was the arresting officer, or read Detective Smit's name typed on the case report, because Lou Smit never once lost a case in court. We also knew Lou Smit would never give up representing a victim, regardless of their race, age, sex, criminal background, or financial status. Every victim held a special place of honor in Lou Smit's eyes.

Lou Smit's faith in God was as enduring for him, as it was contagious for the rest of us who knew him. He would pray at the crime scene asking for God's help in solving this crime, he would pray every night asking for His guidance, mentioned his victims by name and after a conviction was returned in court, he would return to the scene of the crime to say thank you in a prayer. Lou Smit often referred to himself as simply "an ordinary detective, with an extraordinary partner", but it wasn't so much what Lou said, but what he did that demonstrated his faith in God.

Note – I sensed my eulogy to Lou during his funeral service was running a little long so I chose to eliminate this paragraph; however, for the purposes of this writing I thought it might be appropriate to include it: With respect to Lou's attention to detail, I've read hundreds of Lou's reports, but one really stood out to me; I remember reading one of Lou's crime scene supplements, on a murder-suicide case, where his crime scene description alone was 26 pages in length. I asked Lou about his amazingly detailed scene description, commenting at the time that the case seemed rather open and shut; the suspect, a police officer, who had murdered his wife, called 911 to confess, then turned the gun on himself, obviously we would not be going to court. Lou replied since it was a police officer involved, he wanted to ensure the scene was investigated impartially, if anyone ever read this report they would feel as if they there were there and he just wanted to make sure he didn't leave any questions unanswered. Those three investigative principles became part of the foundation so many of us built our careers upon.

Lou and I first met when I was 18 years old; my first real job out of high school was as Police Cadet for the Colorado

Springs Police Department. Working midnight shifts in the ID Bureau, I would read all the solved and unsolved homicide cases and dream that someday I would become Lou Smit's partner and we would forge a partnership equal only to such legendary detective teams as Killa and Trapp, or Spencer and Smit. By the time I was 28, I was living that dream. When I turned 38, I shared another dream with Lou; I somehow knew I was supposed to be the next Sheriff for El Paso County, Colorado.

Lou came to my announcement in the spring of 1994 and sat in the front row; there were only two other people in attendance, Tom Orr, who some of you know, is presently serving a one-year tour of duty in the Army embedded deep in the rugged mountains of Afghanistan, and Ollie Gray, who is here with us today, you will find him where he always is, embedded somewhere in the background, almost out of sight. Only three people were there that day, when I announced my candidacy for Sheriff, no media, not one single camera. I commented to Lou afterwards, "Geez Lou, I didn't exactly have a resounding start to my political career, did I?" Lou stood by my side and reassured me that things would work out the way God intended.

What was it like, to be one of Lou Smit's partners? It was an adventure! Life with Lou was for me a continually evolving series of dreams come true. All Lou's partners are blessed with a lifetime of cherished memories, mine include meeting Miss Lee in Las Vegas atop the Landmark Hotel in the revolving restaurant, Lou buying chicken wings at the Cloud 9 for our lunch as we searched for the spent bullet that killed Jerry Terry, or pointing out to Dave Spencer and me where we would find the killer of Donnie Emmitt.

Andrew Louis Smit died on Wednesday, August 11, 2010 at 4:04 p.m., surrounded by his loving family and friends. Lou's obituary appeared in *The Colorado Springs Gazette* on Wednesday, August 18, 2010. In the week between those two dates, his obituary also ran in the *Washington Post*, the *New York Times*, the *Seattle Times,* and countless other newspapers all across this nation. Lou was known by such notable people as Katie Couric, Barbara Walters, Larry King, Kris Kristofferson, and Kelsey Grammer.

On an individual and deeply personal level, Lou Smit touched a lot of lives and along the way became a law enforcement legend. As a lasting tribute to the memory of this dedicated detective with unparalleled skill, Lou's grandchildren would like to invite the following representatives from each of the four law enforcement agencies Lou worked in to please come forward and accept these plaques to be displayed for future generations of detectives to come:

1. Detective Commander Kurt Pillard, Colorado Springs Police Department

2. Doctor Robert Bux, El Paso County Coroner

3. District Attorney Dan May, 4th Judicial District, State of Colorado

4. Inspector John San Agustin, El Paso County Sheriff's Office

Lou Smit was not just my partner, my hero, my mentor, best man at my wedding; he was also my and many of yours' best friend, and the best man many of us have ever known. Thank you for being here today and sharing in celebrating the life of Lou Smit.

Acknowledgements

I want to express my sincere appreciation to the family of Lou Smit. Cindy Smit Marra and her husband, Kent Marra, have been the driving force behind out team and Mark Smit spent countless hours improving multiple drafts of manuscript. Thank you, working with you to find justice for JonBenét has helped me stay connected to Lou.

I also want to express my sincere appreciation to the Ramsey family for their commitment to do whatever it takes to find the killer of JonBenét.

To my partners: Lou Smit, Dave Spencer, Dick Reisler, and Kurt Pillard, thank you guys; I appreciated you always standing in my corner. I also want to say thank you to Heidi Wigand-Nicely, Karen Rhodes, and my sister Tammy Bodycomb, for the countless hours they invested in proofreading my rough draft manuscripts—this is a far better book because of you.

To my publisher, Steve Jackson, co-owner of WildBlue Press, I want to express my sincere appreciation for your personal support of this book. I am grateful you were able to get to know Lou Smit and were committed to publishing a book that would tell his story.

Lastly, I want to thank my family and friends for their continuing support of me as an author and understanding my need to ensure the legacy of Detective Lou Smit and the life of JonBenét Ramsey are not forgotten.

Thank you,
John

About the Author

John Wesley Anderson, MBA, is a former police detective turned full-time author. He is the recipient of the Friends of the Pikes Peak Library District 2022 Golden Quill Award. John retired after a thirty-year career in law enforcement, including twenty-two years serving with the Colorado Springs Police Department where he worked homicide cases for six years as partners with Lou Smit. John retired from the Police Department in 1995, when he was elected Sheriff for El Paso County, Colorado. After serving eight years as Sheriff, John was term-limited in office and accepted a position with the Lockheed Martin Corporation where he worked homeland and corporate security. After ten years of service, John retired from the corporate world to launch a small consulting business allowing him the freedom to pursue his passion for writing, art, and history. After Lou Smit passed away in 2010, John joined Lou's family and a handful of other retired homicide detectives to continue Lou's efforts to find the killer of JonBenét Ramsey.

Index

Symbols

$118,000   117, 120, 230, 264
911 Emergency Phone Call   107, 109, 228, 264

A

Access Graphics   137, 204, 229
AFIS   101
Ainsworth, Steve Sheriff's
          Detective   129
Alcalde, Diego Olmos   177
Anderson, Margie Meter
          Patrol   31, 32
Arndt, Linda Police
          Detective   115, 120, 135, 264
Arrow Media   247, 248
Autopsy   14, 17, 23, 56, 72, 110, 116, 169, 172, 180, 188, 189, 192, 193, 194, 227, 259, 260, 261, 265, 266

B

Bailie, Robert Wolfgang   231, 232
Barnhill, Betty & Joseph Sr.   173
Barry, Bernie Sheriff   43, 44, 96
Baseball Bat   110, 111, 172, 173, 177, 191
Beck, Peggy   239
Beckner, Mark Police Chief   15, 136, 137, 140, 214
Bjornsrud, Don "BJ"
          Lieutenant   82, 83, 84, 87

Boulder, Colorado   9, 13, 17, 31, 33, 49, 52, 68, 72, 79, 80, 90, 104, 107, 109, 112, 120, 130, 140, 143, 165, 173, 177, 180, 187, 190, 200, 210, 213, 217, 226, 231, 234, 239, 249, 253, 255, 256, 264, 265, 267
Brave, Michael   258
Brennan, Charlie Reporter   204, 205
Broken Window   111, 114, 118, 123, 126, 205, 257, 265
Browne, Robert Charles   100, 218
Bruce, Dad Police Chief   32
Bundy, Ted   71
Busemeyer, Jerry Police
          Sergeant   25, 28, 218, 221

C

Charlevoix, Michigan   122, 169
Chase, Susannah   177
Church, Heather Dawn   93, 97, 99, 100, 102, 127, 215, 218, 225
CODIS   140, 177, 191, 230, 232, 238, 243, 246
Conrad, Janet Kate   40, 231
Corbett, Michael   37, 40, 93
Crystal Springs Estates   87

D

Dabling, Mark Police Officer   48, 51, 52
Davis, Harold "Red" Police
          Sergeant   31, 35, 39, 43
Davis, Les Police Lieutenant   33, 36, 75, 99
Dawes, Donald M., M.D.   259
DeAngelo, Joseph James Jr.   235,

DeMuth, Trip Prosecuting
    Attorney   77, 129, 139,
    144, 197, 225
DNA   14, 29, 72, 123, 127, 140,
    170, 177, 185, 191, 199,
    200, 213, 219, 227, 230,
    240, 249, 252, 262, 266
Dougherty, Michael District
    Attorney   239, 244
Duct Tape   14, 29, 115, 171, 182,
    187, 189, 228, 261, 265
Dying Declaration   212

E

Eller, John Detective
    Commander   15, 129,
    133, 136, 182

F

Flashlight   190
French, Rick Police Officer   109,
    118
Frey, Heather Detective   240

G

Garnett, Stan District
    Attorney   235
Garrote   14, 115, 169, 172, 182,
    184, 190, 192, 193, 246, 265
GEDmatch Genomics
    Website   235
Gelb, Edward L., Ph.D.
    Polygraphs   207
Gentry, Elvin Defense
    Attorney   211
Glenn, Freddie Lee   37, 93
GoFundMe Account   234, 241,
    248, 253
Golden State Killer   235, 239,
    256

Gosage, Ron Police
    Commander   123, 244,
    245, 253
Grammer, Karen   38, 93
Grammer, Kelsey   38, 77, 276
Grand Jury   17, 47, 74, 141, 174,
    176, 197, 200, 206, 235, 256

H

Haddon, Morgan &
    Foreman   201
Harold, Maris Police Chief   247
Hartkopp, Barry Police
    Sergeant   240, 242, 245
Hess, Charlie   99, 207, 218, 219,
    232
Hi-Tec Boot Print   14, 116, 171,
    184, 189
Hofstrom, Peter Deputy
    DA   129, 134, 144, 197
Hoverstock, Father Rol
    Priest   119
Hunter, Alex District
    Attorney   128, 136, 138,
    141, 174, 197, 199, 200,
    201, 213, 235

I

Iuppa, Barney District
    Attorney   71, 74

K

Kane, Michael Grand Jury
    Prosecutor   139, 141, 174,
    197
Kenda, Joe Police Lieutenant   69,
    70, 72, 76, 86, 203
Killa, Harry Police Detective   36,
    61, 219
Koby, Tom Police Chief   90, 133,
    135, 136, 140

Kramer, Lorne Police Chief   90,
        96
Krashoc, Darlene   236
Kristofferson, Kris   201, 203,
        228, 276
Kurtis, Bill Reporter A&E
        Special   136, 204, 205

L

Lacy, Mary District
        Attorney   213, 235
Ligature   170, 182, 186, 187, 192,
        241, 246
Lockheed Martin
        Corporation   137, 219,
        231, 278
Lucas, Henry Lee   58

M

Marietta, Georgia   166, 211
Marra, Cindy Smit   76, 221, 226,
        240, 277
McGarry, Elinor CSI
        Technician   94, 99
McLuen, Cynthia   48, 68
Meyer, John E., M.D.
        Coroner   192
Miss Lee   57, 60, 62, 275
Morrissey, Mitch Denver
        DA   141
Munger, Jim Police Chief   76,
        81, 90

O

Ockham's Razor Theory   118
Oh, Jeffrey D., M.D.   259
Owens, Bill Governor
        Colorado   200

P

Paint Brush Handle   115, 241,
        246, 265
Palmprint   26, 190
Papol, James   238
Parachute Cord   14, 115, 172,
        182, 190, 192, 261, 265
Petechiae   46, 193
Pillard, Kurt Police
        Detective   16, 40, 44, 95,
        221, 231, 251, 276
Polygraph Tests   207
Practice Ransom Note   184
Pubic Hair   182, 190

R

Radabaugh, Richard Police
        Cadet   22, 25, 34
Ramsey, Beth   166
Ramsey, Burke   16, 122, 125,
        175, 182, 188, 199, 206,
        234, 241, 266
Ramsey, John   2, 29, 77, 107,
        120, 125, 130, 137, 171,
        173, 181, 188, 191, 203,
        208, 212, 220, 225, 229,
        234, 255, 264
Ramsey, John Andrew   113, 125,
        168, 173, 199, 204, 225,
        230, 241, 248, 253, 267
Ramsey, John Bennett   167
Ramsey, Melinda   125, 199, 206,
        212, 241
Ramsey, Patsy   29, 40, 107, 121,
        130, 137, 140, 142, 165,
        172, 173, 181, 188, 191,
        198, 200, 204, 206, 211,
        220, 228, 235, 255, 261,
        264, 266
Ransom Note   16, 108, 110, 115,
        116, 125, 169, 171, 181,
        184, 208, 211, 228, 261, 264

Reisler, Dick Police
    Detective   16, 44, 47, 71,
    77, 226, 231, 249, 251, 277
Rhodes, James Lamar   49
Romer, Roy Governor
    Colorado   140, 197
Rope & Bag   113, 168, 185, 190
Russel, Bob District
    Attorney   39, 64, 71, 198,
    224, 273

S

San Agustin, John   207, 239, 248,
    276
Sapp, Art Police Detective   49,
    80
S.B.T.C.   118, 188
Schiller, Lawrence   201
Smit, Mark   224, 226, 251, 277
Spears, Jess Police Captain   32,
    34
Spencer, Dave Police
    Detective   7, 16, 37, 40,
    44, 52, 78, 107, 118, 222,
    226, 233, 240, 242, 249,
    273, 275, 277
Stanton, Melody   170
Stratton, Neal Acting Police
    Chief   75, 76
Stun Gun   14, 17, 29, 116, 131,
    170, 182, 188, 200, 206,
    209, 246, 257, 260, 265

T

Talley, Ad Police Lieutenant   60
Taylor, James Raymond   238
Templeman, Vernon Wayne   49
The Dr. Oz Show   247
Thiede, Bill Police Captain   21,
    35, 82, 87

Thomas, Steve Police
    Detective   120, 123, 129,
    134, 138, 140, 173, 181, 201
Toole, Ottis Elwood   58, 62, 64
Transfer Theory   13, 29, 179
Trujillo, Tom Police
    Detective   134, 138, 189,
    193, 244

U

United Flight 585   86

V

Vialpando, Mary Lynn   238, 243

W

Walker, Ron FBI
    Supervisor   130, 136
Walta, Greg Defense
    Attorney   198, 256
Watson, Winslow Douglas
    III   38, 93
Whyte, Michael   237
Wine Cellar   112, 114, 118, 190
Wood, Lin Attorney   207
Woodward, Paula   123, 125, 197

*For More News About John Wesley Anderson,
Signup For Our Newsletter:*

http://wbp.bz/newsletter

Word-of-mouth is critical to an author's long-term success. If you appreciated this book please leave a review on the Amazon sales page:

http://wbp.bz/louandjonbeneta

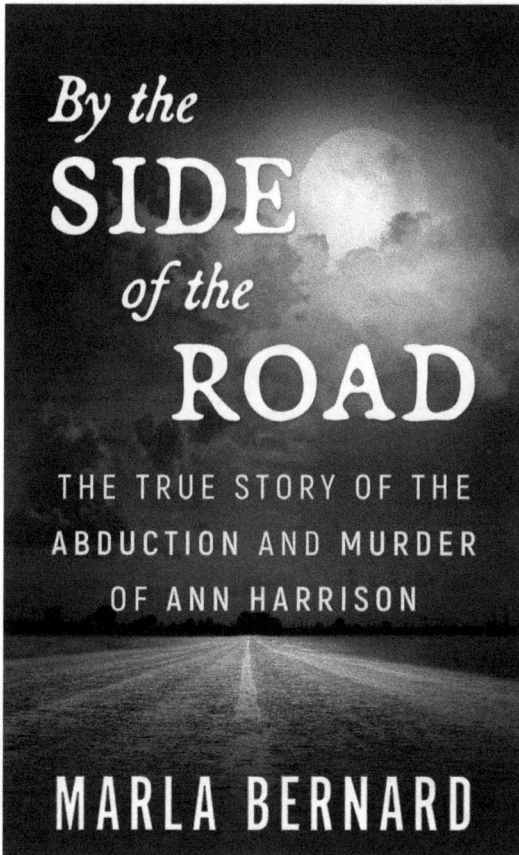

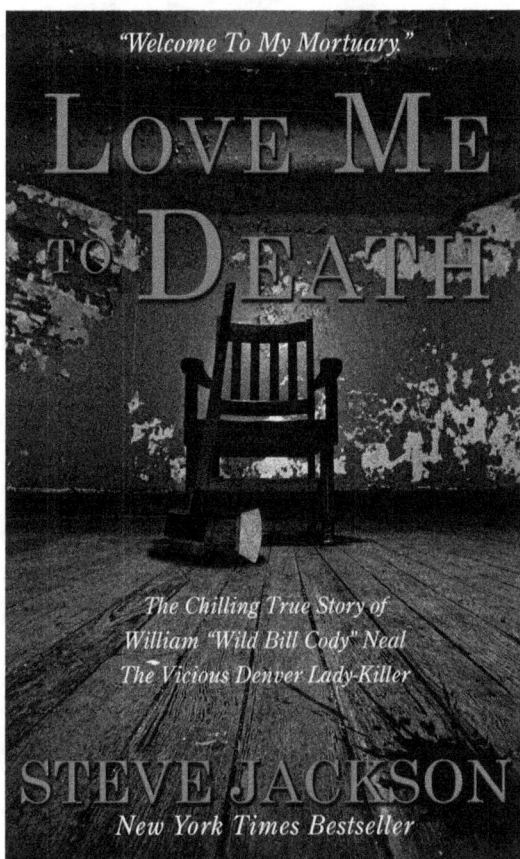

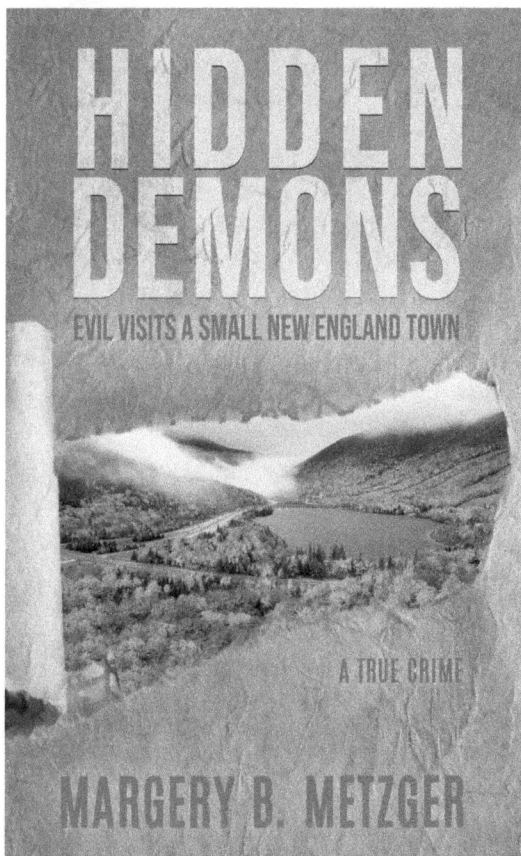

HIDDEN DEMONS by MARGERY B. METZGER

http://wbp.bz/hiddendemons

In chilling, dramatic narrative HIDDEN DEMONS: Evil Visits a Small New England Town, Margery B. Metzger details these events and reveals a savage serial killer, Lewis Lent, Jr., who lurked in the shadows.

www.ingramcontent.com/pod-product-compliance
Lightning Source LLC
Chambersburg PA
CBHW071940260326
41914CB00004B/703